The
HUMANISTIC
PERSONOLOGY
Project

GENETIC PERSONOLOGY:

The Formation, Functioning, and Development of the Person & Personality. *A Humanistic-Ontological Approach*

Author:
Petru Stefaroi

Cover:
Ionut Platon, Petru Stefaroi

ISBN: 9781719967020

Amazon KDP, USA

Includes Bibliography

Printed book : 312 pages

Product Dimensions : 6" x 9" / 15.24 x 22.86 cm

GENETIC PERSONOLOGY

**The Formation,
Functioning and Development
of the
Person & Personality**

*A Humanistic-Ontological
Approach*

Authored and Edited by

Petru Stefaroi

Other books and articles of the author:

* Humanistic Philosophy: Humanistic and Pro-Humanistic Ideas, Values, Orientations, Movements, Methods, and Representatives in Philosophy, Science, Society, and Social Practices, 2016, CreateSpace-Amazon.

* Travail Social Humaniste: La Personnalité et les Relations Humaines - Ressources Principales de la Pratique, 2015, CreateSpace-Amazon.

* Humanistic Personology: A Humanistic-Ontological Theory of the Person & Personality. Applications in Therapy, Social Work, Education, Management and Art (Theatre), 2015, CreateSpace-Amazon.

* Humane & Spiritual Qualities of the Professional in Humanistic Social Work: Humanistic Social Work - The THIRD WAY in Theory and Practice, 2014, CreateSpace-Amazon.

* The Humanistic Approach in Psychology & Psychotherapy, Sociology & Social Work, Pedagogy & Education, Management and Art: Personal Development and Community Development, 2012, CreateSpace-Amazon.

* Humanistic Paradigm of Social Work or Brief Introduction in Humanistic Social Work, Social Work Review, No. 1, 2012, University of Bucharest/ Polirom Publishing House.

* Humanistic Perspective on Customer in Social Work, Social Work Review, No. 1-2, 2009, Polirom Publishing House.

* Happiness Theory in Social Work. From Care Management to Happiness Management), 2009, Lumen Publishing House.

* Socio-Affective Development Disorders of Institutionalized Child. From The Survival Objective towards the Happiness Objective in Social Work for Children, Social Work Review, No. 1-2, 2008, Polirom Publishing House.

* Efficient Management Particularity in Social Work, Social Work Review, No. 3, 2007, University of Bucharest / Polirom Publishing House.

TABLE OF CONTENTS

EDITORIAL NOTICE 11

INTRODUCTION 13

CHAPTER 1. GENETIC PERSONOLOGY. FORMATION AND DEVELOPMENT OF THE PERSON/ PERSONALITY -- THE HUMANISTIC APPROACH AND THE HUMANISTIC-ONTOLOGICAL APPROACH 17

CHAPTER 2. THE FORMATION AND DEVELOPMENT OF THE PERSON/ PERSONALITY -- BASIC SOURCES, FACTORS AND CONDITIONS 75

CHAPTER 3. BASIC CHARACTERISTICS, LAWS, AND PRINCIPLES OF THE PROCESS OF FORMATION AND DEVELOPMENT OF THE PERSON/ PERSONALITY 87

CHAPTER 4. THE PROCESS OF PERSONALIZATION. THE GREAT SUB-PROCESSES OF THE PROCESS OF PERSONALIZATION 101

CHAPTER 5. MATURE, FULLY FUNCTIONING AND HUMANE PERSON/PERSONALITY -- THE TARGET OF THE ONTOGENETIC PROCESS OF PERSONALIZATION. A HUMANISTIC-ONTOLOGICAL MODEL OF THE PERSON & PERSONALITY 119

CHAPTER 6. THE FORMATION OF THE ONTOLOGICAL-PSYCHOLOGICAL SPHERE OF THE PERSON 131

CHAPTER 7. THE FORMATION OF THE PSYCHOLOGICAL-SOCIAL/ RELATIONAL SPHERE OF THE PERSON 179

CHAPTER 8. THE FORMATION OF THE PERSON AS A WHOLE 195

CHAPTER 9. THE INTERNAL JOUISSANCE, THE BEINGNESS AND THE FUNCTIONING OF THE PERSON/ PERSONALITY 213

CHAPTER 10. THE DEVELOPMENT/ FULFILLMENT OF THE PERSON/ PERSONALITY. EDUCATION AND THERAPY/ COUNSELING 229

INSTEAD OF CONCLUSIONS 269

REFERENCES AND CONSULTED BIBLIOGRAPHY 297

The
HUMANISTIC
PERSONOLOGY
Project

CONTENTS

EDITORIAL NOTE 11

INTRODUCTION 13

CHAPTER 1. GENETIC PERSONOLOGY. FORMATION AND DEVELOPMENT OF THE PERSON/ PERSONALITY -- THE HUMANISTIC APPROACH AND THE HUMANISTIC-ONTOLOGICAL APPROACH 17

1.1. INTRODUCTORY ASPECTS 18

1.2. PERSONOLOGY, GENETIC PERSONOLOGY AND *HUMANISTIC* GENETIC PERSONOLOGY 19
1.2.1. PERSONOLOGY. HUMAN BEING. PERSON, PERSONALITY 19
1.2.2. GENETIC PERSONOLOGY 33
1.2.3. GENETIC PERSONOLOGY – THE HUMANISTIC PARADIGM 33

1.3. THE FORMATION AND DEVELOPMENT OF THE PERSON/ PERSONALITY - THE NON-HUMANISTIC AND THE HUMANISTIC APPROACH 34
1.3.1. THE NON-HUMANISTIC APPROACH 34
1.3.2. THE HUMANISTIC APPROACH 35

1.4. THE FORMATION AND DEVELOPMENT OF THE PERSON/ PERSONALITY - A HUMANISTIC-ONTOLOGICAL APPROACH/ THEORY 37
1.4.1. INTRODUCTORY ASPECTS 37
1.4.2. CORE ELEMENTS, CHARACTERISTICS, AND PROCESSES 38
1.4.3. SCIENTIFIC-THEORETICAL, PHILOSOPHICAL, AND CULTURAL SOURCES AND MODELS 54

CHAPTER 2. THE FORMATION AND DEVELOPMENT OF THE PERSON/ PERSONALITY -- BASIC SOURCES, FACTORS AND CONDITIONS 75

2.1. INTRODUCTORY ASPECTS 76

2.2. THE HUMAN BODY/ ORGANISM 77
2.2.1. THE BODY AND THE PERSON 77
2.2.2. PHYLOGENESIS AND ONTOGENESIS 78
2.2.3. THE ORGANISM AND THE PERSON. THE CENTRAL NERVOUS SYSTEM 78

2.3. THE SOCIO-HUMAN ENVIRONMENT 79
2.3.1. THE HUMAN/ PERSONAL ENVIRONMENTAL ONTO-SYSTEM 79
2.3.2. MICRO-COMMUNITY, FAMILY 80
2.3.3. CULTURE, RELIGION, MORALS, EDUCATION 82

2.4. THE MIND 83
2.4.1. THE MIND AND THE PERSON 83
2.4.2. THE COGNITIVE HABILITATION, PERTENTION AND THE EPISTEMIC SUBJECT 84
2.4.3. THE MENTAL APPARATUS, INTELLIGENCE, THE NOETIC ONTOS 85

CHAPTER 3. BASIC CHARACTERISTICS, LAWS, AND PRINCIPLES OF THE PROCESS OF FORMATION AND DEVELOPMENT OF THE PERSON/ PERSONALITY 87

3.1. INTRODUCTORY ASPECTS 88

3.2. PRINCIPLES/ LAWS/ CHARACTERISTICS 89
3.2.1. EMERGENCE AND IMERGENCE 90
3.2.2. TRANSMERGENCE AND TELEGENCE 91
3.2.3. CONMERGENCE AND SINMERGENCE 92

3.3. STAGES/ STEPS / PROCESSES 93
3.3.1. THE CONTACT AND THE ACQUISITION/ ACCUMULATION 93
3.3.2. THE STRUCTURING/ CENTRALIZATION, AND THE CONSTITUTION/ HOLISTIZATION 94
3.3.3. THE ESTABLISHING/ NETWORKING, AND THE ONTIFICATION/ FULFILLMENT 95

3.4. ENERGY, MECHANISMS, RESORTS 96
3.4.1. THE ONTO-PERSONAL ENERGY AND THE PROSTASIS 96
3.4.2. MECHANISMS, MONTAGES, MOTIVATIONAL SOURCES AND RESORTS 97

3.5. THE ONTO-FORMATIZATION, THE PERSOMIZATION, AND THE PROMERGENCE/ DISMERGENCE 98
3.5.1. THE PERSONAL ONTO-FORMATIZATION AND THE PERSOMIZATION 98
3.5.2. THE PROMERGENCE AND THE DISMERGENCE 99

CHAPTER 4. THE PROCESS OF PERSONALIZATION. THE GREAT SUBPROCESSES OF THE PROCESS OF PERSONALIZATION 101

4.1. INTRODUCTORY ASPECTS 102

4.2. THE PROCESS OF PERSONALIZATION 103

4.3. ESSENTIAL CHARACTERISTICS OF THE PROCESS OF PERSONALIZATION 107

4.4. THE TWO GREAT SUBPROCESSES OF THE PROCESS OF PERSONALIZATION. THE FORMATION OF THE PERSON AL A WHOLE 109

CHAPTER 5. MATURE, FULLY FUNCTIONING AND HUMANE PERSON/PERSONALITY -- THE TARGET OF THE ONTOGENETIC PROCESS OF FORMATION AND DEVELOPMENT. A HUMANISTIC-ONTOLOGICAL MODEL OF THE PERSON & PERSONALITY 119

5.1. INTRODUCTORY ASPECTS 120

5.2. MATURE, FULLY FUNCTIONING AND HUMANE PERSON/PERSONALITY -- THE TARGET OF THE ONTOGENETIC PROCESS OF FORMATION AND DEVELOPMENT 121
5.2.1. MATURE PERSON 121
5.2.2. FULLY FUNCTIONING PERSON 122

5.3. HUMANE PERSONALITY AND HUMANE PERSON 124
5.3.1. HUMANE PERSONALITY 124

5.3.2. HUMANE PERSON 125

**5.4. A HUMANISTIC-ONTOLOGICAL MODEL
OF THE PERSON & PERSONALITY 126**
5.4.1. THE ONTOLOGICAL-PSYCHOLOGICAL SPHERE – THE NEED 127
5.4.2. THE SOCIAL-PERSONAL/ PSYCHOLOGICAL-SOCIAL
SPHERE THE NEED 128
5.4.3.. THE PERSON AS A WHOLE 129

**CHAPTER 6. THE PROCESS OF FORMATION OF THE ONTOLOGICAL-
PSYCHOLOGICAL SPHERE OF THE PERSON 131**

6.1. INTRODUCTORY ASPECTS 132

6.2. THE ONTOLOGICAL-PSYCHOLOGICAL SPHERE OF THE PERSON 135
6.2.1. THE PERSONAL ONTOS 137
6.2.2. THE SOUL 164
6.2.3. THE EGO/SELF 159

6.3. THE FORMATION OF THE PERSONAL ONTOS 161

6.4. THE FORMATION OF THE SOUL 166

6.5. THE FORMATION OF THE EGO 175

**CHAPTER 7. THE ONTOGENETIC PROCESS OF FORMATION OF THE
PSHYCHOLOGICAL-SOCIAL/RELATIONAL SPHERE OF THE PERSON 179**

7.1. INTRODUCTORY ASPECTS 180

7.2. THE PSYCHOLOGICAL-SOCIAL/RELATIONAL SPHERE 181
7.2.1. CONSCIENCE 183
7.2.2. CHARACTER 185
7.2.3 THE SOCIO-HUMAN/ HUMANE SKILLS, COMPETENCIES,
HABITUDES AND CONDUCTS 187

7.3. THE FORMATION OF THE (SOCIAL) CONSCIENCE 188

7.4. THE FORMATION OF CHARACTER 190

**7.5. THE FORMATION OF THE SOCIO-HUMAN/ HUMANE SKILLS,
COMPETENCIES, HABITUDES AND CONDUCTS 192**

CHAPTER 8. THE FORMATION OF THE PERSON AS A WHOLE 195

8.1. INTRODUCTORY ASPECTS 196

8.2. THE PERSON AS A WHOLE 197

**8.3. THE FORMATION OF PERSONALITY AND THE PERSOMIZATION/
HOLISTIZATION OF THE PERSON 202**

**8.4. STAGES IN THE HOLISTIC/ GLOBAL PROCESS OF FORMATION OF THE
PERSON AS A WHOLE 209**

CHAPTER 9. THE INTERNAL JOUISSANCE, THE BEINGNESS AND THE FUNCTIONING OF THE PERSON/ PERSONALITY 213

9.1. INTRODUCTORY ASPECTS 214

9.2. THE HUMANE MOTIVATIONAL SYSTEM, THE JOUISSANCE AND ENERGY OF THE PERSON/ PERSONALITY 215
9.2.1. THE HUMANE MOTIVATIONAL SYSTEM 215
9.2.2. THE HUMANE JOUISSANCE 216
9.2.3. THE HUMANE ENERGY 219

9.3 THE INTERNAL BEINGNESS AND FUNCTIONING OF THE PERSON/ PERSONALITY 220
9.3.1. THE INTERNAL BEINGNESS OF THE PERSON/ PERSONALITY 221
9.3.2. THE INTERNAL FUNCTIONING OF THE PERSON/ PERSONALITY 222

9.4. THE EXTERNAL BEINGNESS AND FUNCTIONING OF THE PERSON/ PERSONALITY 226
9.4.1. THE SOCIO-HUMANE BEHAVIOR OF THE PERSON 227
9.4.2. THE SOCIO-HUMANE ADAPTATION AND
INTEGRATION OF THE PERSON 228

CHAPTER 10. THE DEVELOPMENT/ FULFILLMENT OF THE PERSON/ PERSONALITY. EDUCATION AND THERAPY COUNSELING 229

10.1. INTRODUCTORY ASPECTS 230

10.2. THE DEVELOPMENT AND FULFILLMENT OF THE PERSON/ PERSONALITY 231
10.2.1..THE DEVELOPMENT OF THE PERSON/ PERSONALITY. PERSONAL DEVELOPMENT 231
10.2.2. THE FULFILMENT OF THE PERSON/ PERSONALITY. PERSONAL ACCOMPLISHMENT 232

10.3. THE EDUCATION AND THE THERAPY/ COUNSELING OF THE PERSON/ PERSONALITY 240
10.3.1. HUMANISTIC PEDAGOGY AND EDUCATION 240
10.3.2. HUMANISTIC PSYCHOTHERAPY AND COUNSELING 258

INSTEAD OF CONCLUSIONS 269

1 THE INTRODUCTORY SECTIONS OF THE SUBCHAPTERS 271

2 THE INTRODUCTORY SECTIONS OF THE CHAPTERS 287

REFERENCES AND CONSULTED BIBLIOGRAPHY 297

EDITORIAL NOTE

T his book is published under the aegis of *"The HUMANISTIC PERSONOLOGY Project"*, launched, by the author, with the assumed purpose to contribute to the development – particularly from a humanistic-ontological perspective – of a coherent, unitary and comprehensive theoretical system, representing the human person and personality both structurally and functionally but also genetically, ontogenetically.

Humanistic Personology is defined, in the book with the same title, published in 2015, *"as the theoretical domain/ discipline that researches, theorizes, and represents the person, the human personality, in a complex and ideothetical manner, incorporating knowledge, ideas, theories from the humanistic-existentialist and spiritual-transpersonal spheres of thought/ philosophy and culture, from humanistic psychology, humanistic sociology, and other disciplines, sciences and practices of humanistic orientation/ approach, developing, consequently, a multidisciplinary, interdisciplinary, transdisciplinary and profound humane, spiritual and existential-positive perspective on the individual human phenomenon, on the personal human being, on the human as a individual, individuality, personality and PERSON."*

According to Petru Stefaroi, humanistic personology, as humanistic science of the concrete person, can studies the person, and implicitly the human personality, principally, from the following points of view:

- structurally – internal organization and composition,
- functionally – dynamics, functioning, beingness, networking, etc., and
- genetically – factors and processes of formation.

This new paper of the author focuses on this last aspect, on the factors and the processes that determine, conditionate and favour, ontogenetically, the formation and consolidation of what has been consecrated in literature – as personological concept and theory – Plenary and Accomplished Person.

For this purpose, he operates with a theoretical-psychological and conceptual apparatus with important philosophical valences, proposing an ontological-humanistic model of interpretation and research of the factors, processes, stages, and mechanisms that lead to the formation of the personality and, especially, of the *Person as a Whole.*

The work is carried out – after a technical introduction referring to the situation and the presence of the subject in the context of the contemporary literature – throughout 10 chapters, passing gradually, from an introductory theoretical exposition opener of operational frameworks of analyze to applied and detailed approaches relating to the formation and development of the person/ personality (the humanistic approach and the humanistic-ontological approach), basic sources, factors and conditions, basic characteristics, laws, and principles of the process of formation and development of the person/ personality, the holistic process of personalization.

A particular attention is paid in the book to the great subprocesses of the holistic process of personalization, of formation of mature, fully functioning and humane person/ personality, to the formation of the psychological-social/ relational sphere of the person, and, finally, of formation of the person as a whole, therefore.

Other aspects approached by the author are the beingness, the functioning and the development/ fulfillment of the person/ personality, the education and the therapy/ counseling (in relation to the core theme of the paper).

In the end of the work, it is placed, with summative and conclusive purpose, the introductory sections of the chapters and subchapters.

Regarding **the destination** of this paper, its design, content and bibliography are made in such a way that to be useful both to the academic community, to students and teachers, and also to the professional community, to psychotherapists, educators, managers, social workers, artists, etc.

Happy reading !

INTRODUCTION

Speaking of **Genetic Personology,** it is placed, brought to the foreground not only the factors and the processes of formation of the psychic/ psychological system, so it happens in *Genetic Psychology,* or of the intellect, so it happens in *Genetic Epistemology,* but, especially, the factors and processes of formation, ontogenetical construction of the ***Person.*** In this sense, in this book the defining ontogenetical approach it is the one *humanistic,* with a focus on the *humanistic-ontological* factors and processes, but, also, its specific definition is realized through the opposition to the structural-functionalist and instrumentalist-objectualist paradigm of formation of the person, and personality.

In this sense, Genetic Personology is approached and represented, in the present book, as the theoretical domain/ science that researches, theorizes and represents the processes of formation of the person, of the human personality, in a complex and ideothetical manner, incorporating knowledge, ideas, theories from the humanistic-existentialist and spiritual-ontological spheres of thought/ philosophy and culture, from humanistic genetic psychology, humanistic sociology, and other disciplines, sciences and practices of humanistic orientation/ approach, developing, consequently, a multidisciplinary, interdisciplinary, and profound *humane, spiritual* and *existential-positive* perspective on the complex and profound process of formation, ontogenetical construction of the PERSON.

The humanistic-ontological paradigm prioritizes especially the importance and the processes of formation of the self, of the ego, and of the soul, of the psychological-existential/ experiential, psychological-spiritual- ontological and socio-human factors, in combination with the ones cultural, moral, etc., representing the process as a successive and concomitant, emergent and imergent, phenomenological and ideothetical constructions of personal onto-formations, spheres, etc., and less as a simple activation and enabling of certain existing structures, of certain universal patterns (less variable), recognizing, therefore, the self-determination, the ontogenetical autonomy, the role of the subject and of the will, or the importance of some phenomenological, imergent and emergent psychological-ontological constructions as the ego the and the soul.

Crucial there are, so, in the process of **formation** and **development**, in **the structure/ structuration** and **the beingness/ functioning** of the person/ personality, the unique existential/ ontological experiences of the subject, the feelings, the emotions or the ontological ego and the free will, the existential and the psychological-spiritual factors/ formations (especially the ego and the soul, the self-generative internal dynamics, through culturalization and humanization, through emergence and superization, through spiritual/ human generalization/ abstraction of the psychological-compathetical (socio-humane) subjective experiences.

The processes are of infinite complexity, these transcend the contingent, entail the past and the future, exceeding the spatial and temporal limitations, working simultaneously in the same "space" and time, having unpredictable evolutions, arising, emerging, randomly, some from others.

In this theoretical model of person/ personality the formation, the beingness, and the functioning of any living being imply some properties, processes, laws, characteristics of forming, beingness and functioning, stages, phases, as well as some kinds of energies, mechanisms, resorts which support, "feed", determine, facilitate both the formation as well the beingness or the functioning of some formations, spheres, persoms, or of the person/ personality as a whole.

In contrast to the processes of formation, to the laws, stages and the energetic resorts from the inorganic physical world level the processes of formation, the laws, the steps and the energetic resorts from the biological, psychological, or spiritual world level are of infinite complexity; these transcend the contingent, entail the past and the future, exceeding the spatial and temporal limitations, working simultaneously in the same "space", having unpredictable evolutions, arising, emerging, randomly, some ones from others.

These properties, laws, processes make possible the appearance of new entities, structures, properties etc. from the previous ones, defined as sources, factors, premises, (pre-)conditions, entities which, usually, are more complex and better adapted to the internal and environmental factors; the resulting entities incorporating features of the *source-entities* but are presented yet as new existences, with their own features and ways of relating, adapted also to an environmental context, in turn, usually reformed.

According to these properties/ laws principles the processes of formation, establishment and functioning of the onto-formations, persoms, spheres, etc. transcend the structures, the organizations, and the entities already constituted, they attract and involve them in the processes of forming, constituting and establishing of the new formations, without altering them. The degree of freedom/ action is very large, the number of combinations and the facilities of structuring and "formatization" being almost unlimited. This property/ law is explained, in part, by the structural, generic, and genetic unity/ cohesion of the living and spiritual world, the multiplication to infinit of the informational/ spiritual systems/ entities, and through the extraordinary quality of the living, psychological, noetic and spiritual environments, systems to permit the transcendence.

Despite appearances, these processes, laws, stages, and resorts are, in our opinion, normal, natural dimensions, valences, properties of the objective existence, these do not originate and do not belong to another world, but, still, must to be understood, modeled in a scientific-epistemological framework much wider than permit the rules of the sciences of physicist type, applied, often, almost mechanically to the biological, psychological, and spiritual processes and phenomena.

In the humanistic-ontological paradigm of formation, beingness and functioning of the person/ personality - of the human being - we will speak, therefore, about characteristics, properties, processes, principles such as onto-formatization, persomization and promergence, emergence and imergence, transmergence and telegence, conmergence and sinmergence, about stages of evolution, formation, development, establishment of the personal ontological-psychological formations, of the person as a whole, such as of contact, of acquisition/ accumulation, of structuration/ centralization, of constitution/ holistization, of establishing/ networking, of ontification/ fulfillment, and about ontological-subjective humane and spiritual experiences that represent the main "substance", motivational-energetical sources and resorts of forming of the personality/ person's formations and spheres, driven in mechanisms and assemblies from where the formations are "fed", with genetic/ formative or functional/ existential purpose - some categories of experiences being destined, with a great accuracy, to certain formations.

Regarding the global ontogenetical formation, the structure/ composition, the beingness and the functioning of the person, in this ontological-humanistic paradigm/ theory, we operate mainly with two perspectives.

One it is the systemic-atomistic perspective, in which the person is represented as *a bio-psycho-social system, a unitary assembly of relatively autonomous formations,* the other it is the spherical perspective, where the person is represented as *a multi-spherical bio-psycho-social construction.*

In our paper we will refer/ relate both to the systemic-atomistic perspective, where will do punctual references at every important formation of the personal system/ assembly, respectively the personal ontos, the soul, the ego, personality, and conscience, as well as to the multi-spherical perspective, where we will refer mainly at two major (sub)spheres of the personal macro(sphere), of the person as a whole, respectively the ontological-psychological sphere, and the social-personal/ psychological-social sphere.

So, in the paper, the person, the formation, the structure, and the functioning/ beingness of the person, of the human personality, are conceived and described both as a whole, in relation to the environment as a whole, through the formations and subsystems that compose them, but also through two large (sub)spheres - the ontological-psychological sphere and the psychological-social/ personal-social sphere. Of course, both, the structure/ composition of the ontological psychological sphere, but also of the social-personal sphere, are descriptive constructions with theoretical-epistemological and didactical assumed purpose; actually the personal assembly operating as a unitary/ whole system, entity, being almost impossible to pinpoint spheres, formations that to be or to work, existentially/ ontologically distinctly, or strictly framed in some structures, systems, assemblies, formations, etc. This is the defining characteristics of the ontological approach, of the genetic personology presented in the humanistic-ontological paradigm.

Petru Stefaroi,

2017

CHAPTER 1

GENETIC PERSONOLOGY. FORMATION AND DEVELOPMENT OF THE PERSON/ PERSONALITY -- THE HUMANISTIC APPROACH AND THE HUMANISTIC-ONTOLOGICAL APPROACH

1.1. INTRODUCTORY ASPECTS 18

1.2. PERSONOLOGY, GENETIC PERSONOLOGY AND HUMANISTIC GENETIC PERSONOLOGY 19

1.2.1. PERSONOLOGY. HUMAN BEING. PERSON, PERSONALITY 19

1.2.2. GENETIC PERSONOLOGY 33

1.2.3. GENETIC PERSONOLOGY – THE HUMANISTIC PARADIGM 33

1.3. THE FORMATION AND DEVELOPMENT OF THE PERSON/ PERSONALITY - THE NON-HUMANISTIC AND THE HUMANISTIC APPROACH 34

1.3.1. THE NON-HUMANISTIC APPROACH 34

1.3.2. THE HUMANISTIC APPROACH 35

1.4. THE FORMATION AND DEVELOPMENT OF THE PERSON/ PERSONALITY - A HUMANISTIC-ONTOLOGICAL APPROACH/ THEORY 37

1.4.1. INTRODUCTORY ASPECTS 37

1.4.2. CORE ELEMENTS, CHARACTERISTICS, AND PROCESSES 38

1.4.3. SCIENTIFIC-THEORETICAL, PHILOSOPHICAL, AND CULTURAL SOURCES AND MODELS 54

1.1. INTRODUCTORY ASPECTS

The humanistic paradigm/ way of representation of the person and personality prioritizes the role of the self and of the ego, of the psychological-existential/ experiential, psychological-spiritual/ transpersonal and socio-*humane* factors, in combination with the ones concrete social, cultural, moral factors, representing the process of **formation** of the person as a successive and concomitant, emergent and imergent, phenomenological and ideothetical constructions of personal onto-formations, spheres, etc., and less as a simple activation and enabling of certain existing structures, of certain universal patterns (less variable), recognizing, therefore, the self-determination, the ontogenetical autonomy, the role of the subject, or the importance of some ideographical, imergent and emergent psychological-ontological constructions as the ego, the conscience, or the soul.

Crucial there are, so, in the process of **formation** and **development**, in **the structure/ structuration** and **the beingness/ functioning** of the person/ personality, the unique subjective experiences of the subject, the feelings, the emotions or the ontological ego and the free will, the existential and the psychological-spiritual factors/ formations (especially the ego and the soul – affective, spiritual, humane), the self-generative internal dynamics, through culturalization and humanization, through emergence and superization, through spiritual/ human generalization/ abstraction of the psychological-compathetical (socio-humane) subjective experiences.

1.2. PERSONOLOGY, GENETIC PERSONOLOGY AND HUMANISTIC GENETIC PERSONOLOGY

Core Fragment

Humanistic genetic personology could be defined as the theoretical domain/ discipline that researches, theorizes and represents the processes of formation of the person, of the human personality, in a complex and ideothetical manner, incorporating knowledge, ideas, theories from the humanistic-existentialist and spiritual-transpersonal spheres of thought/ philosophy and culture, from humanistic genetic psychology, humanistic sociology, and other disciplines, sciences and practices of humanistic orientation/ approach, developing, consequently, a multidisciplinary, interdisciplinary, and profound humane, spiritual and existential-positive perspective on the complexe, profound and unique process of formation, ontogenetical construction of the PERSON, theories, means, methods of theHumanistic personology,Humanistic genetic psychology, Positive psychology, Transpersonal psychology, Humanistic sociology, Existential philosophy, Cultural anthropology, etc.

1.2.1. PERSONOLOGY. HUMAN BEING. PERSON, PERSONALITY

Personology, as term, is used, mostly, in/for two epistemological meanings, purposes, goals. One it is that identical with *physiognomy,* which highlights the idea that *the outward appearance, especially the face, is the main means/method to interpret a person's character, personality, conduct.* It is a discipline that has as founders, promoters, and authors names as Johann Kaspar, Lavater Edward Jones, Naomi Tickle, or Yoshito Mizuno. The other, which we adopt especially in this book, in our project, it is the one, simple, of *Science of the Person, of the Personality* (Murray, 2007).

As it was consecrated as theory, especially in psychology, personology is represented, implicitly or explicitly, directly or indirectly, by its founders, theoreticians and practitioners, respectively William Stern, Henry Murray, William James, Mary Whiton Calkins, Abraham Maslow, Gordon Allport, Carl Rogers, and others, as the science, discipline, theoretical and practical area that researches and theorizes the human personality and the person, reflected in a complex and holistic manner, incorporating, therefore, knowledge, ideas, theories from psychology but also from sociology, philosophy, anthropology, and other sciences and domains, developing, therefore, a multidisciplinary and interdisciplinary perspective on the individual human phenomenon, on the personal human being, on the human as individual, individuality, personality, and person.

Speaking, therefore, about *person*-ology we put, in our book, in the foreground not the personality, as it happens in most of the definitions of personology, but *the person,* the person both as subject as well as object, both as concrete existence as well as ideal, where, still, as it was previously mentioned, personality, structurally and compositionally, has a very important role.

As science of the person, personolology can study the person, and implicitly the human personality, ontogenetically - the factors and ways of forming, structurally - the internal organization and composition, as well as functionally and existentially - the dynamics, functioning, beingness, networking; with means, methods of the psychology, sociology, psychosociology, but also of the philosophy, anthropology etc.

What differentiates and particularizes, amongst other things, personology compared to psychology is its concentration on the person as a whole, on the personality as a complex, multidimensional and emergent system (Murray, 2007; Kirsley, 2010).

So, in comparison to psychology which represents, as a consecrated and experimental science, the person and personality in a preponderant technical, analytical and nomological way, through measurable psychological-behavioral characteristics, issues, items, framed in standards of universality and generality (Fiske, 2009, p.24-25), personology, in its authentic definition, represents, as a discipline with profound philosophical origins and valences, the person/ personality in a preponderant ontological, ideographic and holistic way, as a being, as a human being, as unicity.

Another important difference between personology and psychology is that the main object of study of the personology it is the person and personality while psychology mainly investigates the human psyche, the mind (Murray & Clyde, 1953). From the psychology's field personology it is closest of humanistic psychology, having connections also with humanistic social work, humanistic education, humanistic management, etc.

As has been stated, the dominant approach and representation of the person and personality in this book is the one *humanistic,* with a focus on the *humanistic-ontological paradigm,* but its specific definition is realized through the opposition to the structural-functionalist and instrumentalist-objectualist approach/ representation.

Humanistic personology could be defined as the theoretical domain/ discipline that researches, theorizes and represents the person, the human personality, in a complex and ideothetical manner, incorporating knowledge, ideas, theories from the humanistic-existentialist and spiritual-transpersonal spheres of thought/ philosophy and culture, from humanistic psychology, humanistic sociology, and other disciplines, sciences and practices of humanistic orientation/ approach, developing, consequently, a multidisciplinary, interdisciplinary, and profound *humane, spiritual* and *existential-positive* perspective on the individual human phenomenon, on the personal human being, on the human as individual, individuality, personality and PERSON.

The sphere of applicability of the knowledge and solutions that it promotes is very wide but the focus is oriented especially to areas such as therapy, social work, education, management, art, etc. (Rogers, 1977).

Humanistic personology, as humanistic science of the *concrete person* (Murray & Clyde, 1953; Maslow, 1970), can studies the person, and implicitly the human personality, principally, from the following points of view:

> ➢ genetically - factors and the way/ process of forming,

> ➢ structurally - internal organization and composition, and

> ➢ functionally - dynamics, functioning, beingness, networking, etc.

With theories, means, methods of the:

- Humanistic psychology,

- Positive psychology,

- Transpersonal psychology,

- Humanistic sociology,

- Existential philosophy,

- Cultural anthropology, etc.

From the perspective of approach and the sphere of personality which is studied/ investigated with predilection we can talk of:

> Humanistic-Existential/Positive Personology, and,

> Humanistic-Ontological/Spiritual/Transpersonal Personology.

The humanistic-existential/positive personology studies the person/ personality focusing on concepts, paradigms and issues as strong personality, personal development, high level of self-control, optimal experiences, hope and optimism, full consciousness, happiness, well-being, satisfaction (Seligman & Csikszentmihalzi, 2000), resilience, self-determination (Binswanger, 1947), self-efficacy, strength of character, perseverance, creativity, emotional intelligence, positive emotions, sense in life and engagement to a goal, success, performance, professional achievement, etc.

The central concept of the humanistic-existential/ positive personology is *strong personality*, that, in our opinion, is a coherent and durable construction, but also a set of formations of the person/ personality high developed as the ego/ self, the conscience, the abilities, the skills and the behavioral habits - constitutional-structural psychological and intellectual sources of the qualities and the behaviors of adaptation of the person.

Closely linked to the concepts of humanistic-existential/ positive personology and strong personality is the concept of *personal development* (Erikson, 1968).

The humanistic-ontological/spiritual personology - which we approach especially in this work - studies the person/ personality focusing on concepts, paradigms and issues as:

- Humane Development;

- Humane Personality;

- Spirituality;

- Ideographical Approach;

- Soul;

- Ego;

- Ontogenesis;

- Ontology;

- Imergence and Constructionism:

- Altruism;

- Empathy/ Compathie;

- Love;

- Qualitative Methods;

- Introspection;

- Existence in Itself;

- Emergence, Transmergence, Telegence, Conmergence, Sinmergence;

- Chaos Theory, Complex Systems Theory (Bickhard, 2012), etc.

The central concept of the humanistic-ontological (spiritual) personology is *humane/ spiritual personality*, which, in our opinion, is determined of the high development of a set of formations of the person/ personality as the soul (affective/ social, spiritual, humane), the humane ego, the humane consciousness, the humane character, and others – structural-constitutional onto-psychological and intellectual sources of the humane and spiritual traits and behaviors of the person. Closely linked to the concepts of humanistic-ontological personology and humane personality is the concept of *humane/ spiritual development.*

If in the structural-functionalist paradigm, implicitly the one instrumentalist-objectualist, the person is, nomologically, represented, as a mere individual, as a mere element in the social machinery, subjected to the structures and the processes of group, community, society, etc, placing in the background its subjectivity, ego, soul, the particular ontology as existence, as being, as uniqueness, as destiny, in the humanistic personology, the humanistic paradigm, especially the humanistic-ontological personology (paradigm) bring them in the spotlight, articulating a model of person/ personality of humanistic and spiritual type (Maddi & Costa, 1972).

In the assessment activity, in therapy, social work, education etc, the professional will represent the client/ student mainly in terms of undeveloped, disturbed, misappropriated, or unadjusted humane personality, in terms of socio-humane, cultural and morale maladjustment, non-integration, exclusion, marginalization, finding the sources and explications, mainly, therefore, within the compathetical, cultural and moral socio-humane disorders and anomies, within the insufficiently or improperly humanized, cultured, spiritualized personality of the evaluated person.

Even if at first glance the humanistic approach in personology seems somewhat incompatible with the scientific research and methodology in fact their finds can represent very useful knowledge, means and resource. The researches and studies from the broad sphere of personology, particularly of the humanistic personology, use with preference, the qualitative methods, but without disdaining the resources of the quantitative methods.

These researches combine the rigor with the complexity, the general with the particular, leading to more relevant and useful results for the specific characteristics of the psycho-human phenomena and processes, taking both from the rigor of the quantitative methods but also from the deepness, flexibility and comprehensivity of the qualitative methods (Seligman & Csikszentmihalzi, 2000). The main goal of research being that, through analysis, analogies, comparisons, exclusions, similarities, differences, observations of great extension and profoundness, to extract, with great caution, several relevant regularities, to serve eventually to the formulation of some minimal empirical statistical laws, evaluative predictions or intervention projects.

The specifics of the qualitative, interpretative and comprehensive researches is mainly that these focuses largely on capturing the *phenomena* more than the essences, universal laws; the object of observation and investigation being most often the sentiment, the socio-human context, the event, the concrete attitudes, feelings and reactions (Znaniecki, 1969).

The advantage is that through this methodology is obtained the access to psychological and and human aspects which would escape to an eminently positive, nomological, scientific approach, more focused on capturing the structural, universal and repeatable evidences, by modelations of mathematical type (Denzin & Lincoln, 2005).

The philosophical concept, idea, category of **Human Being** is established with two principal meanings

- individuality, personality, uniqueness, entity, subject of existential law, limited temporally and spatially, of determined ego and experience, determined interaction and cohabitation, with the attribute of agency, free will, freedom and responsibility;

- entity, value with the attribute of humanity, spirituality, species and superior existence, having qualities as rationality, intelligence, empathy, altruism, love, creativity, activity, etc.

As is well known, Ontology is the domain of philosophy that has in its center of interest/ research/ knowledge the category of *being, the existence in-itself*. Most often, the domain being opposed to Epistemology, which studies the knowledge in himself and the things mainly scientifically and categorically, opposed to the ontological approach (Reichmann, 1985).

Human Ontology favors the interest for the real, unique, concrete person and social community, with their particular, specific, unique feelings, emotions and socio-human contexts and relationships, imposing an idiographic-empirical/ emergentical paradigm on the human being, whereas Epistemology favors the representation of the human being through universalization, globalization, through scientific categories such as structure, system, function, institution, social control, recurrence, nomological approach.

Ontology has consecrated/ established/ proposed, among others, the paradigmatic ontological triad: *being-existent-existence (being in itself - being for itself - being outside-itself)*.

In humanistic-ontological perspective **the being** (being in itself) of an entity represents the essence, the original content, the invariable, the ontological-metaphysical foundation of the entities, of the existent and of the existence, **the existent/ existing** (being for itself) represents the organization, the concrete form, unique, part of a context, the exposed side of the being, acquiring the characteristics of form of the concrete environment where it exists, while **the existence**, or **the beingness** (being outside-itself), represents the processual, contingental, situational-contextual side, exposed time, dynamic, experiential, the feeling and the thinking. (Maritain, 1956; Hegel, 1977).

In agreement with the metaphysical-ontological paradigm outlined above, regarding the representation of the human being we will consider that ***the ontological-psychological sphere*** (the self, the ego) represents *the being* of the person, ***the psychological-personal***

sphere (the conscience, personality, the skills) represents *the existent/ existing*, while ***the experiential-behavioral sphere*** (the functioning, the beingness, the current life/ activity/ experience of the person, its jouissance, feelings, concrete processual thinking) represents *the existence*.

The humanist-existentialist Ontology favors the interest for the concrete person, for his unique experiences, for his emotions and his concrete social context, imposing a philosophical-theoretical paradigm of ideographic-contextualist and constructivist type, while the humanistic-spiritual Ontology focuses on the inner aspects of the person, on his Self, faith, love, transcendence, immortality, etc., reflected and approached, to a great extent, by qualitative, comprehensive, and intensive paradigms and methodologies, sometimes even from the sphere of meditation, and through transcendental or mystical ways.

In therapies, education, and recuperative social practices, the epistemological foundation in the representation of the person, in the humanistic perspective, it is, in fact, its approach as human being, personality, spiritual being, existing in a complex socio-humane, compathetical system/ community (Frankl, 1976). Therefore, it is required the settlement, in the forefront of the intervention strategies, of the objective of satisfying his psychological-personal and humane and spiritual needs represented as human being.

Humanistic psychotherapy and counseling, humanistic education, humanistic social work, as suggest also the origins of the term *humanism*, in which to the knowledge and science are given a privileged role, closely linked to the idea of human rights, emancipation and affirmation, promotes the scientific training, and, in conclusion, multilateral and complex, of the professional represented but as complex human being.

Associated with the philosophical concept of *human being* are found, very often, in literature, the concepts of **Human Nature, Human Essence**, Person, and Personality, defining categories of the humanistic philosophy, imposing some very prolific dichotomical debates, especially with respect to the classical "dialectical" matter-spirit contradiction, humanistic philosophy, in its large, comprehensive meaning, not having here a rigid positioning, theorizing and promoting both the thesis of materiality (objectivity) of the human being, of the person (the secularist approach), but also the thesis of spirituality (subjectivity) of the human being, person and personality (the idealistic-subjective approach and the spiritualistic/ metaphysical approach) (Reichmann, 1985).

Humanistic personology theorizes and represents **the person** in a complex and ideothetical manner, incorporating knowledge, ideas, theories from the humanistic-existentialist and spiritual-transpersonal spheres of thought/ philosophy and culture, from humanistic psychology, humanistic sociology, and other disciplines, sciences and practices of humanistic orientation/ approach, developing, consequently, a multidisciplinary, interdisciplinary, and profound *humane, spiritual* and *existential-positive* perspective on the individual human phenomenon, on the personal human being, on the human as individual, individuality, personality and PERSON.

As humanistic science of the *concrete person* (Murray & Clyde, 1953; Maslow, 1970), humanistic personology can studies the person genetically - factors and the way/ process of forming; structurally - internal organization and composition, and functionally - dynamics, functioning, beingness, networking, etc., with theories, means, methods of the humanistic philosophy, humanistic psychology, positive psychology, transpersonal psychology, humanistic sociology, existential philosophy, cultural anthropology, spiritual philosophy, etc.

The humanistic-existential/positive personology studies the person focusing on concepts, paradigms and issues as strong person, personal development, high level of self-control, optimal experiences, hope and optimism, full consciousness, happiness, well-being, satisfaction (Seligman & Csikszentmihalzi, 2000), resilience, self-determination (Binswanger, 1947), self-efficacy, strength of character, perseverance, creativity, emotional intelligence, positive emotions, sense in life and engagement to a goal, success, performance, professional achievement, etc.

The central concept of the humanistic-existential/ positive personology is *strong personality*, that, in our opinion, is a coherent and durable construction, but also a set of formations of the person high developed as the ego/ self, the conscience, the abilities, the skills and the behavioral habits - constitutional-structural psychological and intellectual sources of the qualities and the behaviors of adaptation of the person.

Closely linked to the concepts of humanistic-existential/ positive personology and strong person is the concept of *personal development* (Erikson, 1968).

The humanistic-ontological/spiritual personology - which we approach especially in this work - studies the person focusing on concepts, paradigms and issues as Humane Development; Humane Personality; Spirituality; Ideographical Approach; Self; Ego; Ontogenesis; Ontology; Emergence and Constructionism: Altruism; Empathy/ Humanity; Love; Qualitative Methods; Introspection; Existence in Itself; Transmergence, Telegence, Conmergence, Sinmergence; Chaos Theory, Complex Systems Theory (Bickhard, 2012), etc.

If in the structural-functionalist paradigm, implicitly the one instrumentalist-objectualist, the person is, nomologically, represented, as a mere individual, as a mere element in the social machinery, subjected to the structures and the processes of group, community, society, etc, placing in the background its subjectivity, ego, Self, the particular Ontology as existence, as being, as uniqueness, as destiny, in the humanistic personology, the humanistic paradigm, especially the humanistic-ontological personology (paradigm) bring them in the spotlight, articulating a model of person of humanistic and spiritual type (Maddi & Costa, 1972).

The Humanistic Existential/ Positive Approach focuses, especially, on personal development and social adaptation by using the psycho-volitional and cognitive-adaptive resources of the social personality, will and conscience. It highlights and promotes personality traits and qualities such as free will, liberty, autonomy, self-determination, self-realization, optimism, energy, hope, positive thinking, activity, consciousness, responsibility, etc.

This perspective prioritizes the role and the importance of the psychological-social/relational/behavioral sphere/ content of the person, which, in our opinion, includes mostly the social ego, active conscience, and the system of the socio-human aptitudes, skills, competencies, habitudes, conducts.

The humanistic-ontological/ spiritual approach to person highlights especially the inner-ontological psychological-spiritual and psychological-humane sphere/ content of the personality, of the spiritual self, of the Self, their aesthetic, playful, moral or religious resources.

This perspective gives, as is natural, so, to the ontological-spiritual sphere the primary etiological, structural and existential role in formation, structure, beingness and functioning of the person. It highlights and promotes personality traits and qualities such as spirituality, virtue, humanity/ humanness, altruism, empathy, love, faith, etc.

Rogers affirms that, from the humanistic psychology's position, the essential and structural instance and structure of the person is *the self*. He says that the self is an important part of the human existence and experience, and the goal of the personality training and development of each individual should be to determine/ facilitate the client to become *truly him-self* by expressing and developing its inner biological, psychological and spiritual potential, its own authentic self (Rogers, 1980).

Maslow, in the book "Toward A Psychology of Being", published in 1962, reprinted in 2011, indicates an important gap in the academic/ scientific psychology theory and methodology, namely the relatively lack in the scientific representation of the structure and composition of the person of its ontological-spiritual content, of its *Being*.

In psychology the term/ concept **Personality** is used primarily to refer to the ensemble of constant psychological and behavioral characteristics of an individual, of a concrete/ determined person, highlighting, with preference, the aspects of invariability and unity of the behavior in different situations. Some definitions make reference to the dominance/ consistency of certain features, traits, qualities, especially from the temperament and character spheres, in the personal structure and constitution of an individual (Allport, 1961; Maslow, 2011).

The philosophical approaches highlight the importance of the self/ ego as core/ central instances and formations in the internal structure and functioning/ economy of personality (Friedman & Schustack, 2010; McAdams, 2009). This orientation is called as well *ego-psychology*.

Depending on the perspective of approaching, or other criteria, in psychology and philosophy were outlined few major paradigms, theories, and models of personality, among which we note:

- The humanistic paradigm (C. Rogers, G. Allport, R. May, A. Maslow, V. Frankl, H. Murray, etc.);

- The psychodynamic and analytical theory (S. Freud, C. Jung, A. Adler, J. Lacan, etc.);

- The functionalist and behaviorist paradigm (W. James, B.-F Skinner, E. Thorndike, J. Dollard, N. Miller, etc.);

- The structuralist and typological paradigm (R. Cattell, H. Eysenck, K. Leonhard, A. Liciko, W. Sheldon, E. Kretschmer, etc.);

- The cognitive and social-cognitive theory (E. Kelly, J. Atkinson, A. Bandura, W. Mischel, etc.);

- The biological-temperamental theory (M. Zuckerman, E. Kretschmer, Mary K. Rothbart, etc.);

- The cybernetic model, the electronic-virtual model (J. Suler, N. Badler, R. Zheng, etc.), etc.

The structural-functionalist, or cognitive-behavioral approaches and guidelines, in psychology, emphasize, in formation and functioning, either the role of the body structure or the structural neuro-cognitive factors, either that of the structural societal, cultural, educational factors, representing the human personality mostly in a cybernetical way (Zheng, 2012), either as a reflection of the structure and physiology of the body or brain, or as a automatic product of the socio-cultural environment wherein was formed the personality, through learning, imitation and internalization of the dominant/ characteristic social roles and behaviors (Burkitt, 1991), which imprints itself ontogenetically as characteristic patterns of thought and conduct, thus marking constitutionally the structure, dynamics and functioning of the personality.

The structural-functionalist and instrumentalist-objectualist paradigm prioritize the role of the genetic factors, of the body, of the neuro-cognitive factors, in cooperation with the structural social, cultural, educational factors, representing the process of personality and person formation and development as an activation and enabling of certain existing structures, of a less variable social or biological universal pattern, not recognizing the self-determination, the ontogenetic autonomy, the role of the subject, or the importance of certain ideographic psychological-ontological constructions such as the soul or the ego.

Crucial it is so the cognitive and the technical-behavioral process of learning of conducts, roles, models (Burkitt, 1991), of maximal exploitation of the body's resources, of the mind and institutional environment, putting in the background the importance of the subjective (heuristic) experiences, the importance of the feelings, the emotions, or of the will, putting in background the role of the psychological-spiritual factors, of the self-generative internal dynamics, through an autonomous emergence and superization, through compathetical, subjective-experiential, spiritual generalization/ abstraction.

The simplistic, bidimensional, cybernetical, biological, even "electronical" structural-functional and objectual-instrumental representation of the personality, of the human person, propose reductionist, immanent structural and functional models, where prevail formations and instances of biological, material, informational order, where the subject has little freedom, but also less responsibility, where prevail biological and psychological forces as the body and the mind (intellect), also psychological-behavioral functions such as attention, intelligence, technical performance, etc. (McAdams, 2009).

As theoretical-epistemological paradigms/ frameworks/ models the structural-atomistic theories, the general systems theory, and the structural-functionalist theory explains in the most appropriate way that approach of the personality.

In the structural-atomistic theories and the structural-functionalist theories, also in the classical general systems theory's perspective/ light personality is, on the one hand, socially, an invariable element into a system, and, on the other hand, biologically and psychologically, itself a structured system, with dominant attribute s of invariability, generality and universality (Kellerman, 2012).

Instead, the **humanistic representation of personality** is imposed, after our observation, through two main currents/ paradigms/ theories; it is about *the humanistic-existential/positive current/*

paradigm/ theory (Carl Rogers, Abraham Maslow, Rollo May, and others.), and *the humanistic-ontological/spiritual current/ paradigm/ theory* (Thomas Plante, Rosemarie Anderson, Viktor Fankl, Abraham Maslow, and others), speaking, therefore, on the one part, of a

> ➢ *psychology of the ego, consciousness and will,*

and, on the other part, of a

> ➢ *psychology of the spiritual self and of the soul.*

The Humanistic-Existential/Positive Approach/ Paradigm/ Theory of Personality focuses, especially, on personal development and social adaptation by using the psycho-volitional and cognitive-adaptive resources of the ego-personality, will and conscience.

It highlights and promotes personality traits and qualities such as:

> ➢ free will, liberty, autonomy, self-determination, self-realization,
> ➢ optimism, energy,
> ➢ hope, positive thinking,
> ➢ activity, consciousness, responsibility, etc.

The Humanistic-Spiritual/Ontological Approach/ Paradigm/ Theory of Personality highlights especially the inner-ontological psychological-spiritual and psychological-humane content/ valence/ dimension of the personality, of the spiritual self, of the soul, their aesthetic, playful, moral or religious resources. The humanistic-ontological psychological perspective on the personality gives, as is natural, so, to the ontological-spiritual sphere the primary etiological, structural and existential role in formation, structure, beingness and functioning of the person. It highlights and promotes personality traits and qualities such as:

> ➢ spirituality, virtue,

> ➢ humanity/ humanness, altruism,

> ➢ empathy, love,

> ➢ faith, etc.

1.2.2. GENETIC PERSONOLOGY

Speaking about genetic personology we put in the foreground not only the formation of psychic system or personality, so it happens in humanistic (genetic) psychology, or of the intellect, so it happens in genetic epistemology, but, especially, the processes of formation, ontogenetical construction of *the person*; the person both as subject as well as object, both as concrete existence as well as ideal/ project, where, still, personality, ontogenetically, structurally, and functionally, of course, has a very important role.

Therefore, in this book the defining ontogenetical approach is the one *humanistic*, with a focus on the *humanistic-ontological processes*, but its specific definition is realized through the opposition to the structural-functionalist and instrumentalist-objectualist paradigm of the formation of the person/ personality.

1.2.3. GENETIC PERSONOLOGY – THE HUMANISTIC PARADIGM

Humanistic Genetic Personology could be defined as the theoretical domain/ discipline that researches, theorizes and represents the processes of formation of the person, of the human personality, in a complex and ideothetical manner, incorporating knowledge, ideas, theories from the humanistic-existentialist and spiritual-transpersonal spheres of thought/ philosophy and culture, from humanistic genetic psychology, humanistic sociology, and other disciplines, sciences and practices of humanistic orientation/ approach, developing, consequently, a multidisciplinary, interdisciplinary, and profound *humane, spiritual* and *existential-positive* perspective on the complexe, profound and unique process of formation, ontogenetical construction of the PERSON, theories, means, methods of the:

- Humanistic personology,
- Humanistic genetic psychology,
- Positive psychology,
- Transpersonal psychology,

- Humanistic sociology,

- Existential philosophy,

- Cultural anthropology, etc.

1.3. THE FORMATION AND DEVELOPMENT OF THE PERSON/ PERSONALITY - THE NON-HUMANISTIC AND THE HUMANISTIC APPROACH

Core Fragment

The humanistic paradigm/ way of representation of the person and personality prioritizes the role of the self and of the ego, of the psychological-existential/ experiential, psychological-spiritual/ transpersonal and socio-humane factors, in combination with the ones concrete social, cultural, moral, etc., representing the process of **formation** *of the person as a successive and concomitant, emergent and imergent, phenomenological and ideothetical constructions of personal onto-formations, spheres, etc., and less as a simple activation and enabling of certain existing structures, of certain universal patterns (less variable), recognizing, therefore, the self-determination, the ontogenetical autonomy, the role of the subject, or the importance of some ideographical, imergent and emergent psychological-ontological constructions as the ego, the conscience, or the soul.*

1.3.1. THE NON-HUMANISTIC APPROACH

The structural-functionalist and instrumentalist-objectualist paradigm prioritize the role of the genetic factors, of the body, of the neuro-cognitive factors, in cooperation with the structural social, cultural, educational factors, representing the process of personality and person formation and development as an activation and enabling of certain existing structures, of a less variable social or biological universal pattern, not recognizing the self-determination, the ontogenetic autonomy, the role of the subject, or the importance of certain ideographic psychological-ontological constructions such as the soul or the ego.

Crucial it is so the cognitive and the technical-behavioral process of learning of conducts, roles, models (Burkitt, 1991), of maximal exploitation of the body's resources, of the mind and institutional environment, putting in the background the importance of the subjective (heuristic) experiences, the importance of the feelings, the emotions, or of the will, putting in background the role of the psychological-spiritual factors, of the self-generative internal dynamics, through an autonomous emergence and superization, through compathetical, subjective-experiential, spiritual generalization/ abstraction.

The simplistic, bidimensional, cybernetical, biological, even "electronical" structural-functional and objectual-instrumental representation of the personality, of the human person, propose reductionist, immanent structural and functional models, where prevail formations and instances of biological, material, informational order, where the subject has little freedom, but also less responsibility, where prevail biological and psychological forces as the body and the mind (intellect), also psychological-behavioral functions such as attention, intelligence, technical performance, etc. (McAdams, 2009).

As theoretical-epistemological paradigms/ frameworks/ models the structural-atomistic theories, the general systems theory, and the structural-functionalist theory explains in the most appropriate way that approach of the person/ personality.

In the structural-atomistic theories and the structural-functionalist theories, also in the classical general systems theory's perspective/ light the person/ personality is, on the one hand, socially, an invariable element into a system, and, on the other hand, biologically and psychologically, itself a structured system, with dominant attributes of invariability, generality and universality (Kellerman, 2012).

1.3.2. THE HUMANISTIC APPROACH

The humanistic paradigm/ way of representation of the person and personality prioritizes the role of the self and of the ego, of the psychological-existential/ experiential, psychological-spiritual/ transpersonal and socio-*humane* factors, in combination with the ones concrete social, cultural, moral, etc., representing the process of **formation** of the person as a successive and concomitant, emergent and imergent, phenomenological and ideothetical constructions of personal onto-formations, spheres, etc., and less as a simple activation and enabling of certain existing structures, of certain universal patterns (less variable), recognizing, therefore, the self-determination, the ontogenetical autonomy, the role of the subject, or the importance of some ideographical, imergent and emergent psychological-ontological constructions as the ego, the conscience, or the soul.

Crucial there are, so, in the process of **formation** and **development**, in **the structure/ structuration** and **the beingness/ functioning** of the person/ personality, the unique subjective experiences of the subject, the feelings, the emotions or the ontological ego and the free will, the existential and the psychological-spiritual factors/ formations (especially the ego and the soul – affective, spiritual, humane), the self-generative internal dynamics, through culturalization and humanization, through emergence and superization, through spiritual/ human generalization/ abstraction of the psychological-compathetical (socio-humane) subjective experiences.

As theoretical-epistemological paradigm/ framework/ model, **the emergent systems theory** explains in the most appropriate way the ontological-humanistic approach to the person/ personality.

In the emergent systems theory's perspective/ light the person/ personality is, on the one hand, socially, a variable and dynamic element into a system, and, on the other hand, biologically and psychologically, is itself a dynamic and emergent system, with dominant attributes of variability, particularity and unicity (Bickhard, 2012).

The central ideas of the emergent systems theory in humanistic personology it is that the person/ personality (particularly the soul and the ego), is an existential product and not an ancestral given.

The process of ontogenetical formation of the person/ personality combines, synthesizes through emergence, in a unique, irrepetible way, the three great, fundamental factors:

- the organism,
- the mind, and
- the socio-human/ humane environment.

The processes are of infinite complexity, these transcend the contingent, entail the past and the future, exceeding the spatial and temporal limitations, working simultaneously in the same "space" and time, having unpredictable evolutions, arising, emerging, randomly, some from others.

1.4. THE FORMATION AND DEVELOPMENT OF THE PERSON/ PERSONALITY - A HUMANISTIC-ONTOLOGICAL APPROACH/ THEORY

Core Fragment

In our ontological-humanistic paradigm of formation, beingness and functioning of the person/ personality - of the human being - we will speak, therefore, about characteristics, properties, processes, principles such as onto-formatization, persomization and promergence, emergence and imergence, transmergence and telegence, conmergence and sinmergence, about stages of evolution, formation, development, establishment of the personal ontological-psychological formations, of the person as a whole, such as of contact, of acquisition/ accumulation, of structuration/ centralization, of constitution/ holistization, of establishing/ networking, of ontification/ fulfillment, and about ontological-subjective humane and spiritual experiences that represent the main "substance", motivational-energetical sources and resorts of forming of the personality/ person's formations and spheres, driven in mechanisms and assemblies from where the formations are "fed", with genetic/ formative or functional/ existential purpose - some categories of experiences being destined, with a great accuracy, to certain formations.

1.4.1. INTRODUCTORY ASPECTS

The theoretical **MODEL OF PERSON/ PERSONALITY** that it is used in this paper, developed by us, greatly during the last fifteen years, respectively **HUMANIST-ONTOPERSONOLOGICAL**, wherein *the personal ontos, the soul, and the humane/ spiritual personality* and *development* have central roles, has been used before in other our paper appearances, respectively in the books "Humane & Spiritual Qualities of the Professional in Humanistic Social Work: Humanistic Social Work - The THIRD WAY in Theory and Practice", 2014, CreateSpace, Charleston SC, Amazon.com Company, USA, and "The Happiness Theory in Social Work: From Care Management to Happiness Management", (title translated, here, from Romanian in English), Lumen Pubthelishing House, 2009, but also in paper articles such as "Humanistic Perspective on Customer in Social Work", nr. 1-2,

2009, "Socio-Affective Development Disorders of Institutionalized Child. From the Survival Objective towards the Happiness Objective in Social Work for Children", nr. 1-2, 2008, published in *Social Work Review* (Faculty of Sociology and Social Work - University of Bucharest), published by Polirom Publishing House (titles translated, here, from Romanian in English), as well in electronic appearances and eBooks grouped and published, the most significant, in three collections, namely: "Psychology and Humanistic Social Work Electronic Collection", "Sociology and Humanistic Social Work Electronic Collection", and "Philosophy and Humanistic Social Work Electronic Collection". Among these works we mention: "Humanistic Social Work Theories and Methods: Personality – Core Resource of Practice", and "Spiritual Qualities of the Professional in Humanistic Social Work Practice". The vast majority of the works were taken and displayed by bookstores, libraries, Websites from the virtual space.

1.4.2. CORE ELEMENTS, CHARACTERISTICS, AND PROCESSES

In this theoretical model of person/ personality, that we use in the paper and project, the formation, the beingness, and the functioning of any living being imply some **PROPERTIES, PROCESSES, LAWS, CHARACTERISTICS of forming, beingness and functioning, stages, phases,** as well as some kinds of **energies, mechanisms, resorts** which support, "feed", determine, facilitate both the formation as well the beingness or the functioning of some formations, spheres, persoms, or of the person/ personality as a whole.

In contrast to the processes of formation, to the laws, stages and the energetic resorts from the inorganic physical world level the processes of formation, the laws, the steps and the energetic resorts from the biological, psychological, or spiritual world level are of infinite complexity; these transcend the contingent, entail the past and the future, exceeding the spatial and temporal limitations, working simultaneously in the same "space", having unpredictable evolutions, arising, emerging, randomly, some ones from others.

These properties, laws, processes make possible the appearance of new entities, structures, properties etc. from the previous ones, defined as sources, factors, premises, (pre-)conditions, entities which, usually, are more complex and better adapted to the internal and environmental factors; the resulting entities incorporating features of the *source-*

entities but are presented yet as new existences, with their own features and ways of relating, adapted also to an environmental context, in turn, usually reformed.

According to these properties/ laws principles the processes of formation, establishment and functioning of the onto-formations, persoms, spheres, etc. transcend the structures, the organizations, and the entities already constituted, they attract and involve them in the processes of forming, constituting and establishing of the new formations, without altering them. The degree of freedom/ action is very large, the number of combinations and the facilities of structuring and "formatization" being almost unlimited. This property/ law is explained, in part, by the structural, generic, and genetic unity/ cohesion of the living and spiritual world, the multiplication to infinit of the informational/ spiritual systems/ entities, and through the extraordinary quality of the living, psychological, noetic and spiritual environments, systems to permit the transcendence.

Despite appearances, these processes, laws, stages, and resorts are, in our opinion, normal, natural dimensions, valences, properties of the objective existence, these do not originate and do not belong to another world, but, still, must to be understood, modeled in a scientific-epistemological framework much wider than permit the rules of the sciences of physicist type, applied, often, almost mechanically to the biological, psychological, and spiritual processes and phenomena.

In our ontological-humanistic paradigm of formation, beingness and functioning of the person/ personality - of the human being - we will speak, therefore, about characteristics, properties, processes, principles such as onto-formatization, persomization and promergence, emergence and imergence, transmergence and telegence, conmergence and sinmergence, about stages of evolution, formation, development, establishment of the personal ontological-psychological formations, of the person as a whole, such as of contact, of acquisition/ accumulation, of structuration/ centralization, of constitution/ holistization, of establishing/ networking, of ontification/ fulfillment, and about ontological-subjective humane and spiritual experiences that represent the main "substance", motivational-energetical sources and resorts of forming of the personality/ person's formations and spheres, driven in mechanisms and assemblies from where the formations are "fed", with genetic/ formative or functional/ existential purpose - some categories of experiences being destined, with a great accuracy, to certain formations.

Regarding **the global ontogenetical formation, the structure/ composition, the beingness and the functioning of the person**, in our ontological-humanistic paradigm/ theory, in the book and project, we operate mainly with **two perspectives**.

One it is the **SYSTEMIC-ATOMISTIC PERSPECTIVE**, in which the person is represented as *a bio-psycho-social system, a unitary assembly of relatively autonomous formations*. The other it is **THE SPHERICAL PERSPECTIVE**, where the person is represented as *a multi-spherical bio-psycho-social construction*.

In our paper we will refer/ relate both to the systemic-atomistic perspective, where will do punctual references at every important formation of the personal system/ assembly, respectively the **personal ontos, the soul, the ego, personality**, and **conscience**, as well as to the multi-spherical perspective, where we will refer mainly at two major (sub)spheres of the personal macro(sphere), of the person as a whole, respectively

1) the ontological-psychological sphere, and

2) the social-personal/ psychological-social sphere.

So, in the paper and the project, the person, the formation, the structure, and the functioning/ beingness of the person, of the human personality, are conceived and described both as a whole, in relation to the environment as a whole, through the formations and subsystems that compose them, but also through two large (sub)spheres, nominated above - therefore the ontological-psychological sphere and the psychological-social/ personal-social sphere.

Of course, both, the structure/ composition of the ontological psychological sphere, but also of the social-personal sphere, are descriptive constructions with theoretical-epistemological assumed purpose; actually the personal assembly operating as a unitary whole/ system, being almost impossible to pinpoint spheres, formations that to be or to work distinctly, or strictly framed in some structures, systems, assemblies, etc.

The two major sub-spheres of the person reflect two relatively distinct existential statuses, fundamental characteristics, needs and realities of every being, the more of the *human* being: *to be, to exist, on the one hand, in itself, inside, in its own bio-psychic and spiritual world*, and, on the other hand, *to exist outside, in environment, in community, culture, nature, among people, values, rules, institutions, etc.*

For each one, ontogenetically, are being built and function specific structures, spheres, constructions, formations, even if, as we have seen above, one cannot speak of rigid boundaries or locations, clearly distinct - these coexisting, transmergently, in the wide, large framework of the person/ personality as a dynamic, functional system, as a whole.

The formation, **the structure, the beingness, and the functioning of the ONTOLOGICAL-PSYCHOLOGICAL SPHERE** reflects principally three cardinal needs of the person: 1) of interior good, pleasure, happiness, security, existence, beingness, continuity, 2) of compathetical coexistence among people, humans, in communities and culture, 3) of self/inner-accomplishment - comprising so, as responses at these needs, three great ontological-psychological formations: *the personal ontos* (the hedonic ontos, the phobic ontos-formation, the projective ontos, the prosentic ontos-formation, the malsentic ontos-formation), *the soul* (the compathetic ontos, the affective/ social/ interpersonal soul, the spiritual soul, the humane soul), and *the ego* (the self and the ontic subject/ ego, the onto-projective and the spiritual ego).

So, into the ontological psychological sphere of the person three great formations are essential: the personal ontos, that could be considered "the being" of the person, the soul, that can be represented as the formation which represents/ reflects, psychological-ontologically, the other's interest and feelings in the person's internal jouissance, economy and functioning, and the self / the ontic ego, that represents/ reflects, psychological-ontologically, the inner's interest and feelings in the subject's internal jouissance, economy and functioning.

The personal ontos, in its broad and comprehensive acceptation, comprises, mainly ontos-formation as the hedonic ontos and the phobic ontos-formation, the projective ontos, the prosentic ontos-formation and the malsentic ontos-formation, but also, in its large acceptance, the soul and the ego/ self. The soul and the ego will be presented, due to the importance and very great weight, but also because of the fact that they have a great degree of autonomy, separated, in distinct sections in the book.

The personal ontos, this ontic-metaphysical "medium" cannot be located, nor technically delimited, because of the fact that it is not an existent and do not actually exists, it is, however, the *sphere of the being* – "space" where it is established the indetermination, and it is, ultimately, the metaphysical source of the intentionality and liberty, it is a prime foundation, principle, element of the person which gives ontological-psychological "substance" to the person. The sensation and the internal bio-psychological living are not content of the personal ontos, nor forms of manifestation, but the specific internal environment of existence, source, "feed".

The personal ontos is the place, the frame, the source, the environment, the premise of forming and beingness of some of the most important formations and constitutional spheres of the person, especially of the soul and the ego; the soul, as experiential "internalizing" of the other (person, value etc.), and the ego, as experiential "internalizing" of the ontic and social self, of the socialized subject.

Regarding **the soul**, in the book, and the project, we see, define it, in a simple representation, as a *set of psychological-ontological formations, ontogenetically formed and established, in the context of some objective premises and factors such as the human body, sensations, feelings, needs, subjective and social experiences, the natural and cultural context, and, especially, of some factors such as the characteristics of the nearest persons, the continuity and consistency of the social interactions, of the particular human/ humane relationships of attachment, communication, coexistence, love.* In other words, the main source of forming and functioning of the person's soul is THE MAN/ HUMAN, with all the bio-psychological-anthropological, cultural-historical, and natural-contextual systems that implies, involves, includes it. Therefore, in our view, the soul is not necessarily something metaphysical, though, probably, it has and such dimensions or interferences, but an existential very deep and complex spiritual-objective entity/ instance/ formation of the individual human being, alongside the body, personality, self/ ego, conscience, character or intellect, representing, in this context, what one might call *the place, the source, and the personal-psychological receptor, recipient of the feelings, of social and spiritual emotions, particularly human.*

Depending on their nature, location or source one can speak of sub-spheres such as *affective (social) soul, spiritual soul, humane soul,* etc.; the affective (social) soul determining the attachment, social sensitivity and interpersonal/ contingent empathy, the spiritual soul determining the spiritual richness and virtue, and the humane soul determining empathy/ compathy and humanity/ humaneness/ humanism, the human/ transhuman solidarity/ unity. The soul, as sphere, content, cumulates/ unites/ synthesizes, psychological-ontologically, the subjective-sensorial experiences with those intellectual and socio-affective, generating superior miraculous unique emergent psychical-spiritual phenomena as well the passions, loves, faiths, the altruism, the empathy, the authentic happiness, the virtue - characteristics only of the human being. All of these must to have a place in the sphere of personality/ person, from where to come, to originate, to be produced by something - that *something* can only be, thus, primarily, the soul, the human soul.

Thus, by forming the soul each person assimilates, internalizes, emergentely, transmergentely and subjective-experientially, potentially, the whole human, personal/ psychological, social, cultural experience of the humanity (community), the ancestral matrix of the human being, of the generalized other, acquiring, just so, the supreme quality of MAN, HUMAN, the psychological-ontological belonging to the HUMAN community, with the well known existential characteristics that differentiates it to the other modes of existence, facilitating, indirectly, mediated, also, the access to the experience (pain, happiness, etc.) of the other, concrete or generalized, generating inexhaustible psychological resources for social adaptation and helping others through the qualities they imprint to personality and behavior such as empathy, spirituality, virtue, happiness and eudaimonical-altruistic energy/ motivation, humanity, agreeableness, optimism, enthusiasm, sociability, altruism, etc.

Another crucial part of the psychological-ontological sphere of the person, as we have seen, it is **the ego, the self**. According to the humanistic-ontological perspective, the ego, in a simple interpretation, is the projection of the subject's (humane and spiritual) needs and jouissance in the subject's cognition and conscience. It can also be represented as a synthesis of ontological-subjective formations constitutionally oriented to the self, but being also a product of the interaction whit the (social) environment, community, society, values, where there are many of the resources and means by which the subject can fulfill it both psychologically and socially.

If the soul, as we have seen above, is a set of psychological-ontological formations, ontogenetically formed and established, in the context of some, mostly, *external* objective premises and factors the ego can be represented as a set of psychological-ontological formations, ontogenetically formed and established, in the context of some, mostly, *internal* objective premises and factors.

In humanistic personology very important is the *humane ego*, which, in the internal economy and structure of the personality, meets both ontological and instrumental functions. Essentially, the ontological-noetic content of the humane ego is supported by perceptual-attitudinal patterns like: "I'm a man"; "1 belong to humanity"; "the common good is also my good, and vice versa"; "I'm a good man"; "I'm selfless, generous"; "I am perceived as an altruistic citizen"; "I have dominant traits and conducts such as tolerance, compassion, humanness"; "I am happy through the happiness of the others, and vice versa "; "I like to help, to be useful", etc.

As we have seen, the main role, function, aim of the ontological-psychological sphere is so to ensure, to confer the fundamental, constitutional, ontological support of the person - to be, to exist in itself, inside, in its own bio-psychic and spiritual world, to maintain and ensure the link with the biological, ancestral and metaphysical worlds of the person, even if through socialization, culturalization, humanization the ontological-psychological sphere acquires a great opening, orientation to the exterior, values, rules, institutions, organizations, people, to the concrete, actual (socio-cultural) environment where the person lives, coexists.

So, despite appearances, the ontological-psychological sphere of the person is not a simple extension, product or emanation of the existence and functioning of the body; it exists in the general context of the personal structure, economy and functioning under the influence/ determination of the environmental factors, in the conditions of the internal action of the emergence, transmergence, telegence, sinmergence, conmergence, imergence principles/ laws/ properties; it could be represented also as a distemporalizat space and, relatively, protected of the action of the so-called *objective* (mechanical) laws; the biological and psychological elements and structures can be easily translated noetically, spiritually or sympathetically, and vice versa; the possibilities of transformation and combination becoming practically limitless.

The process of formation of the ontological-psychological sphere of the person/ personality includes mainly the formation of the personal ontos, of the soul, and the ego/self, through the processes of ontosfication, spiritualization, individualization, and holistization/ persomization, while, as we will be seen below, the formation of the social-personal, psychological-social sphere of the person, of the person as a whole, is conditioned mainly by the formation of the (social) conscience (comscience, culture, the humane conscience), character, and (social) competences, skills, abilities, qualities and habitudes, through the process of social autonomization through profession, own family, and community life, etc.

The entire **process** begins from the ***formation of the personal ontos***, from the permanentization of some profound, fundamental constitutional-ontological structure of the person, from the establishment of some formations, instances with great ontological-psychological consistency as the soul and the ontological ego - as we have seen the soul as experiential "internalizing" of the other (person, value etc.) jouissance, and the ego as experiential "internalizing" of the internal, inner, jouissance and needs, of the ontic and social self.

The process implies, in addition to the formation of the personal ontos as formation, as a whole, also the formation of some constitutional component formations, or very dependent to the personal ontos. Mainly it is about the processes of formation of the hedonic ontos, of the phobic ontos-formation, of the projective ontos, of the prosentic ontos-formation, of the malsentic ontos-formation, of the soul (the compathetic ontos, the affective/ social soul, the spiritual soul - mystical, intellectual, playful, aesthetical, ethical, the humane soul), of the ontic subject/ ego, the projective ego and the spiritual ego, the humane ego, etc.

In the complex, profound and long process of ontosfication crucial roles have the inner activity of the organism, of the mind and of the environment, especially the socio-human and cultural environment. So, crucial roles have the central nervous system, the sensitive jouissance, the endocrine system, the neuro-vegetative apparatus, the mechanisms of production, storage, processing and superization of the emotions, and more.

In the process of forming of the personal ontos and its sub-formations the *emergence* is the quality/ capacity/ property of the processes that makes possible the appearance of new entities, structures, properties etc. from the previous ones, defined as sources, factors, conditions. The emergence generates new realities and qualities. Usually the new entities are more complex and better adapted to the environmental factors. The *imergence* represents the property and capacity of the process of ontosfication to forming, developing, evolving it in themselves, in itself, from nothing, of inertia, "subversively", simultaneously with the developments, evolutions, changes caused by the determined, objective identified factors.

Transmergence represents the property and capacity of the processes to carry out without limitations and physical barriers of space and organization. while telegence means much the same thing, but concerns the temporal aspect of the processes of formation, bengness and functioning.. *Conmergence* entails the transmergence, the telegence, the imergence and the promergence and represents the tendency of the processes to organize, function and concentrate it "thematically" in ontos-formations, ontos-structures, etc., reflecting the inherence of some functions, beyond any limitations of "logistic" or temporal order. *Sinmergence* is the quality/ capacity/ property of the ontological-psychological processes which makes possible the coexistence, simultaneously, of some ontos-personal entities in the same personal "space", the functioning and beingness of some distinct ontos-entities, structures, relationships, processes on/ through the same material, biological, informational, spiritual support.

These properties, laws, principles characterize/ determine also **the process of formation of the soul, the process of spiritualization**. The soul formation, establishment and beingness in the structure, the composition of personality is an objective necessity, the soul being constitutional, ancestral, genetic, and emblematic part of the being, of the human/ humane personality, mainly through its adaptive function, through the experiential-ontological internalization of the social-contextual, spiritual-cultural, and human-existential environmental characteristics.

The humanization of the soul, of the personality, and, by this, the humanization of the person as a whole, is, so, an emergent holistic integrator process more pronounced in people/ professionals that, through the specific activity, should engage or work with/or for broad categories of people, especially in difficulty, in formation, crisis etc., such as the teachers, the workers in social, political, cultural areas, the artists, the priests, etc.

Constitutionally, the soul is formed in the general context of the existence and functioning of the specific human organism, in the overall process of forming and developing of personality, under the influence of the environmental factors and internal action of the principles/ laws of emergence, imergence, transmergence, telegence, conmergence, etc.

The gradual process of forming of the soul passes through the following stages: of contact; of acquisition/ accumulation; of structuration; of constitution; of institution/ establishment in the constitution of the personality; and, finally, of endemization/ ontification.

The soul formation process is not automatically, simple and linear, through the mere presence of the body in the socio-human environment, in society and culture. The biological, sensorial, cognitive, affective experiences, the successes, failures and traumas marks significantly the process, the structure, organization, architecture/ composition and orientation (hedonic, emotional, social, intellectual, spiritual, artistic, religious, etc.) of the soul.

In this respect, the strong, deep, altruistic, humane personality is described also in the context of a consistent and structurally balanced soul - this becoming a fundamental source of spiritual, moral, humane energy for the person, also for the ontogenetic process of developing of the personality as a whole.

The interaction with the other real person, dear, with the nearest persons, with the significant groups, with the near physical/ objectual environment leads to the formation of the affective (social) soul, also to the personal system/ relationships of attachments, reflecting the personal contingental interaction, and appurtenance of the person to the group or to the particular socio-human context.

The interaction with the world of spirit, culture, education, art, etc., leads, by the mental and soulful capacity of idealization, projectivity, symbolization, and superior emotional resonance to the formation of the spiritual soul, to virtue and spirituality as personal qualities.

The mental, emotional, and spiritual interaction with the universal, the generalized, the concept other, with the "status" other, by mental and soulful facilities of generalization, idealization, projectivity, symbolization, abstractization, through superior emotional resonance leads to the formation of the humane soul and to the empathy, empathetic capacity of the person. It reflects the abstract interaction and affiliation of the person to society, humanity, as well as his human condition and nature. Once being established, the soul works like all the other formations, but will need of affective, spiritual and humane experiences, feelings, sentiments in order to exist, to be, to function.

A crucial **subprocess** of the great process, general, of personalization is the one **of individualization and of formation of the ego**. The formation of the ego and the individualization are a necessity, together with the processes of culturalization and humanization, with which it completes and interacts, even if, at least in the psychoanalytic perspective, they are somewhat opposite; the processes of culturalization and humanization are guided by the other's interests, the common good, while the individualization process is guided by the personal-endemic motivational resorts, by the individual intrinsic jouissance, by the impulse and unconscious, by the self.

Regarding **of the SOCIAL-PERSONAL / PSYCHOLOGICAL-SOCIAL SPHERE OF THE PERSON, its structure, beingness and functioning** reflect principally the needs and functions of the person *to exist outside, in environment, in community, culture, nature, among people, values, rules, institutions, etc.* For their meeting, fulfillment, ontogenetically, are being built, and function specific formations, structures, spheres, constructions; even if, as we have seen, one cannot speak of rigid boundaries or locations, clearly distinct, coexisting, transmergently, in the wide, large framework of the person/ personality as a dynamic, functional system, as a whole.

The social/ humane ego incorporates the need, the tendency, the quality of the self, subject, ego of role-statuses, the need, the tendency to adapt at the social/ human/ environmental/ community characteristics; the conscience reflects the need/ function of the person to reflect, assimilate, knowledge, unitarily, epistemological-axiologically, the world, the community, the other, the culture, the society, the history, the mankind, the people, etc.; the character reflects the need/ function of the personality/ person to have a structure, a unitary organization, reflecting in the same time, simultaneously, axiologically, the structure of the interior ontological-psychological world and the structure of the exterior world, especially the one socio-cultural; the socio-human aptitudes, skills, competencies, habitudes, conducts reflects the need of the personality/ person to have a system of relational-behavioral instruments/ facilities/ means with which to can have psychological-human and social relations/ interactions with the (social) environment, with the other, with people, etc.

In our paradigm, ontological-humanistic, of the person/ personality, **the social/ humane ego** represents, mostly, the projection of the (social/ human) other's image and jouissance in the subject' cognition and jouissance. It is a syntesis/ conmergence of subjective, mental and emotional, formations constitutionally oriented both to the inside and to the outside, where there are many of the resources and means by which the subject can fulfill it psychological-ontologically and socially - the social ego having a great link with the person's roles and statuses.

The (social/ human/ humane) conscience could be considered the reflexive-intellectual-axiological "being" of the person. It is the synthetic, conmergent intellectual reflectation of the (social/ human) generalized other in the ego's cognition and thinking. The (social/ human/ humane) conscience is so an ensemble of epistemological-reflexive-axiological formations constitutionally oriented to the outside, the generalized other.

The (social/ humane) character can be represented as the personal macro-structure which reflects, psychologically-attitudinally, the generalized other's interests, needs and feelings in the person's internal jouissance, economy, thinking, functioning, and behavior, being, so, in a large interpretation, a product of the interaction between ego and conscience.

The socio-human aptitudes, skills, competencies, habitudes, conducts represents the system of relational-behavioral instruments of the person, the praxeological-technical relation with the (social) environment/ other.

Just like at the ontological-psychological sphere level, at the social/ personal sphere level the social/ humane ego, the conscience, the character, the socio-human aptitudes, competencies, skills, abilities, qualities, habitudes exist and operate together and interdependently, forming, in the great frame of the personal ensemble, a structural-functional unity. Also, these can be represented as an operationalization of the ontological-psychological sphere, of its elements, of the personal ontos, of the soul, of the ego, at the level of person, in relation with the (social) environment.

The main *role, function, aim* of the personal-social sphere is to ensure, to confer the psychological-axiological and psychological-praxeological tools to person in relation with the (social) environment, to be, to exist in outside, in the natural, human and socio-cultural world, to maintain and ensure the link with the world of people, values, institutions, rules, with the communities where the person lives, coexists. So, the social-personal sphere can be represented also as a link between the ontological-psychological world of the person, its authentic/ irreducible existence, and the socio-human environment where there are its "food", means, resources and resorts of existence, survival, love, happiness, fulfillment, etc.

Regarding **the formation of the social-personal / psychological-social sphere of the person,** here, must to be highlighted the crucial contribution of the environmental, socio-cultural, factors.

The essence of the humanistic-ontological conception regarding the person/ the human personality is given by the idea that these are ontological products of some gradual and stadial processes held with the crucial contribution of the concrete/ contextual/ contingent socio-human, cultural and institutional factors where the person grows and lives. Very important are also the personal-human/ humane factors, with the crucial contribution of the individual persons, concrete people from the proximate environment with intense and constant psychological-moral presence and influence, especially the significant members from its family/ significant group. Important are so the socio-cultural factors. Therefore, even if in the child rearing are important the material conditions, the organism, still the socio-human/ humane, cultural and moral conditions are, in fact, those that contribute crucially to the formation of a harmonious social personality, fulfilled and, socio-humanly, effective.

Each of the two major spheres of the person, is, as we have seen, the product of the interaction of the subject with specific factors, even if cannot be traced strict boundaries between them. The social, cultural, institutional, morale conditions of learning and training are, therefore, essential for the formation of the social-personal sphere.

In humanistic personology, the humanistic-ontological perspective on the person, the micro-community, the family, in special, is very important, even crucial factor in the formation and beingness of the person, especially through their human and personal compathetical dimensions. In this perspective each member of a community is a product of a unique interaction, depending on the personalities of the others, the place, time, cultural niche, hazard. Each person is so actually part of a particular compathetical system. This is, in turn, part of a comprehensive system. The most common compathetic system and most consistent is the family. This empathetic community works, through its organizational-compathetical culture, as a system of symbols or values that are rooted in the individuals' personalities (souls) or activism. These symbols and values are imposed as links and unitary resorts between the two parties. Their existence and function give the sense of belonging, familiar, known, give comfort, safety and happiness. Between the empathetic community and the individuals which it constitutes it is established an ontological-socio-human balance, an existential and functional optimum, in which is satisfied, in principle, in a harmonious and non-confrontational way, both the personal and the collective necessities.

The empathetic community and the compathy, as common, collective background of feelings and ideas, can also have a negative influence, may be an area of non-value, of conflict, hostility or social exclusion, or can have a coherent organization and functioning but founded on non-value, on antisocial attitudes, or may be poorly organized, dysfunctional, immature. In the both cases, the members are exposed to personal/ humane/ spiritual underdevelopment, marginalization and social/ moral maladjustment. Consequently, the optimal conditions for the construction and functioning of a humane personality, a strong, equilibrate, adaptable and happiness person, are the opposite thereof - namely compathy, solidarity, love, unity, communication, cooperation in the family and community.

Returning, as we have asserted above, in the ontogenetic process of forming of the person we distinguish two main sub-processes, steps, periods: the formation of the ontological-psychological sphere, and the formation of the social-person/ sphere.

If the formation of the ontological-psychological sphere/ personality is done especially during childhood and adolescence, the formation of the social-personal sphere is done especially together with, and after, the subject acquires social autonomy, profession, its own family etc. The process being, as we have seen, conditioned mainly by the formation of the (social) conscience, character, and competences/ habitudes, and the process of social autonomization. Through the construction of the social-personal / psychological-social sphere takes place not only a simple formation of some new psychological-social entities, but also take place a complex, deep and global process of socialization, humanization and culturalization, the person becomes aware of its own social, moral and human situation, condition, of its own ontogenetical processes of autonomization - in relation to itself and, especially, in relation to the environmental factors.

The process of personalization implies, as we have seen, the formation of new spheres and levels but also and general, holistic re-structurations re-dimensionations, retrievable at the level of all the formations, after the "completion" of the socialization process (social maturation), that could be "located", in our opinion, statistically, somewhere after the age of 40 years. The person, later, after completing the two major sub-processes, and establishing of the two macro-spheres - the ontological-psychological sphere and the social-personal sphere, will be, largely, a new construction, not only the overlapping, the coexistence of the two.

Thus, we may speak, also, about a third process, and a third sphere, a mega-, pan-sphere - **THE SPHERE OF THE PERSON, THE PERSON AS A WHOLE,** where the two sub-processes and spheres will merge, unify, leading to what will be, ultimately, a certain human individual, a person, reflected, finally, in what could be considered *the unitary/ global beingness and functioning of the person.*

So, after the construction of the great formations and spheres and crossing the great phases, process, of forming of the person/ personality, of properly personalization, one can speak of PERSON, in the complex, ancestral, social and human meaning of the word; therefore, with meaning of human, of social being, but also of being in itself, with **characteristics** of *unicity, authenticity,* properly of *human being.*

Unicity and authenticity which are given both by the genetic inherited biological characteristics, results of the phylogenetical evolution, as well as by the environmental characteristics of the ontogenetic process. Important role having also some factors which are related to the subjective-metaphysical indeterminism, to the free will, the learning trial-error mechanism, to the world of ego, of will, to the abyssal world of the spirit and subjectivity, to the interior energy and resorts of great depthness and complexity that determine us to consider the ontological process of forming of the person, largely, as unpredictable and never ended, and the person as never perfect, never identical with the themselves or with the social role that it meets.

All this leads us to consider that, at any age, the person is an opened bio-psycho-social system, fragile, influential, flexible, dynamic, in formation, change, progress and regress, with frequent changes of the internal hierarchical economic, structural, axiological relations. So, it would be simplistic to consider the process of personalization as "standard", predetermined, it would be against the ontological paradigm which we assume in this paper. Beyond an inherent pattern, the ontogenetic process of forming of the person is carried out at the confluence of some conditions and factors described through a great complexity, infinite variety, diversity, dynamics, which confers it accentuated characteristics of unicity and authenticity, aspect reflected in the way it is presented the product, the result of the process - THE PERSON.

In the humanistic personology paradigm, the humanistic-ontological perspective on the person/ personality, the attention/ interest is mostly concentrated to the **HUMANE AND SPIRITUAL DIMENSION,**

VALENCE AND ORIENTATION, to the way in which, axiologically, was formed, exists and function the person by a number of features of human/ humane, moral orientation, of spiritual richness and virtue, of humanism, but also of humane and spiritual maturity, functionality, fulfillment and conduct such as empathy, generosity, helpfulness, agreeability, amiability, charity, charisma, compassion, confidence, cooperation, decency, honestity, selfless, sociability, paternalism, solidarity, humanism, openness, peace of soul, spirituality, patience, allocentricity, passion, humane energy, genuinity, idealism, culture, humanistic intelligence, romanticism, sensitivity, sentimentalism, wisdom, femininity, emotionality, impressionability, invisibility, purity, self-consciousness, unaggressivity, adaptability, elegance, humor, incorruptibility, loyalty, moderation, modesty, nonauthoritarism, persuasivity, respect, responsibility, confidentiality, optimism, happiness, balance, calm, enthusiasm, faith, responsivity, flexibility, profoundness, creativity, etc.

To this end, the humanistic-ontological paradigm of the person's beingness and functioning highlights, with poignancy, the determinant role of some psychological-ontological spheres, formations such as the soul, with its the three large spheres (affective, spiritual, humane), the humane ego, the humane conscience and the humane character, profiling, the dimension, pan-sphere, called, by us, *humane personality*.

From the holistic, unitary, teleological perspective on the person, the humane personality, as entity, is part of the personal assembly, but a part with crucial role, largely determining the humane, humanistic dimension of the person, of its conduct. In our opinion, very important is the "weight" that has one or other of the soul's spheres in its architecture, in the beingness and functioning of the soul as a whole, as extended part of the personal ontos, but as well of the humane personality.

For example, the more pronounced development of the affective soul (social/ personal) will profile a personal structure oriented predominantly to the jouissance of the dear/ close/ relative people, the more pronounced development of the spiritual soul will orient the personal assembly toward a development, as the case, of artistic, mystical, scientific type, while a greater development of the humane soul will imprint to person's personality and behavior features such as altruism, empathy, humanism, human solidarity, disinterested love, etc.

Of course, seeking to highlight what it would mean *the humane configuration/ structure/ orientation of the person,* we should approach the holistic perspective, where to remark the importance of some configurations of system or global type, the crystallization and ontification of some internal hierarchies, related but to the environmental factors, with whom are in a permanent feed-back and feed-before; the humane configuration, orientation, but also the humane development and traits of the person profilating itself, therefore, only through the dialectical conjugation of the two universes: the personality and the environment.

The activity of the professionals in areas such as therapy, education, social work/ welfare, culture, religion, etc. cannot be conceived without humane and spiritual development - very important resources and crucial factors of the activity effectiveness and achieving the specific objectives. The personal humane development confers to professionals characteristics which help to operate both with the soul and with the mind. Through the great development of the professional's humane personality his personality and personal ensemble as a whole is reformed and is defined through solidarist-humanistic qualities and humane behavioral traits such as altruism, empathy, agreeableness, tolerance, humanity, human/ humane sensitivity, etc.

The "humanization" of the professional's personality and behavior is a very complex and profound process and phenomenon, an ontogenetical emergent, holistic and integrator process more pronounced to those who have grown and lived in social environments based on love, altruism, happiness, solidarity and empathy/ compathy, to the employees whose current activity requires continuous and prolonged work/ interaction with people (clients) in difficulty and/ or suffering, being achieved thus an adaptation of the professional's personality and behavior to the specific of activity, imposing, developing traits and qualities with strong humanistic, humane, prosocial, altruistic valences.

1.4.3. SCIENTIFIC-THEORETICAL, PHILOSOPHICAL, AND CULTURAL SOURCES AND MODELS

Ontology, with its the triad *being-existent–existence,* humanism, humanistic psychology and psychotherapy, transpersonal psychology, positive psychology, microsociology, humanistic sociology, and the emergent/ complex systems theories represent, in our opinion, the most important theoretical-scientifical, philosophical and cultural sources and models of humanistic personology, with its the two cardinal approaches/ paradigms: *humanistic-positive/ existential* and *humanistic-ontological/ spiritual.*

THE EMERGENT AND COMPLEX SYSTEMS THEORIES

The emergent and complex systems theories (which include, among others, the chaos theory), regarding the process of personalization, the formation of the person/ personality, of the human being, but also the composition, the beingness and functioning, involve characteristics, properties, processes, principles such as onto-formatization, persomization and promergence, emergence and imergence, transmergence and telegence, conmergence and sinmergence, and aspects regarding the ontological stages of evolution, development, establishment of the personal ontological-psychological formations, of the person as a whole, such as of contact, of acquisition/ accumulation, of structuration/ centralization, of constitution/ holistization, of establishing/ networking, of ontification/ fulfillment, etc.

In the light of these theories the processes take place, largely, without limitations and physical barriers of space and organization (Waldrop, 1993), transcending the structures, the organizations, and the entities already constituted, attracting and involving them in the processes of forming, constituting and establishing of the new formations, without altering them.

In humanistic personology, the ontological-humanistic perspective on the processes of forming and functioning of the person/ personality the degree of freedom/ action is very large, the number of combinations and the facilities of structuration and formatization being almost unlimited; one of the most important explanation is given by the fact that in the emergent and complex systems the processes have the extraordinary quality to permit the transcendence and the multiplication to infinit to the informational/ spiritual entities (Bickhard, 2012), taking place without time limitations and barriers, by the fact/ explanation that in the emergent and complex systems the processes have the tendency to organize and concentrate them "thematically" in formations, persoms, structures, spheres etc., reflecting the inherence, the objective necessity of some functions, beyond any limitations of "logistic" or temporal order, by the fact that the entities coexist, simultaneously, in the same personal "space", the functioning and beingness of some distinct entities, structures, relationships, processes on/ through the same material, biological, informational, spiritual support, framework.

The humane and spiritual experiences and the promergent processes are involved in complex, emergent, dynamic mechanisms and entities, every formation, persom, personality, the person as a whole being so a product of the ontogenetical-emergent incorporation, union, synthesis, of the conmergent, emergent, transmergent unitary organization of the sub-entities/ formations, structures, energies, mechanisms, of the processes of organization in new structures, formative entities, formations, persoms, usually upper structurally and axiologically (Stefaroi, 2014, 2015).

ONTOLOGY. THE ONTOLOGICAL TRIAD <u>BEING-EXISTENT–EXISTENCE</u>

Ontology is a fundamental and constitutional domain of philosophy, and has in its center of interest/ research the category of *being, the existence in-itself.*

Most often, the domain is opposed to epistemology, which studies the things mainly scientifically and categorially.

From the ontological point of view the things, even the spiritual things, really exist, these have a nature, a beginning, a processual, determined, unique, unrepeatable existence (Harvey, 2006), also a *the end*, while epistemology, in its purely position, claims that the things are rather representations and products of some intellectual or sensory-cognitive processings, and, if the things and phenomena actually exist, are multiplications of some immutable structures, patterns, epistemologically subjected to certain intellectual and scientific processes of generalization, categorization universalization.

Ontology is a conceptual-philosophical system yet underutilized in the modeling of the processes of formation, or in understanding and modeling the mode of functioning/ beingness of the person/ personality. It could provide thus a framework for a lot of explanations and for solving many human problems.

We are talking about an ontological-phenomenological paradigm but also dynamic, with its central theme: the theory of being, (especially of the human being) and of existence, of the concrete fact, and namely of the concrete, unique human being, in process, in beingness and functioning.

Ontology favors the interest for the real, unique, concrete person, with its particular, specific, unique feelings, emotions and socio-human context, imposing an idiographic-empirical/ *emergentical* paradigm, whereas epistemology favors the representation of the person or the community where this lives, in general the socio-human phenomenon, through universalization, globalization, through scientific categories such as structure, system, function, institution, social control, recurrence, nomological approach.

Therefore, regarding the representation of the person and personality, their formation, the ontological theory/ paradigm highlights, mostly, the following aspects:

- the person, the personality, the soul, the ego, the conscience, etc. are unique, emergent products of the individual, particular, contextual ontogenesis, and not simple "embodiments" of some universal, transpersonal patterns, structures, models;

- as existence the person lives, coexists, firstly, among complex, unpredictable men, persons, living beings, with soul, with specific and unique needs, dramas, attachments, and personality, and only indirectly in social structures, institutions, systems.

Ontology has consecrated, among others, the paradigmatic ontological triad: *being-existent-existence.*

In ontological perspective **the being** (being in itself) of an entity represents the essence, the original content, the invariable, the ontological-metaphysical foundation of the entities, of the existent and of the existence, **the existent/ existing** (being for itself) represents the organization, the concrete form, unique, part of a context, the exposed side of the being, acquiring the characteristics of form of the concrete environment where it exists, while **the existence**, or **the beingness/ functioning** (being outside-itself), represents the processual, contingent, situational-contextual side, exposed to time, dynamic, experiential, the feeling and the thinking (Maritain, 1956; Hegel, 1977).

In agreement with the metaphysical-ontological paradigm outlined above we will consider that **the ontological-psychological sphere** (the personal ontos, the soul, the ego) represents *the being* of the person, **the psychological-personal sphere** (the conscience, personality, the skills) represents *the existent/ existing*, while **the experiential-behavioral sphere** (the functioning, the beingness, the current life/ activity/ experience of the person, its jouissance, feelings, concrete processual thinking) represents *the existence*.

HUMANISM

As it is well known, in the social and human sciences, the term/ terms *humanist/ humanistic/ humanism* has been consecrated through many meanings. We hold mainly two:

1) regarding the *human* condition, the idea of ancestral human unity and solidarity; the representation of the person as ontological part of a human community, mutual conditioned by the human-ontogenetic interpersonal interaction (Confucius, 1979) - theoretical-axiological sources of the social/ human solidarity, humanism, socio-human adaptation, and concern/ care for each other;

2) regarding to the intrinsic resources and capacities of the man, as individual, as person, of affirmation, self-actualization, self-determination, personal accomplishment and development; the representation of the person as *Me*, personality, with the attribute of will and freedom, creativity, responsibility and dignity (Davies, 1997) - the sources of the personal and social change and empowerment, of the individual and the community.

The first meaning is, with predilection, exploited and stated by philosophy, religion, transpersonal psychology and anthropology, while the second by the humanistic and positive psychology, pedagogy, psychotherapy and humanistic sociology.

In agreement with the two established theoretical-axiological meanings also the humanistic orientation from personology, especially with applicability in practice, generates two relatively distinct theories, forms, i.e. the solidarist-humanistic personology, and the positive-humanistic personology.

Although, strictly analytic, seems somewhat opposite, in fact, the two forms, solidarist-humanistic and positive-humanistic, are "two faces of the same coin", two sides and dimensions of the same process, subsumed to a unitary theory and practice of the humanistic personology, within the larger theoretical-methodological framework of the *science of man as a whole* (Stefaroi, 2013).

Undoubtedly, the humanism, with its phenomenological and existentialist philosophical foundations, through all its artistic, social, philosophical, scientific, ideological, political, educational dimensions, manifestations and concerns, through the multitude of themes and meanings by which it was consecrated, as system or mode of thought and action predominating the human interests, the human values and dignity, as variety of ethical theories and practices that emphasize the human fulfillment through knowledge and social development, focusing on the person/ individual/ self, centering on the person's resources, the self-determination, human solidarity, humanity, human sensitivity, philanthropy, happiness, promoting the person's welfare, through the constitutional concern for researching the human being, his nature, essence, condition, through the interest for promoting of some great general human values and ideals in the evolution and development of society, through the interest for change and new, for truth, beautiful, good, represents one of the most important foundation and essential source of the humanistic personology, of an authentic humanistic theory of the person, represented not only with the theoretical apparatus of biology, psychology and cybernetics but with all what created the humanity in his history in domains as philosophy, art, science, anthropology (Lamont, 1997; Fromm, 2013).

Referring to the role that it plays the humanism in the fundamentation of the humanistic social work theory, axiology and practice Malcolm Payne affirms:

„Humanism brings together rational thinking, through science, with artistic creativity and imagination; one is not more important than another. The aims of that constellation of human skills are the development of thought-out value systems, innovation, and critical evaluation of ideas and actions. Democracy, human rights, and personal liberty go alongside one another in helping us achieve personal fulfillment in our lives" (Payne, 2011, p. 5).

PHENOMENOLOGY, EXISTENTIALISM, AND EXISTENTIAL PHILISOPHY

Phenomenology and **existentialism** was released, promoted and developed by thinkers such as Kierkegaard, Husserl, Heidegger, Sartre, de Beauvoir, Merleau-Ponty, Nietzsche etc., with their concerns for:

- The human condition and nature;

- The person-society relationships;

- Emphasis on real, lived life;

- Interest in topics such as happiness and distress;

- The limit experiences;

- The existential crises and impasses;

- The willpower and ability to self-determination;

- Freedom and responsibility;

- The limits of the personal freedom;

- The ontological congruence between person and environment;

- The concrete social existence;

- The displacement of the interest from the abstract, metaphysical themes, towards the existential, phenomenological themes;

- From the speculative philosophy towards the philosophy of the concrete, determined, existing, particular man;

- The primacy of the man as an individual, person, ego, and uniqueness in society;

- The limits of the human being, the human being's fragility;

- Interest for personal growing and autonomy;

- The power of reason, the self-knowledge, the self-realization, the self-actualization, etc. (Heidegger, 1962; E. Husserl, D. Moran, 2012)

In sociohuman plan phenomenology and existentialism bring in foreground concepts, ideas, and values as the human-individual (personal) condition and nature, emphasis on real, lived life, interest in topics such as the limit experiences, the existential crises and impasses, the willpower and ability to self-determination, freedom and responsibility, the limits of the personal freedom, the ontological congruence between person and environment, the concrete social existence, the displacement of the interest from the abstract, metaphysical themes, towards the existential, phenomenological themes, the primacy of the man as an individual, person, ego, and uniqueness in society, the limits of the human being, the human being's fragility, interest for personal growing and autonomy, the power of reason, the self-knowledge, the self-realization, the self-actualization, etc. (Heidegger, 1962; Husserl & Moran, 2012). Crucial concepts and syntagms of existentialism and phenomenology as humanistic approaches are *anthropo-centrism* and *human-centered approach* - reveled and applied in social work through techniques or methods as client-centered intervention, intervention centred on concret human relationships etc.

If phenomenology, existentialism and humanism are some doctrines, orientations, currents, schools of thought, **existential philosophy**, or the philosophy of existence, is a domain of philosophy - without ideological-doctrinal temptation - which has as object of study, in the philosophical-ontological triad existence - existence - existence, the latter, the study of the existence, with emphasis on aspects of unicity, dynamics, process and phenomenon, detached from aspects of structure or essence, without unilateralisation but, and in the context of structural-functional correlation with the other two elements of the ontological triad.

This philosophical domain has, as importants representatives, philosophers as Kierkegaard, Heidegger, Sartre, Simone de Beauvoir, Maurice Merleau-Ponty, etc., and studies, philosophically, aspects as:

- the real, lived life;
- happiness and distress;
- the experiences of limit;
- the existential crises and impasses;
- the individual/ personal human condition and nature;
- the particular person-society relationships;
- freedom and responsibility;
- the limits of the personal freedom;
- the existential/ phenomenological congruence between person and environment;
- the concrete social existence;

- the concrete, determined, existing, particular man;

- the man as an individual, person, ego, and uniqueness in society;

- the limits of the human being, the human being's fragility;

- the personal growing and autonomy;

- the power of reason, the self-knowledge, the self-realization, the self-actualization, etc.

PHILOSOPHY OF MAN. HUMANISTIC PHILOSOPHY

In the theoretical-philosophical fundamentation/ substatiation of the (humanistic) genetic personology, important concepts, ideas and models come from the Philosophy of Man, and from the Humanistic Philosophy.

Philosophy of Man, represents, so, an important theoretical and methodological foundation and theoretical source for a humanistic theory of the ontogenetical formation the concrete man, of the person (Reichmann, 1985), of a person with ego, personality and soul, of a person who lives and suffers and not of a person who is a simple element into social system/ mechanism (Kainz, 1981; Husserl, 2012).

This is also an important these of **Humanistic Philosophy**, that as a sub-discipline, as a branch, as a area, domain, section, part of (general) Philosophy, is focused on, and brings in attention, especially, the category, the value-concept of *Human Being*, with the meaning of individuality, subject, the person with the attribute of *freedom* and *self-determination*, the category, value-concept of *agency*, the respect for the human as individual, as a Person, in opposition to the approaches that represent the person, the individual human being as a simple statistical element in a social structure, system, mechanism. In the second meaning, crucial concepts, syntagms, and ideas-values that are bring to attention, when we speak, therefore, of (general) philosophy as a *humanistic discipline* are *Anthropo-Centrism* and *Person-Centered Approach.*

Essentially, philosophy as a *humanistic* discipline, through all its branches, orientations, schools, and methods, is an ethics of the phenomenon, process and act of knowledge in general, and of the philosophical knowledge in particular, an ethics of the human, of the man, of humanity, and, especially, ultimately, a philosophy of the human as an objective, values, ideal, principle of all the demarches, acts of knowledge and action, epistemologically and methodologically speaking.

In general, the humanistic methodology, in philosophy, but also in sociology, psychology and other socio-human sciences, in theory and practice, give to human, to person and to the human relationships crucial roles, examining with priority the humanistic fundamental resorts of the micro-groups and particular socio-human contexts, focusing on the subjective/ human/ socio-human processes, on the inter-personal/ inter-human relationships and phenomena of cooperation, attachment, solidarity, love, conflict, etc., in everyday life, in communities and organizations. Between other characteristics of the humanistic philosophy's methodology can be also mentioned complexity, emergence, reflection, meditation, revelation, inspiration, introspection, creativity, questioning, humanistic hermeneutics, pro-humanistic deconstruction, heuristic analysis, etc The specifics of the qualitative, interpretative and comprehensive methods in philosophy and the socio-human sciences and practices is mainly that these are focused largely on capturing the *phenomena* more than the essences, universal laws; the object of evaluation, observation and investigation being most often the event, the socio-human context, the sentiment, the concrete attitudes, feelings and reactions of people being in determined social and human relationships and processes. The advantage is that through this methodology is obtained the access to social and human aspects which would escape to an eminently positive, nomological, scientific-technical approach, more focused on capturing the structural, universal and repeatable evidences, by modelations of mathematical type.

Undoubtedly, the theoretical foundation of the humanistic philosophy must starts from the concept-value of HUMAN, consequently from that of *humanism*, then follows the concentration on the phenomenological, existential, spiritual, cultural and moral mark on the specific theory and methodology, everything, consequently, in the context and on the basis of a very comprehensive perspective, approach, including many trends, orientations, thinking schools or methods, some of them even appearing to be in opposition, in contradiction.

As sub-discipline, area, and dimension of the philosophy as a whole, humanistic philosophy, in its broad sense, is grounded and defined at the same time on and by a large number of concepts, themes. ideas, values such as human freedom, agency, human being, person, human relationships, human nature/ essence, happiness and dignity, self-determination, responsibility, human development, spirituality and culture, empathy, love, faith, attachment, etc. (Williams, 2008).

So, under its broad umbrella are found, congruently but also competitively, even antagonistically, concepts, themes, ideas, values afferent both to the existentialist, phenomenological, contextualist, interactionist, constructivist or realistic orientations, as well as to the spiritual, cultural, ethical, and humanitarian orientations, found sometimes together, sometimes separately, in the ideologies, doctrines, and methods that underpin, theoretically-philosophically and methodologically, the great contemporary social, cultural, and political movements of humanistic inspiration, or the social sciences and practices called *humanistic* as humanistic psychology and humanistic psychotherapy, humanistic sociology and humanistic social work, humanistic pedagogy and humanistic education, humanistic management, etc.

Mainly through the doctrinal-ideological direction/ dimension imprinted by the termination *ism*, in the broad area of the concept, idea of *humanistic philosophy* enter many other concepts, categories, ideas, approaches or debates such as:

- Concentration of the philosophical reflection/ theory on person, individuality, subject;

- Agency – individuals have the constitutional and natural capacity to act independently and to make their own free choices;

- Reflection and promoting, theoretically-philosophically, the respect for the human as individual, as a person, *for each person*;

- Human dignity and social justice (Humanistische Akademie, 1998);

- The idea of human solidarity, humanitarianism, charity, altruism;

- The value-idea of equality, nondiscrimination, tolerance;

- Concentration of the philosophical reflection on promoting with priority of the general/ universal/ ancestral HUMAN interests and aspirations in relation to other beings, entities or forms of existence;

- Highlighting, philosophically, the human nature and essence of the person in the relation to the explanations of cybernetic, biologist or structuralist-mechanicist type;

- Highlighting, philosophically, the human nature and essence of the society and humanity in relation to the explanations of cybernetic, statistical, structuralist-functionalist, structuralist-mechanicistic, or deistic type;

- Reflection and promotion of a relative and contextual Ethics, of a Ethics of happiness and human-personal good, in opposition to the universalistic, functionalist, "oppressive" or divine Ethics, of course, without disregarding the interest, the good and the happiness of the other, the common interest;

- The philosophical reflection/ theory and promotion of an optimistic attitude towards life and towards future;

- The exploitation of the cultural and socio-human resources from the society and social context (Krill, 1978);

- Spiritual empowerment, personal/ human development and self-determination (Payne, 2011);

- Empathy, attachment and human relationships (Payne, 2011, p. 4);

- Secularism, non-theistic approach.

In the last century and also today many philosophers start, in their humanistic philosophical approaches, with the belief that there is no God, believing in situation, relative, contextual Ethics, the primary goal of humanism being the establishment of a one-world government.

But in its essence, beyond any ideological-doctrinaire order, humanistic philosophy is distinguished by its special attitude towards man, towards society and social practices, generating the focus of interest on individuality, person and personality, on micro-community and human interpersonal relationships, on creativity, spirituality and on human resources in the social practices and activities.

The humanistic approach rejects the assumptions of the behaviorist-environmentalist perspectives which are characterized as social/ external-deterministic, focused on stimulus-response behavior, also rejects the biologistic-psychodynamic approaches, because it is mostly biological-deterministic, with unconscious irrational and instinctive forces that are considered to be determinant for the person's thought and behavior (Bugental, 1964).

Instead, from the humanistic theory's position, every healthy individual has, inherently, an Ego and a Personality, will, and through these, freedom, the capacity of self-determination, the capacity to achieve its potential in human, social and spiritual terms; all depending on its internal activism and of the willingness for change, self-fulfillment, and happiness (Plotnik and Kouyoumdjian, 2007).

Person and personality are addressed in humanistic philosophy by the two cardinal guidelines of the humanistic theory, respectively *existential-phenomenological* and *ontological-spiritual/ humane*, speaking, therefore, in humanistic-ontological perspective of *spiritual/ humane personality,* and, in existential-positive perspective of *strong* and *developed personality.*

Core concepts in humanistic-existential philosophy are *Ego, Personal Development* and *Strong Personality,* implying features as freedom, will, personal and social efficiency, socio-emotional development, high control of emotions, emotional intelligence, realism and balance, resistance to failure and frustrations, hope, orientation to future. positive attitude, optimism, active thinking, high degree of awareness, self-knowledge, self-esteem, professional development, personal and social autonomy, interpersonal development, mature personality, adaptability.

One of the most important ways of achieving these humanistic-personal attributes is the emancipation, empowerment and development through spiritualization and humanization, through spiritual and human/ humane empowerment and development. Even if it is a very complex and difficult endeavor, the humanization, spiritualization and humane-spiritual/cultural integration/ development of the person are considered miraculous solutions for many kinds of problems, sufferings, deviances, etc.

Therefore, the humanistic-epistemological foundation in the representation of the person, in humanistic philosophy, is his approach as *complex personality,* promoting the representation of the person as *Ego,* the power of the consciousness and of the will, the freedom, responsibility and self-determination, the development of the person in accordance with his characteristics and choices.

HUMANISTIC PSYCHOLOGY, TRANSPERSONAL PSYCHOLOGY, POSITIVE PSYCHOLOGY, HUMANISTIC SOCIOLOGY

Humanistic psychology, often called "the third force" in psychology after psychoanalysis and behaviorism (Bugental, 1964; Maslow, 1968), promotes mainly the representation of the person as *ego* and *personality*, the power of the consciousness and of the will, the freedom, responsibility and self-determination, the development of the person in accordance with its characteristics and choices.

The humanistic method and approach to psychology rejects the assumptions of the behaviorist perspective which is characterized as social/ external-deterministic, focused on stimulus-response behavior, also rejects the psychodynamic approach because it is biological-deterministic, with unconscious irrational and instinctive forces that are considered to be determinant for the person's thought and behavior (Bugental, 1964).

Behaviorism and psychoanalysis are regarded therefore as dehumanized approaches and methods by the promoters of humanistic psychology, neglecting the importance of the ego, conscience and personality in the person's thinking and behavior.

Instead, from the humanistic psychology's position, every healthy individual has, inherently, an Ego and a Personality, and through these the capacity of self-determination, the capacity to achieve its potential in human, social and spiritual terms; all depending to its internal activism and of the willingness for change or self-fulfillment (Plotnik and Kouyoumdjian, 2007).

These are also some of the main resources of the humanistic psychology and its applications in psychotherapy, which brings in the forefront of clinical knowledge and therapeutic action concepts and ideas such as person-centered approach, self-determination, self-actualization, the power/ force of the ego, personality, and consciousness, strength-based interventions, spirituality, empowerment, personal development, personal accomplishment, holistic assessment and intervention, optimism, creativity, happiness, the individual/ client uniqueness, focus on the particular aspects of the human existence, tolerance, love, etc. (Maslow, 1968; Bugental, 1964; Rogers, 1959).

The theories of development and empowerment, empathy theory and happiness theory support, theoretically, in great measure, the humanistic psychology and psychotherapy.

The Theories of Personality/ Personal Development represent in humanistic psychology/ psychotherapy theoretical models and supports for approaching of the person/ client as human being under development, with the personality and conscience as core resources for growing, with ego, will, character, sensibility and empathy, and not as a simple reply of the human race, or a mere individual being in a simple social, organizational interaction.

In general, in humanistic psychology/ psychotherapy, the humanistic representation of the personality, approached as resource of development and empowerment, is imposed, according to our observations, by two main theories/ orientations/ approaches. One is the *positive/ existential-psychological* theory, another is the *ontological-spiritual* theory.

According to Rogers, Maslow, Allport and other representatives of humanistic psychology and psychotherapy the need to achieving personal fulfillment is a crucial way for social and human rehabilitation of the client. Personal development is, so, one of the key tool of psychological rehabilitation and social adaptation of the person/ client.

Empathy theory is a formative instrument used by the professionals in achieving the specific objectives, mainly in the psychological-human rehabilitation and social empowerment of the client. The professional-client proactive psychological-empathetic relationship is in fact a framework for transfer, a subtle lane that the professional uses, intentionally and professionally, for solve the client's problem (Gerdes, Segal, 2011).

Crucial is the goal of psychological-personal rehabilitation and social/ compathetic integration of the client through its humanization, through spiritual development, through the development of empathetic spheres of his personality and behavior.

About empathy as psychosocial concept and phenomenon have dealt great thinkers like Lipps (to feel himself in something), Allport (understanding and feeling each other), Titchener (ability to think and feel what another person thinks and feels), Rogers (the fourth stage in the emotional-personal development; ability to really sit in the other's place, of seeing the world as he sees it), Batson (disposition/ motivation oriented to the other).

Hoffman (2000) interprets the empathic disposition of the person as effect of cognitive-affective action of the other, resulting so an emotional response closer to the other's interests than the self.

Most of the authors give the following meanings to the concept of empathy: sympathetic projection of the self, emotional fusion, sympathetic intuition, affective union, knowledge by interweaving, introjection, tranzitivism, intropathy, sympathy, transposition into the current other's state, identification with another, transfer, sympathetic projection.

Empathy is a form of knowledge of the environment, so is a cognitive process, is a form of feeling and emotional experience to the other, therefore, an emotional process, is an interpersonal process, so is a social process and, not least, a spiritual process/ phenomenon, through the human capacity to resonate to culture, science, philosophy, religion etc. All these phenomena and processes contribute to the establishment of what might be called the human sensitivity.

The practitioner uses the proactive, formative, educational and inductive valences of the empathy for the reconstruction, human-psychologically and social-compathetically, the personality, as step in the personal development and social/ human rehabilitation of the client.

An important moment in the history of humanistic psychology and its imposition as an autonomous discipline is the postulation of what was consecrated as *the five core principles* of humanistic psychology, in the "Journal of Humanistic Psychology" by James Bugental, in 1964, respectively:

- *Human beings, as human, supersede the sum of their parts. They cannot be reduced to components.*

- *Human beings have their existence in a uniquely human context, as well as in a cosmic ecology.*

- *Human beings are aware and are aware of being aware - i.e., they are conscious. Human consciousness always includes an awareness of oneself in the context of other people.*

- *Human beings have the ability to make choices and therefore have responsibility.*

- *Human beings are intentional, aim at goals, are aware that they cause future events, and seek meaning, value, and creativity.*

*(http://academic.udayton.edu/jackbauer/
Readings%20595/Hum%20Psy%205%20principles.pdf).*

(Humanistic) Onto-Psychology is an interdisciplinary domain of knowledge that is focused on the ontological-psychological sphere of the person. In onto-psychology all the psychological functions, spheres, phenomena, systems, and processes are interpreted in connection to the existence and the manifestation of the ontological spheres and resorts of the personality, especially of the self, the soul, and the ego - core ontological-psychological formation of the personal ontos, that could be considered the *being* of the person.

Transpersonal Psychology represents the person and the personality as a cumulation/ overlapping of personalities, persons and universal, ancestral or cosmic values, highlighting in particular the transcendental, ancestral and spiritual content and, valences and resources of the human personality (Lajoie & Shapiro, 1992).

In transpersonal psychology are used especially terms, concepts, ideas as:

- spiritual evolution;
- religious conversion;
- altered states of consciousness;
- spiritual practices;
- spiritual self-development;
- self beyond;
- the ego;
- systemic trance;
- spiritual crises;
- peak experiences;
- mystical experiences (Anderson, 2011; Lajoie & Shapiro, 1992).

Regarding the specifics of therapy the authors and therapists emphasize that its goals include both traditional outcomes, such as symptom relief and behavior change, as well as action at the transpersonal level, which may transcend psychodynamic issues (Walsh, Vaughan, 1993).

Positive psychology starts from the premise that the human beings have, constitutionally, the capacity and the right to happiness, and they are often, perhaps more often, drawn by the future than they are driven by the past. In this sense the psychologists must use in the therapeutic process of intervention especially the inner psychological-eudaimonical resources of the client, but also of the psychotherapist (Seligman and Csikszentmihaly, 2000).

Essentially, this kind of psychology highlight the importance in the human life, personality and therapy or counseling of some issues and resources as:

- happiness;
- positive emotions;
- orientation to the future;
- positive expectation;
- love;
- appreciation;
- empathy;
- states of pleasure or flow;
- values;
- strengths;
- virtues, talents;
- positive experiences;
- enduring psychological traits;
- positive relationships;
- positive institutions. etc.

Seligman and Csikszentmihalyi (2000) define positive psychology as the scientific study of *positive* human functioning and flourishing on multiple levels that include the biological, personal, relational, institutional, cultural, and global dimensions of life.

The achievement of the therapeutic goals in positive psychotherapy and counseling is so, among others, correlated with the therapist and clients's positive attitudes towards the life, with the degree of internal psychological relaxation, the irony and the personal happiness (Seligman, 2002), qualities and resources that need to be identified, promoted and developed both at the client's level but also at the therapist's level.

Concluding, essentially, the core idea of positive psychotherapy, but also of the positive social work and counseling, is that, in practice, the therapist and counselor aim to increase the positive feelings, the happiness, the psychological wellbeing, but also the positive behaviors and relationships, to increase also the positive cognitions but also the positive expectations, as opposed to focusing on the negative thoughts and expectations.

Happiness Theory, as a psychological-positive theory is based on the assumption that the efficiency and the personal/ professional/ social adaptation of the person in socio-human context is closely related to the degree of happiness, satisfaction and complacency (M.E. Seligman, 2002).

The happiness theory is sustained by the fact that it is based on the following ideas, facts, principles:

- Every person, regardless of age, sex, nationality, race, social status, profession is entitled to a dignified life, to happiness, to personal fulfillment;

- The essential indicator of the human life quality is the internal satisfaction, subjective felt, the happiness and complacency of the person;

- The authentic happiness is a source of personal development, social/ professional efficiency and factor for the acquisition of the autonomous social reintegration capacity (Seligman, Csikszentmihalzi, 2000).

Humanistic Sociology is an important theoretical, heuristical, and futuristical branch of sociology. Among the most important concerns of humanistic sociology are:

- the observation of how individuals as complex and unforeseeable human beings, as persons specifically live, love, suffer, interact;

- what attachment relationships are established between them in relationships of kinship, friendship, enmity, interest, collegiality, power relationships (Mills, 1959; Znaniecki, 1934);

- how persons and groups adjust, interactively, their behaviors and symbolizes, mutually, the social existence (the laws, values, customs, rituals, behaviors, institutions, ideologies) (Znaniecki, 1969);

- the resilience and coping with difficult situations;

- how persons and groups solve the problems;

- how persons and groups adapt to the changes or react to crisis or major events (Merton & Nisbet, 1961).

Essentially, the humanistic approach and method in sociology make the accent on human subjectivity and creativity, highlighting how individuals respond to social constraints and actively assemble social worlds, dealing with concrete human experiences, with their socio-human, inter-personal, inter-human organization. promoting a kind of society in which there is less exploitation, oppression and injustice. From the perspective of humanistic sociology's principles, the person, as being, subject, self matter and prevail in the relationships with the society as a whole and with the man as ancestral entity (Mills, 1959).

In this sense, in humanistic sociology the person is not a simple element, or a tool, means for society or humanity to achieve their objectives, the historical and ancestral goals, but, conversely, the society, the community are the existential frame where the person is fulfilled, where expresses its vocation for freedom and finds the happiness in the unique and irreducible existence and life that it has (Merton & Nisbet, 1961).

Humanistic sociology is also a militant science, this is the reason why one of the most important purposes/ directions is the study of how to make a better world, the key commitment is that *people matter* (Mills, 1959; Znaniecki, 1934).

CHAPTER 2

THE FORMATION AND DEVELOPMENT OF THE PERSON/ PERSONALITY - **BASIC SOURCES, FACTORS AND CONDITIONS**

2.1. INTRODUCTORY ASPECTS 76

2.2. THE HUMAN BODY/ ORGANISM 77

2.2.1. THE BODY AND THE PERSON 77

2.2.2. PHYLOGENESIS AND ONTOGENESIS 78

2.2.3. THE ORGANISM AND THE PERSON. THE CENTRAL NERVOUS SYSTEM 78

2.3. THE SOCIO-HUMAN ENVIRONMENT 79

2.3.1. THE HUMAN/ PERSONAL ENVIRONMENTAL ONTO-SYSTEM 79

2.3.2. MICRO-COMMUNITY, FAMILY 80

2.3.3. CULTURE, RELIGION, MORALS, EDUCATION 82

2.4. THE MIND 83

2.4.1. THE MIND AND THE PERSON 83

2.4.2. THE COGNITIVE HABILITATION, PERTENTION AND THE EPISTEMIC SUBJECT 84

2.4.3. THE MENTAL APPARATUS, INTELLIGENCE, THE NOETIC ONTOS 85

2.1. INTRODUCTORY ASPECTS

Even if, as we'll see in this chapter, in the ontogenetic process of formation of the most important formations, spheres, persoms of the person and personality, are very important the body/ organism, the mind (intellect/ intelligence), the social-economic, material conditions, still, in humanistic perspective, the human/ humane conditions are, in fact, those that contribute crucially to the formation of a harmonious personality, of a strong person, fulfilled and, socio-humanly, effective, adaptable and happy.

Each of the two major spheres of the person is the product of the interaction of the subject with specific factors, even if cannot be traced strict boundaries between them. The contingent-experiential social-personal and socio-affective factors are crucial for the formation of the ontological-psychological sphere, while the cultural, moral, professional conditions of learning, training and working are essential for the formation of the social-personal/ psychological-social sphere. Thus, in a purely humanistic perspective, the human-personal, the human-social, and the human-cultural factors are decisive in the formation and development of a strong, balanced, adaptable and authentic happiness person.

So regarding the formation of the most important formations, spheres, persoms, of the personality and the person as a whole, must to be highlighted, firstly, the crucial contribution of the psychosocial and socio-human/ humane environmental factors.

The essence of the humanistic-ontological conception regarding the person/ the human personality is given by the idea that these are ontological/ ontogenetical products of some gradual and stadial processes held with the crucial contribution of the concrete/ contextual/ contingent socio-human factors where the person grows and lives, mainly the *personal*-human/ humane factors, with the crucial contribution of the individual persons, concrete people from the proximate environment with intense and constant psychological (emotional) and spiritual presence and influence, especially the significant members from its family/ significant group. Important are also the socio-cultural factors.

Of course, as was mentioned, very important are also the contributions of the mind (of the memory, thinking and imagination, intellect and intelligence, of the noetic ontos), or of the conscience; the latter operating with more advanced tools, more developed and more personalized, conditioning, crucially, through feedback, the process of personalization. Very important are also the contributions of the biological/ organic factors (the nervous central system, the humoral and neuro-psychic mechanisms, the neuro-vegetative system, etc.).

2.2. THE HUMAN BODY/ ORGANISM

Core Fragment

In humanistic personology, in the humanistic representation of the person, we operate with the hypothesis that in the consolidated structure of the person the body, as distinct bio-physical entity and as biological organism, retains the functional autonomy and it constitutes their own humoral and neuro-psychic mechanisms of internal control/ regulation and of interaction with the environment, but a substantial dimension (edge) of the organism enters, directly or indirectly, in the process of personalization. The solution of cohabitation which is find by the organism it is a concession, compromise - by which, lastly, the organism "supports" the morpho-physiological personalization, with influences and changes on the majority biological systems and phenomena, in exchange for its survival. In this way they go further and develop mutually both the organism and the person/ personality (Million, 1990).

2.2.1. THE BODY AND THE PERSON

In the genetic, structural and functional humanistic personology the body is not represented as a simple recipient, support, skeleton or pedestal on which is constructed the personal edifice, the personality, and nor as a simple tool, servomechanism of interpersonal communication, but contributes, participates dynamically, dialectically to the ontogenetical formation of the person/ personality, the more so, the organism, meaning as the internal biological organization and dynamics of the body, enters fundamentally, functionally, processually and endemically in the process of personal formation and personal development.

There are, consequently, arguments to consider the human body/ organism determinative, constitutional component of the structure, ontogenesis, beingness and functioning of the person/ personality (Canli, 2006) - reason why we attach it crucial importance both regarding the ontogenetic process of its formation, also regarding the everyday life or the current beingness of the person.

2.2.2. PHYLOGENESIS AND ONTOGENESIS

The (phylo- and onto-) genetic perspective offers the explanation of understanding the way from the cell to the person as *complex transition, process, through successive convergences and synthesis, from inferior to superior* (Chardin, 1959, p. 244) .

The development of the functions and capacities of knowledge, the intellectual leap, the development of the fine motility, of the language, of the domestic habitat, the appearance of the productive and creative activities, and other psycho-behavioral activities are steps in the evolution of the living world, in the transition from the cell to the organism, from the organism to the man as rational, social and spiritual being, and farther, to, what we call in this book, *the person -* as a superior existential entity, product and form of the existence specifically human: expression of the

- phylogenetic biological, social and cultural ancestral evolution; but also expression of the

- ontogenetic development, of the organic development and maturation, of the psychological, spiritual, moral, human, personal development/ ontogenesis, throughout the life.

2.2.3. THE ORGANISM AND THE PERSON. THE CENTRAL NERVOUS SYSTEM

In humanistic personology, in the humanistic representation of the person, we operate with the hypothesis that in the consolidated structure of the person the body, as distinct bio-physical entity and as biological organism, retains the functional autonomy and it constitutes their own humoral and neuro-psychic mechanisms of internal control/ regulation and of interaction with the environment, but a substantial dimension (edge) of the organism enters, directly or indirectly, in the process of personalization.

The solution of cohabitation which is find by the organism it is a concession, compromise - by which, lastly, the organism "supports" the morpho-physiological personalization, with influences and changes on the majority biological systems and phenomena, in exchange for its survival. In this way they go further and develop mutually both the organism and the person/ personality (Million, 1990).

In the formation and beingness of person/ personality crucial roles have the central nervous system, the sensitive jouissance, the endocrine system, the neuro-vegetative apparatus, the mechanisms of production, storage, processing and superization of the emotions, informations, and more (Canli, 2006). The personalization do not being conceivable without their contributions.

2.3. THE SOCIO-HUMAN ENVIRONMENT

Core Fragment

The contingent social-personal and socio-affective factors are crucial for the formation of the ontological-psychological sphere, while the cultural, morale conditions of learning and training are essential for the formation of the social-psychological sphere. The professional climate greatly influencing the formation of the person as a whole. Thus, in a purely humanistic perspective, the human-personal, the human-social factors are decisive in the formation and development of a strong, balanced, adaptable and happiness person. The psychological-human (humane) characteristics of the persons from near environment such as agreeability, soulful warmth, carefulness, empathy, spirituality, their constant presence and consistency, in human, spiritual and moral terms, the human quality of the interpersonal relationships, the compathy, the social relationships as humane relationships are the constitutional determinant factors that marks, crucially, the sense of the personality development, the sense of the person development, the adaptability, the soulful welfare, the happiness.

2.3.1. THE HUMAN ENVIRONMENTAL ONTO-SYSTEM

As we have seen in the book, even if in the child rearing are important the material conditions, the HUMAN conditions are, in fact, those that contribute crucially to the formation of a harmonious personality, of the soul of the ego, of the character, of the person as a whole, fulfilled and, socio-humanly, effective (Cusick, 2011; Moore, 1994).

Each of the two major spheres of the person, of the ontological-psychological sphere and of the psychological-social sphere, of the personality, and properly of the person, is the product of the interaction of the subject with specific factors, even if cannot be traced strict boundaries between them.

The contingent social-personal and socio-affective factors are crucial for the formation of the ontological-psychological sphere, while the cultural, morale conditions of learning and training are essential for the formation of the social-psychological sphere. The professional climate greatly influencing the formation of the person as a whole.

Thus, in a purely humanistic perspective, the human-personal, the human-social factors are decisive in the formation and development of a strong, balanced, adaptable and happiness person (Jung, 1981)..

The psychological-human (humane) characteristics of the person such as agreeability, soulful warmth, carefulness, empathy, spirituality, their constant presence and consistency, in human, spiritual and moral terms, the human quality of the interpersonal relationships, the compathy, the social relationships as humane relationships are the constitutional determinant factors that marks, crucially, the sense of the personality development, the sense of the person development, the adaptability, the soulful welfare, the happiness.

2.3.2. MICRO-COMMUNITY, FAMILY

The micro-community, in general, and the family, in special, are very important, even crucial, in the formation, functioning and beingness of the person, in humanistic personology - the humanistic-ontological perspective, especially through their socio-human/ humane and personal-relational compathetical dimensions (Cusick, 2011; Jung, 1981; Moore, 1994).

In this sense, any social group, community or organization is so, a compathetical community as well. Many human sufferings, tragedies or social problems are rooted in its underdevelopment, in weaknesses or serious compathetical problems.

The knowledge of this aspect by the educator (parent, teacher, caregiver, etc.) is a necessity and, moreover, the compathy, the empathetic community, the social-humane/ humane system of sympathies and empathies can be very effective tools for the personality formation/ development.

The empathetic community and compathy are build and specifically define through the common, collective, inter-/ trans-personal emotional, affective, sentimental, cognitive circumstances, characteristics and behaviors of the individuals who compose it. So, these consist mainly of three types of sub-processes or phenomena:

- emotional/ affective/ sentimental,
- cognitive/ intellectual, and
- spiritual/ cultural/ moral.

In this perspective each member of a community is, inter alia, a product of a unique and but also of a common, collective interaction, depending on the personality of the others, place, time, cultural niche, hazard. Every person being actually part of a particular compathetical system. This is, in turn, part of a comprehensive system. The most common compathetical system and most consistent is the family.

Into any micro-community, into the family, the compathetical consistency is given by the fact that the individual's personalities are composed of common emotional, cognitive, and cultural experiences, by the fact that in each individual personality exists, through empathy and projection, the others. It is established a mutual existential dependence between the persons and between the persons and the community as a whole.

This compathy, empathetic community works, through the organizational culture, also as a system of symbols or values that are rooted in the individual's personality or activism. These symbols and values are imposed as links and unitary resorts between the two parties. Their existence and operation give the sense of belonging, familiar, known, give comfort, safety and happiness.

Between the empathetic community and the individuals which it constitutes it is established a ontological-socio-human balance, an existential and functional optimum, in which is satisfied, in principle, in a harmonious and non-confrontational way, both the personal and the collective necessities. The empathetic community and the compathy can also have a negative influence, may be an area of non-value, of conflict, hostility or social exclusion, or can have a coherent organization and functioning but founded on non-value, on antisocial attitudes, or may be poorly organized, dysfunctional, immature. In both cases, the members are exposed to personal/ humane/ spiritual under-development, marginalization and social/ moral maladjustment.

The optimal condition for the construction and functioning of a strong, developed, equilibrate personality, a adaptable and happiness person, are the opposite thereof, namely positive, functional compathy, social/ human solidarity, unity, communication, cooperation, in the family, community, organization etc.

2.3.3. CULTURE, RELIGION, MORALS, EDUCATION

As is well known, the role of the culture, religion morals, and education in the process of forming and beingness, of proper functioning of the person, is more than important. In the process these bring simultaneously spiritual, ontological, and axiological inputs, mainly through their systems of knowledge, values, beliefs and ideals.

Thus, the **culture** offers both an axiological model, but represents also an inexhaustible reservoir of spiritual and epistemological resources in the processes of forming of the superior formations and spheres of the person/ personality, mostly of the social-personal sphere, of the social ego, of the conscience and character.

Religion, morals and **education**, as well, through their psychological-axiological dimensions and contents (beliefs, convictions attitudes, knowledge etc.), but also through the ones social/ moral (rituals, ethics rules, etc.) can be considered important spiritual and ethical factors/ sources in the ontogenetic process of forming to what we call, in humanistic personology, *the person as a whole*, with its principal spheres - the ontological-psychological sphere and, especially the social-personal sphere.

The role of the culture, religion morals, and education being so more important in the formation, beingness and functioning of the latter one, of the social-personal / psychological-social sphere because these provide models, values, knowledge, cultural and moral frames of forming and developing (Jung, 1981; Moore, 1994).

The humanistic-ontological conception on the person/ the human personality is so given, as well, of the idea that these are ontological products of some gradual and stadial processes held with the crucial contribution of the biological and intellectual factors, but very important role and contribution have the axiological and moral factors, the concrete/ contextual/ contingent socio-cultural factors where the person grows and lives, mainly the moral-humane factors, with the crucial contribution of the moral conducts of the individual persons, concrete people from the proximate environment with intense and constant psychological-moral presence and influence, especially the significant members from its family/ significant group.

Important are also the structural, institutional socio-cultural and the socio-moral factors expressed in the systems of dominant norms and values, in community and society as a whole (Baker, 2004).

2.4. THE MIND

Core Fragment

Each of the two major spheres of the person - the ontological-psychological sphere and the social-personal sphere - is conditioned and is, inter alia, the product, of the existence, beingness and functioning of the mind as a whole but also of the existence, beingness and functioning of certain mind substructures, formations, processes, etc. For example, in the processes of formation, beingness and functioning of the ontological-psychological sphere of the person more important are the sensations, memory and thinking, while in the processes of formation, beingness and functioning of the social-psychological sphere more important are some emergent upper structures as the noetic ontos, intellect, culture or the conscience/ comscience.

2.4.1. THE MIND AND THE PERSON

In the process of forming of the person/ personality the role of the mind, of the cognitive, intellectual factor is, along of the body and of the environment, constitutional and, even, determinant (Jung, 1981).

We are talking, in particular, of the role of memory, thinking and imagination, intellect and intelligence, but, in extension, also, of some emergent upper structures as the noetic ontos or consciousness - these operates with more advanced tools, more developed and more personalized, conditioning, crucially, through feedback, the process of personalization.

Each of the two major spheres of the person - the ontological-psychological sphere and the social-personal sphere - is conditioned and is, inter alia, the product, of the existence, beingness and functioning of the mind as a whole but also of the existence, beingness and functioning of certain mind substructures, formations, processes, etc.

For example, in the processes of formation, beingness and functioning of the ontological-psychological sphere of the person more important are the sensations, memory and thinking, while in the processes of formation, beingness and functioning of the social-psychological sphere more important are some emergent upper structures as the noetic ontos, intellect, culture or the conscience/ comscience.

So regarding the forming of the most important formations, spheres, persoms, of the personality and the person as a whole, must to be highlighted, firstly, the crucial contribution of the mind as a whole but also of the existence, beingness and functioning of certain mind substructures, formations, processes

The essence of the humanistic-ontological conception regarding the person/ the human personality is given, inter alia, by the idea that these are ontological/ ontogenetical products of some gradual and stadial processes carried out with the crucial contribution of the concrete/ contextual/ contingent socio-human factors where the person grows and lives, mainly the personal-human/ humane factors, with the crucial contribution of the individual persons, concrete people from the proximate environment with intense and constant psychological (emotional) and spiritual (soulful) presence and influence, especially the significant members from its family/ significant group, but also of the mental, cognitive, intellectual factors.

2.4.2. THE COGNITIVE HABILITATION, PERTENTION AND THE EPISTEMIC SUBJECT

From the mental point of view the process of personalization begins with **the sensitive-cognitive habilitation**, namely with the activation of the elementary functions and capacities of knowledge and cognitive reflection of the environment in the mind, in the cognitive sphere of the person (Piaget & Inhelde, 1969; Jung, 1981).

Crucial roles in process have also **the pertention** (the structural-functional synthesis, emergence *perception-attention*) (Jing et al., 2006, p.238), but also **the epistemic subject** (the psychological-ontological and biological-constitutional need of knowledge). The last one accompanying and actively supporting the whole process of personalization, especially the processes of formation of the ontological-psychological sphere of the person/ personality – the personal ontos, the soul, the ontic ego.

2.4.3. THE MENTAL APPARATUS, INTELLIGENCE, THE NOETIC ONTOS

The *memory, thinking, imagination* and *language*, as principal reflexive-cognitive functions and processes, represent the four cardinal points among which is carried out the fundamental mental activities of the person, constituting, at the same time, the skeleton, the frame of reference of the mind as personal formation and as **mental apparatus/ resort/ factor** for the ontogenetical processes of personalization, of formation and functioning of the personality (Baker, 2004).

In the process of ontogenetic forming of the personality and the person very important roles having also the cognitive **intelligence** (the capacity of processing the informations) (Jung, 1981). and the **noetic ontos** (the autonomous mental universe of the ideas) but also other forms of intelligence such as *emotional intelligence, spiritual intelligence, social intelligence,* etc. Whole these accompanying and actively supporting the superior processes of personalization, especially the processes of formation of the social-psychological/ personal-social sphere of the person/ personality – the social ego, the conscience, the character.

The
HUMANISTIC
PERSONOLOGY
Project

CHAPTER 3

BASIC CHARACTERISTICS, LAWS, AND PRINCIPLES OF THE PROCESS OF FORMATION AND DEVELOPMENT OF THE PERSON/ PERSONALITY

3.1. INTRODUCTORY ASPECTS 88

3.2. PRINCIPLES/ LAWS/ CHARACTERISTICS 89

3.2.1. EMERGENCE AND IMERGENCE 90

3.2.2. TRANSMERGENCE AND TELEGENCE 91

3.2.3. CONMERGENCE AND SINMERGENCE 92

3.3. STAGES/ STEPS / PROCESSES 93

3.3.1. THE CONTACT AND THE ACQUISITION/ ACCUMULATION 93

3.3.2. THE STRUCTURING/ CENTRALIZATION, AND THE CONSTITUTION/ HOLISTIZATION 94

3.3.3. THE ESTABLISHING/ NETWORKING, AND THE ONTIFICATION/ FULFILLMENT 95

3.4. ENERGY, MECHANISMS, RESORTS 96

3.4.1. THE ONTO-PERSONAL ENERGY AND THE PROSTASIS 96

3.4.2. MECHANISMS, MONTAGES, MOTIVATIONAL SOURCES AND RESORTS 97

3.5. THE ONTO-FORMATIZATION, THE PERSOMIZATION, AND THE PROMERGENCE/ DISMERGENCE 98

3.5.1. THE PERSONAL ONTO-FORMATIZATION AND THE PERSOMIZATION 98

3.5.2. THE PROMERGENCE AND THE DISMERGENCE 99

3.1. INTRODUCTORY ASPECTS

The formation, beingness, functioning and development of any living being imply, obligatory, some processes, laws, and characteristics, as well as some energies, mechanisms, resorts which support, feed, determine, facilitate both its formation as well its beingness, functioning and development. These characteristics are extremely important and relevant in the case of the *human* beings, in the context of formation and functioning of some specific very complex formations, spheres, persoms, or of the person/ personality as a whole.

So, in contrast to the processes of formation, to the laws, stages and the energetic resorts from the inorganic physical world level the processes of formation, the laws, the steps and the energetic resorts from the organic, psychological, or spiritual world level are of infinite complexity, these transcend the contingent, entail the past and the future, exceeding the spatial and temporal limitations, working simultaneously in the same "space", having unpredictable evolutions, arising, emerging, randomly, some from others.

However, despite appearances, these processes, laws, stages, and resorts are, in our opinion, normal, natural dimensions, valences, properties of the objective existence, do not originate and do not belong to another (parallel, metaphysical) world, but, still, these must to be understood, modeled in a scientific-epistemological framework much wider and dialectical way than permit the rules of the sciences of physicist type, applied, often, almost mechanically to the biological, psychological, and spiritual processes and phenomena.

In our ontological-humanistic paradigm of formation, beingness and functioning of the person/ personality, of the individual human being, we will talk so about characteristics, properties, processes, principles such as onto-formatization and persomization, promergence and dismergence, emergence and imergence, transmergence and telegence, conmergence and sinmergence, about stages of the evolution, development, establishment of the personal ontological-psychological formations, of the persoms, of the person as a whole, such as of contact, of acquisition/ accumulation, of structuration/ centralization, of constitution/ holistization, of establishing/ networking, of ontification/ fulfillment, and about psychological-ontological-subjective human and spiritual experiences and jouissances that represent the main "substance", motivational-energetical sources and resorts of forming of the personality/ person's formations, persoms and spheres, motivational-energetical sources and resorts from where these are "feed", with genetic/ formative or functional/ existential purposes and energies. Some categories of experiences and jouissances being destined, with a great accuracy, to certain formations, persons, spheres, or to the personality or the person as a whole.

3.2. PRINCIPLES/ LAWS/ CHARACTERISTICS

Core Fragment

In humanistic personology, according to our opinion, transmergence represents the property and capacity of the personal onto-subjective, bio-psychological, and noetical-spiritual processes and phenomena to carry out without limitations and physical barriers of space and organization. According to these properties/ laws/ principles the processes of formation, establishment and functioning of the onto-formations, persoms, spheres, etc. transcend the structures, the organizations, and the entities already constituted, it attract and involve them in the processes of forming, constituting and establishing of the new formations, without altering them. The degree of freedom/ action is very large, the number of combinations and the facilities of organization, structuration, "formatization" and "persomization" being almost unlimited. This property/ law is explained, in part, by the structural, generic, and genetic unity/ cohesion of the living and spiritual world, the multiplication at infinit of the informational/ spiritual systems/ entities, and through the extraordinary quality of the living, psychological, noetic and

In our humanistic-ontological/spiritual paradigm of formation, beingness, functioning and development of the person/ personality, of the individual human being, we speak, here, in this section, of characteristics, properties, processes, principles such as *emergence* and *imergence, transmergence* and *telegence, conmergence* and *sinmergence.*

3.2.1. EMERGENCE AND IMERGENCE

Emergence is the quality/ capacity/ property of the physical, biological, and (especially) of the psychological and spiritual processes that makes possible the appearance of new entities, formations, spheres, structures, properties, etc. from the previous ones, from their interaction, defined as sources, factors, generative elements, premises, (pre-) conditions (Hubbard, 2012).

Therefore, emergence, in the context of action of the other principles/ laws/ characteristics/ qualities generates or contributes to the formation, beingness and functioning of new entities, structures, formations, realities and qualities which, usually, are more complex, more developed, and better adapted to the internal and (especially) to the environmental factors (Bickhard, 2012).

As process and phenomenon, emergence is based mainly on the dynamic, transmergent, telegent, imergent, conmergent and sinmergent interaction of the (pre-)existing entities, on its intrinsic law-like developmental and transformative properties and qualities, manifested in the context of the specific environmental processes, as well as of the upper systems which it belongs.

The resulting entity incorporates features, qualities and elements of the *source-entities* but is presented yet as a (relative) new existence, new entity, new construction, with its own (new) features, qualities, components/ elements, structures and ways of relating, adapted to an environmental context, in turn, its own, usually, reformed.

In close connection with the emergence, **imergence** represents the property and capacity of the physical, organic, psychological, spiritual systems to forming, developing, evolving it in itself, from nothing, from inertia, "subversively", simultaneously with the developments, evolutions, changes caused by the determined, objective identified factors.

Just as the emergence, the imergence generates or contributes to the formation, beingness and of new entities, structures, formations, realities and qualities which, usually, are more complex and better adapted to the internal and environmental factors (Khan, 1981;

Hubbard, 2012). However, unlike the emergence, the imergence, operating predominantly from the inside, with inner resources, contributes to a greater extent to increasing the complexity of the existing formations than to the appearance of new ones.

3.2.2. TRANSMERGENCE AND TELEGENCE

In humanistic personology, according to our opinion, **transmergence** represents the property and capacity of the personal onto-subjective, bio-psychological, and noetical-spiritual processes and phenomena to carry out without limitations and physical barriers of space and organization.

According to these properties/ laws/ principles the processes of formation, establishment and functioning of the onto-formations, persoms, spheres, etc. transcend the structures, the organizations, and the entities already constituted, it attract and involve them in the processes of forming, constituting and establishing of the new formations, without altering them. The degree of freedom/ action is very large, the number of combinations and the facilities of organization, structuration, "formatization" and "persomization" being almost unlimited (Khan, 1981).

This property/ law is explained, in part, by the structural, generic, and genetic unity/ cohesion of the living and spiritual world, the multiplication at infinit of the informational/ spiritual systems/ entities, and through the extraordinary quality of the living, psychological, noetic and spiritual environments, systems to permit the transcendence.

Telegence means, much, the same thing, but concerns the temporal and teleological-projective aspect of the processes and phenomena, representing, so, the property and capacity of the personal onto-subjective bio-psychological processes and phenomena to carry out without time limitations and barriers (Waldrop, 1993; Bickhard, 2012), and in accordance with a project, goal, aim, scope, direction.

3.2.3. CONMERGENCE AND SINMERGENCE

Conmergence entails the transmergence, the telegence, the imergence and the promergence, and represents the tendency of the personal ontological-psychological formations and processes to organize and concentrate them "thematically" in formations, persoms, structures, etc., reflecting the inherence, the objective necessity of apparition, establishment and beingness of some (new) functions, beyond any limitations of "logistic" or temporal order, through the integrative convergence, conjugation of some disparate elements already existing (Chardin, 1959, p. 106). It is so the quality/ capacity/ property of the physical, biological, and (especially) of the psychological and spiritual processes that makes possible the appearance and functioning of new entities, formations, spheres, structures, properties, etc. from the previous ones, defined as constitutive elements.

Usually, the new entities are more complex, more developed, and better adapted to the environmental factors. The conmergent processes are based mainly on the dynamic, emergent, transmergent, telegent, imergent, sinmergent interaction manifested in the context of the specific environmental processes, as well as of the upper systems which it belongs. The resulting entity incorporates features, qualities and elements of the *source-entities* but is presented yet as a (relative) new existence, new entity, new construction, with its own (new) features, qualities, components/ elements, structures and ways of relating (Waldrop, 1993; Khan, 1981; Hubbard, 2012).

Sinmergence is the quality/ capacity/ property of the physical, biological and spiritual processes which makes possible the coexistence, simultaneously, of the onto-personal, psychological-spiritual entities in the same personal "space", the formation, functioning and beingness of some distinct entities, formations, persoms, spheres, structures, relationships, processes on the same material, biological, informational, spiritual support, phenomenological framework (Waldrop, 1993; Bickhard, 2012).

3.3. STAGES/ STEPS/ PROCESSES

Core Fragment

The transition to the stage of formation, constitution/ holistization, as formation, persom, person, etc., is essentially conditioned, among others, by the appearance, imposing of a new "nature". It is about, for exemple, of the ancestral leap from the biological to the psychological or human nature/ level, from the material or biological formations to the spiritual, human formations. In the global processes of personalization, now is carried out the jump from structure to system, from organism + personality + environment to (=) person as a whole, as unique, individual human being. An important role they meet processes and mechanisms such as the feed-back, feed-before, etc. In this stage occurs, including by means of these processes and mechanisms, a consistent symbiosis personality-community - it is the point from where, properly, one can speak of person, of social and relatively autonomous human being.

In the humanistic-ontological paradigm of formation of the person/ personality, of the individual human being, we operates with stages such as *of contact, of acquisition/ accumulation, of structuration/ centralization, of constitution/ holistization, of establishing/ networking,* and *of ontification/ fulfillment.*

3.3.1. THE CONTACT AND THE ACQUISITION/ ACCUMULATION

In the phase of **contact** occurs the primary junction between the main elements which will come in the constitution of the probable future entity, formation, structure, sphere, persom, etc. One of the elements can be considered the specific function (role), but also the body/ organism as a whole, or certain organs or neuro-vegetative, physiological or psycho-physiological systems.

In the complex and profound processes of perso-formatization, persomization etc. the stage of contact imply, among others, at macroscale level, the interaction, the primary junction *body/organism-*

community/ socio-human environment, especially the junction *organism/ sensations – family/ mother.*

After the stage of contact follows a period of **acquisitions** and **accumulations,** intrinsic, consubstantial to the incipient links and connections which have already been realized. These represent "the seeds" of the future formations, and around them begin to gravitate the elements which will be part of the probable future entity, formation, structure, sphere, persom, etc. It is a prolonged period, difficult, adversarial and sinuous of accumulation of knowledge and experiences, essential premise for the optimal completion of the genetic steps that follows. It is a period that takes place by sub-processes as experimentation, learning, and "experientialization", in other words, of acquisition in cascade, largely uncritical, of new knowledge and experiences.

3.3.2. THE STRUCTURING/ CENTRALIZATION AND THE CONSTITUTIONS/ HOLISTIZATION

In the context of the connections and acquisitions from the stages of contact, acquisitions and accumulations, after a prolonged period, difficult, adversarial and sinuous of accumulation of knowledge and experiences, after many sub-processes of experimentation, learning, and "experientialization", of acquisition in cascade, largely uncritical, of new knowledge and experiences, begins to unfold, gradually, some processes of **structuring/ centralization** and internal organization of the new entity, formation, persom, etc. which, sporadically and schematically, makes its appearance. It is so the third preparatory stage, with very important role in laying the foundations of the new entity, formation, persom etc.

In the global process of personalization, in this period/ process the knowledge and experiences acquired in the phase of accumulation, unorganized or only punctually organized, or structured around of some poles, formations, persoms, more or less representative in the sense and goal of the process of personalization, are now holistically structured, at the level of personal assembly.

The transition to the stage of **formation, constitution/ holistization**, as formation, persom, person, etc., is essentially conditioned, among others, by the appearance, imposing of a new "nature". It is about, for exemple, of the ancestral leap from the biological to the psychological or human nature/ level, from the material or biological formations to the spiritual, human formations. In the global processes of personalization, now is carried out the jump from structure to system, from organism + personality + environment to (=) person as a whole, as unique, individual human being. An important role they meet processes and mechanisms such as the feed-back, feed-before, etc. In this stage occurs, including by means of these processes and mechanisms, a consistent symbiosis personality-community - it is the point from where, properly, one can speak of person, of social and relatively autonomous human being.

3.3.3. THE ESTABLISHING/ NETWORKING AND THE ONTIFICATION/ FULFILLMENT

At the stage of **establishing/ networking** the formation, persom etc. are, internally well organized, permanentizated, established in the personal assembly and plays, largely, the role according to the function which had formed, establishing stable connections with the formations and with the environmental spheres, becoming autonomous part of a superior, comprehensive system. At this level the formation, the persom, personality, or the person as a whole becomes already an entity, an existential unit, finally a person, in determined socio-human context.

If the phase of constitution is defined through formatization and internal functioning, the phase of establishment is defined by consolidation, function and role within the personal assembly, the final stage, the **ontification**, means the completion of the process and identification with goal, function, means the transition to the stage of entity, *being,* of formation, and, consequently, to its **fulfillment**. At the personal ensemble level, at the person as whole level the environment and the personality are merged, unified, being found, constitutionally, ontologically, in structures, formations subordinated almost exclusively to the person's functions, occurring, so, during the properly personal ontogenesis, a process of *in-beingness*, of apparition of a new existential entity, process at the end of which is established *the being* and starts the beingness as person in the socio-human community.

At the level of person, as a whole, this stage is reached only after it has been established the persomic assembly/ the personality, and was constituted the conscience and other person's superior formations/ instances, assimilating but a large part from their dimensions and contents - because we talk of *human* ontification, even if the deepest ontic resorts and mechanisms are described in organical-functional, physiological, neuro-vegetative, neuro-psychical terms.

3.4. ENERGY, MECHANISMS, RESORTS

Core Fragment

The ontological-psychological subjective human/ humane and spiritual experiences represent the main "substance", motivational sources and resorts, driven in mechanisms and assemblies from where the formations are "feed", with genetic/ formative or functional/ existential purposes. In this sense, we believe that some categories of experiences are destined, with a great accuracy, to certain formations, persoms, spheres, structures, etc., also, we believe that one can speak of experiences with polyvalent motivational-energetic qualities/ valances/ functions, so motivational-ontological sources for more formations or assemblies, or for formation, beingness and functioning of the personality, or of the person as a whole, as individual in relation.

3.4.1. THE ONTO-PERSONAL ENERGY AND THE PROSTASIS

The **onto-personal energy** probably conditionates, determine largely, the emergence, the promergence, the formation, the functioning and beingness of the ontos-formations, persoms, of personality and the person as a whole.

There may be an ontic-psychological mechanism of production of the specific energies required for perso-genesis, so, of transformation of the emotions, of the subjective experiences in energy of formatization, persomization, and finally of personalization, assimilated in onto-formations, persoms, structures, etc., then, by the internal ontic mechanisms/ processes of the formations and persoms, of release of other forms of energy, as propeller source for self-development, imergence and autonomous continuation of the process of onto-personalization.

This energy probably acts as a synthesizer, processor in the process of personalization (the construction of the perso-project, personality, self, character), and supports, especially energetically, the construction of the personal assembly and the social functioning/ beingness of the person, both internally and externally, ontological-psychologically and social-behaviorally (Khan, 1981; Hubbard, 2012).

Prostasis means, in our opinion, the trend, property, capacity of the formations, persoms, personality, of the person as macro-formation, as a whole, to preserve, energetically-ontogenetically, its tendency of growing and developing, its nature, structure and function, the existential continuity, its specific beingness and functioning. It is essentially a state of genesis, having a consistent dynamic dimension, being an important mechanism of the persogenetical process, alongside promergence and homeostasis.

Unlike the *homeostasis* that has a "passive" nature the prostazis acts both for internal conservation but also has functions of protecting against regress, against the destabilizing, disturbing actions that come from the inside or the outside of the formation, persom, personality, person a whole, as an individual.

3.4.2. MECHANISMS, MONTAGES, MOTIVATIONAL SOURCES AND RESORTS

At the basc of the processes of personal onto-formatization, persomization, and personalization stand innumerable **mechanisms, montages**, motivational sources and resorts, internal onto-formative loops that "work" in combination and according to some laws, rules which we cannot say, at the moment, many things (Chardin, 1959; Khan, 1981; Hubbard, 2012).

Their role being, mainly, that to process and assimilate the experiences, feelings, emotions, knowledge both in formative aim as well as in functionally and adaptive aim.

The ontological-psychological subjective human/ humane and spiritual experiences represent the main "substance", **motivational sources and resorts**, driven in mechanisms and assemblies from where the formations are "feed", with genetic/ formative or functional/ existential purposes.

In this sense, we believe that some categories of experiences are destined, with a great accuracy, to certain formations, persoms, spheres, structures, etc., also, we believe that one can speak of experiences with polyvalent motivational-energetic qualities/ valances/ functions, so motivational-ontological sources for more formations or assemblies, or for formation, beingness and functioning of the personality, or of the person as a whole, as individual in relation.

The way in which the mechanisms and processes "extract" the human/ humane, spiritual "sap", the "protein" of formatization, persomization, personalization, of humanization of the person, we cannot say that we know, but we must assume that there exist some specialized ontological-psychological resorts which operate to this end.

3.5. THE ONTO-FORMATIZATION, THE PERSOMIZATION, AND THE PROMERGENCE/ DISMERGENCE

Core Fragment

The promergence and the dismergence are opposite ontological-procesual properties, qualities of the processes and phenomena of formatization, persomization and personalization, of the processes of construction or development of the formations, persoms, structures, spheres, reflecting the objective-emergent tendencies of the living and spiritual systems of conservation, development, growing, or entropy, degradation, decrease. At any moment a number of formations, dimensions or processes are in trends of growing, advancement, formation, are promergent, and others are in degradation decline, involution, are dismergent.Both the formation and the beingness/ functioning of every formation, person, structure, sphere, of the personality and the person as a whole are cucially determined by the predominance and the intensity of the promergence, by the promergent processes, by the positive tendencies of conservation, development, growing, progress.

3.5.1. THE PERSONAL ONTO-FORMATIZATION AND THE PERSOMIZATION

The personal onto-formatization is the genetic psychological-ontological process which implies the ontogenetical incorporation, union, synthesis, the conmergent, emergent, transmergent unitary organization of some entities/ formations, energies, mechanisms, processes in new structure, formative entities, formations, usually upper, superior, more complex and more integrated, structurally, functionally, and axiologically.

The personal onto-formation, once constituted, is imposed as a qualitative leap to a new structural and functional existence, and necessary precondition for the overall personal genesis and imposing of the person, socially and culturally, accepted as such.

The formative pressure of the environment (especially the organism and the social community) is fundamental, constitutional, and determinant, and is more intense exercised in the lower stages of the process of personalization.

On the one part act the internal factors, and on the other part act the external factors. To start the role of the internal factors is more important, and determine the emergence, the establishment of the fundamental, constitutional ontic formations, but, along with the ontogenetic development and social exposing, the personal formatization, even the personal higher formatization, are conditioned, influenced and even determined by the action of the external (socio-personal, cultural, moral, economic) factors - the formatization developing itself, ontogenetically, in persomization (Khan, 1981).

Persomization, therefore, is the genetical/ developmental psychological-ontological process which implies the incorporation, union, synthesis, the conmergent, emergent, transmergent unitary, global, holistic organization of the formations, energies, mechanisms, of the sub-personal processes in structures and constructions at the level of personality, person, as stable holistic structural and functional entities, characteristical for the person as human and individual, usually upper, superior, more complex and more integrated, structurally, functionally, and axiologically, in contradiction to the psychological formations, which are, many of them, circumstantial, contextual, fluctuate, relational.

3.5.2. THE PROMERGENCE AND THE DISMERGENCE

The promergence and dismergence are opposite ontological-procesual properties, qualities of the processes and phenomena of formatization, persomization and personalization, of the processes of construction or development of the formations, persoms, structures, spheres, reflecting the objective-emergent tendencies of the living and spiritual systems of

> ➢ conservation, development, growing, or

> ➢ entropy, degradation, decrease (Davis, 2012).

At any moment a number of formations, dimensions or processes are

> ➤ in growing, advancement, formation, are **promergent**, and others are

> ➤ in degradation decline, involution, are **dismergent**.

Both the formation and the beingness/ functioning of every formation, person, structure, sphere, of the personality and the person as a whole are cucially determined by the predominance and the intensity of the promergence, by the promergent processes, by the positive tendencies of conservation, development, growing, progress (Agassi, 1999).

CHAPTER 4

THE PROCESS OF PERSONALIZATION.

THE GREAT SUBPROCESSES OF THE PROCESS OF PERSONALIZATION

4.1. INTRODUCTORY ASPECTS 102

4.2. THE PROCESS OF PERSONALIZATION 103

**4.3. ESSENTIAL CHARACTERISTICS OF
THE PROCESS OF PERSONALIZATION 107**

**4.4. THE TWO GREAT SUBPROCESSES OF THE PROCESS OF
PERSONALIZATION. THE FORMATION OF THE PERSON AL A
WHOLE 109**

4.1. INTRODUCTORY ASPECTS

In humanistic perspective, even if are also important the economic, material conditions, *the socio-personal, the human/ humane,* and *the cultural conditions* are, in fact, those that contribute crucially to the process of personalization, to the formation of soul, ego, personality, to the formation of the person as human being, those that have the determinative contribution in the psychological-ontogenetical process of spiritualization and humanisation, those that contribute, consequently, at forming of a harmonious and developed, ontological-psychologically and socio-humanly, personality/ person.

Each of the major spheres and formations of the person/ personality is, in great measure, the product of the interaction with specific human, social, cultural, moral factors, even if cannot be traced strict boundaries between them. Thus, in a purely humanistic perspective, the human-personal and the human-social factors are decisive in the formation and development of the person as a whole, in the process of *human/ humane* personalization, thtough the two great sub-processes, of formation of the ontological-psychological sphere and of the social-personal/ psychological-social sphere. The formation of the ontological-psychological sphere, of the (ontological) personality, is done especially during childhood and adolescence, while of the social-personal/ psychological-social sphere, of the person, is done especially together with, and after, the subject acquires social autonomy, profession, its own family etc.

The formation of the ontological-psychological sphere, of the (ontological) personality includes mainly the formation of the personal ontos, soul, and ego/self, while the formation of the ontological-psychological sphere implies the ontogenetical construction of the (social) conscience co**m**science, culture, the humane conscience), the character, and the (social) competences, skills, abilities, qualities and habitudes, through processes as ontosfication, spiritualization, individualization, holistization/ persomization, socialization, autonomization etc. All, therefore, as sub-processes of the general, teleological process of personalization.

4.2. THE PROCESS OF PERSONALIZATION

Core Fragment

At any moment a number of formations, dimensions or processes are in growing, advancement, forming, are promergent, and others are in degradation decline, involution, are dismergent; both the formation and the beingness/ functioning of every formation, person, sphere, of the personality and the person as a whole being crucially determined by the predominance and the intensity of the promergence, of the promergent processes, the humane and spiritual experiences representing the main "substance", motivational sources/ resources and positive factors of promergence, of the promergent/ functional processes, of the process of personalization

The mature person, socially integrated, able to manage its own destiny, fulfilled and happy, is one of the main goals of the individual psychological-ontological evolution, throughout life, especially in childhood, adolescence and youth, and target of the complex process of personalization.

But these targets can be achieved only if the ample process, global, teleological of personalization is preceded, doubled, completed, assisted of other processes. It is about, inter alia, of the processes of ontosfication, spiritualization, individualization, persomization/ holistisation, autonomization, finalized with the formation of the person, of the person as a whole, and the properly process of personalization.

In humanistic personology, the humanistic-ontological paradigm, the main psychological-ontological resort and "matter" of almost all processes of personalization is the current inner living, the current, existential, bio-psycho-spiritual experience of the person.

The process of formation unfolds on multiple plans and levels; aspect that involves to take in consideration at least a systemic-atomistic perspective, but also a spherical perspective, the construction in this last approach of two great sub-spheres (with which we will operate, mostly, in the book):

- the ontological-psychological sphere, and
- the social-personal sphere.

The process of formation of this sub-spheres of the person reflect two relatively distinct existential statuses, fundamental characteristics, needs and realities of every being, the more of the *human* being:

- *to be, to exist, on the one hand, in itself, inside, in its own bio-psychic and spiritual world*, and, on the other hand,

- *to exist outside, in environment, in community, culture, nature, among people, values, rules, institutions, etc.*

For each one, ontogenetically, are being built and function specific structures, spheres, constructions, formations, even if, as we have seen above, one cannot speak of rigid boundaries or locations, clearly distinct - these coexisting, transmergently, in the wide, large framework of the person/ personality as a dynamic, functional system, as a whole.

As we have highlighted in other sections of the book, the humanistic-ontological paradigm prioritizes the role of the psychological-spiritual and socio-humane factors, in collaboration with the ones cultural, moral, etc., representing the process of forming of the person as a successive and concomitant, transmergent and emergent, phenomenological and ideographic constructions of personal onto-formations, persoms, spheres, etc., and less as a simple activation and enabling of certain existing structures, of certain universal patterns, less variable; recognizing, so, the self-determination, the ontogenetic autonomy, the role of the subject, or the importance of some ideographic/ emergent psychological-ontological constructions as the soul (affective, spiritual, humane) or the ontological ego.

Crucial there are, so, in the process of forming, in the structure/ structuration and the beingness/ functioning of the person/ personality, the unique subjective experiences of the subject, the feelings, the emotions or the ontological ego and the free will, the psychological-spiritual factors/ formation (especially the soul – affective, spiritual, humane), the self-generative internal dynamics, through culturalization and humanization, through emergence and superization, through spiritual/ human generalization/ abstraction of the psychological-compathetic (socio-humane) subjective experience.

In the spirit of the emergent systems theory (which involves, among others, the chaos theory and the complex systems theory) regarding the formation of the person/ personality, of the human being, we speak about characteristics, properties, processes, principles such as onto-formatization, persomization and promergence, emergence and imergence, transmergence and telegence, conmergence and sinmergence, and about ontological stages of evolution, development, establishment of the personal ontological-psychological formations, of the person as a whole, such as of contact, of acquisition/ accumulation, of structuration/ centralization, of constitution/ holistization, of establishing/ networking, of ontification/ fulfillment.

In the light of the emergent systems theory's principles the processes of formation of the person/ personality, in humanistic personology – the ontological-humanistic perspective, make possible the appearance of new entities, structures, properties, etc. from the previous ones, defined as sources, factors, premises, (pre-)conditions, the processes being based mainly on the dynamic, transmergent, telegent, imergent, conmergent and sinmergent interaction of the existing entities, on its intrinsic law-like developmental and transformative properties, manifested in the context of the specific environmental processes and phenomena, as well as of the systems which the subject belongs.

According to the emergent systems theory the resulting entities incorporate features of the *source-entities* but are presented yet as new existences, with them own features and ways of relating, adapted also to an environmental context, in turn, usually reformed.

The processes take place, largely, without limitations and physical barriers of space and organization, transcending the structures, the organizations, and the entities already constituted, attracting and involving them in the processes of forming, constituting and establishing of the new formations, without altering them.

In humanistic personology, the ontological-humanistic perspective on the process of forming of the person/ personality the degree of freedom/ action is very large, the number of combinations and the facilities of structuration and formatization being almost unlimited; one of the most important explanation is given by the fact that in the emergent and complex systems the processes have the extraordinary quality to permit the transcendence and the multiplication to infinit to the informational/ spiritual entities, taking place without time limitations and barriers, by the fact/ explanation that in the emergent and complex systems the processes have the tendency to organize and concentrate them "thematically" in formations, persoms, structures, spheres etc., reflecting the inherence, the objective necessity of some functions, beyond any limitations of "logistic" or temporal order, by the fact that the entities coexist, simultaneously, in the same personal "space", the functioning and beingness of some distinct entities, structures, relationships, processes on/ through the same material, biological, informational, spiritual support, framework.

At any moment a number of formations, dimensions or processes are in growing, advancement, forming, are promergent, and others are in degradation decline, involution (Bickhard, 2012), are dismergent; both the formation and the beingness/ functioning of every formation, person, sphere, of the personality and the person as a whole being crucially determined by the predominance and the intensity of the promergence, of the promergent processes, the humane and spiritual experiences representing the main "substance", motivational sources/ resources and positive factors of promergence, of the promergent/ functional processes.

The humane and spiritual experiences and the promergent processes are involved in complex, emergent, dynamic mechanisms and entities, every formation, persom, personality, the person as a whole being so a product of the ontogenetical incorporation, union, synthesis, of the conmergent, emergent, transmergent unitary organization of the sub-entities/ formations, structures, energies, mechanisms, of the processes of organization in new structures, formative entities, formations, persoms, usually upper structurally and axiologically.

Finally, as result of the global process of personalization, of the processes of ontosfication, spiritualization, individualization, persomization/ holistisation, autonomization, the person, as a whole, incorporates, unifies, synthesizes, emergently, conmergently, transmergently in a unitary organization the formations, energies, mechanisms, the processes, structures and constructions on the global/ maximal level, forming a holistic entity, with unique characteristics, qualities and conducts; in humanistic personology, the ontological-humanistic perspective on the person, very important being its humanistic/ humane and spiritual dimensions/ valences/ contents.

All, as we see, therefore, begins, personologically, in ontogenesis, with the process of formation of the personal ontos, with the complex and miraculous process of ontosfication.

4.3. ESSENTIAL CHARACTERISTICS OF THE PROCESS OF PERSONALIZATION

Core Fragment

The unicity of the person, and of the process of personalization, is given both by the genetic inherited biological characteristics, result of the phylogenetic evolution, as well as by the environmental characteristics of the ontogenetic process, but important roles have also some factors which are related to the subjective-metaphysical indeterminism, to the free will, the learning trial-error mechanism, to the world of ego, of will, to the abyssal world of the spirit and subjectivity, to the interior energy and resorts of great depthness and complexity, that determine us to consider the ontological process of forming of the person as unpredictable and never ended, and the person as never perfect, identical with himself or with the social role that it meets.

It would be simplistic to consider the process of personalization as "standard", predetermined; it would be against the ontological paradigm which we assume in this paper.

Beyond an inherent pattern, the ontogenetic process of forming of the person is carried out at the confluence of some conditions and factors described through a great **complexity, infinite variety, diversity, dynamics**, which confer accentuated characteristics of unicity; issue reflected in the way it is presented the product, the result of the process - THE PERSON.

The **unicity** of the person is given so both by the genetic inherited biological characteristics, result of the phylogenetic evolution, as well as by the environmental characteristics of the ontogenetic process (McAdams, 2009), but important roles have also some factors which are related to the subjective-metaphysical indeterminism, to the free will, the learning trial-error mechanism, to the world of ego, of will, to the abyssal world of the spirit and subjectivity, to the interior energy and resorts of great depthness and complexity, that determine us to consider the ontological process of forming of the person as unpredictable and never ended, and the person as never perfect, identical with himself or with the social role that it meets.

All this lead us to consider that, at any age, the person is an opened bio-psycho-social system, fragile, influential, flexible, dynamic, in formation, change, progress and regress, with frequent changes of the internal hierarchical, economic, structural, axiological reports (Khan, 1981).

In the humanistic personology paradigm, the humanistic-ontological perspective on person/ personality, we are interested mostly in the way in which it was formed and exists the person by a number of features of human/ humane, moral, orientation, of spiritual richness and virtue, of humanism, but also of maturity, functionality, fulfillment and conduct such as empathy, generousity, helpfulness, agreeability, amiability, carity, charisma, compassion, confidence, cooperation, decency, honestity, honorability, selfless, sociability, paternalism, solidarity, humanism, openness, peace of soul, spirituality, patience, allo-centricity, passion, humane energy, melancholy, genuinity, idealism, culture, humanistic intelligence, romantism, sensitivity, sentimentalism, wisdom, femininity, emotionality, impressionability, invisibility, purity, self-consciousness, unaggressivity, adaptability, courage, dynamism, efficiency, elegance, humor, incorruptibility, independence, assertivity, invulnerability, loyalty, moderation, modesty, non-authoritarism, openness, persuasivity, protectivity, prudence, respect, responsivity, responsibility, confidentiality, informalism, vivacity, optimism, happiness, balance, calm, enthusiasm, faith, flexibility, intuitivity, profoundness, rationality, realism, creativity, reflectiveness, relaxation, self-criticism, self-reliance, seriosity, stability, stoicism, resistance, youthfulness, complexity, etc.

4.4. THE TWO GREAT SUBPROCESSES OF THE PROCESS OF PERSONALIZATION. THE FORMATION OF THE PERSON AS A WHOLE

Core Fragment

Each of the three major areas of the soul - affective (social), spiritual, and humane - is the product of the interaction of the subject with specific factors, even if cannot be traced strict boundaries between them. The contingent social-personal and socio-affective factors are crucial for the formation of the affective (social) soul, the cultural conditions of learning and training the spiritual abilities and sensibility are essential for the formation of spiritual soul, while the altruistic, solidaristic, humanitarian, morale climate greatly influences the formation of the humane soul. Thus, in a purely humanistic perspective, the human-personal, the human-social factors are decisive in the formation and development of the person's soul.

Throwing an overview, we can see that in the ontogenetical process of forming of the person we distinguish two main sub-processes, steps, periods:

- the formation of ontological-psychological/spiritual sphere, of the (ontological/spiritual) personality, and

- the formation of the social-personal/ psychological-social sphere, of the person.

The formation of the ontological-psychological sphere, of the (ontological) personality, is done especially during childhood and adolescence, while of the social-personal/ psychological-social sphere, of the person, is done especially together with, and after, the subject acquires social autonomy, profession, its own family etc.

The formation of the ontological-psychological sphere, of the (ontological) personality includes mainly

- the formation of the

- ➢ personal ontos,

- ➢ soul, and

- ➢ ego/self;

- • through the processes of

  - ➢ ontosfication,

  - ➢ spiritualization,

  - ➢ individualization, and

  - ➢ holistization/ persomization.

The formation of the social-personal / psychological-social sphere, of the person, is conditioned mainly by

- • the formation of the

  - ➢ (social) conscience (co**m**science, culture, the humane conscience),

  - ➢ character, and

  - ➢ (social) competences, skills, abilities, qualities and habitudes;

- • through socialization and the process of social autonomization through profession, own family and community life, etc.

THE FORMATION OF THE ONTOLOGICAL-PSYCHOLOGICAL/ SPIRITUAL SPHERE – THE   ONTOSFICATION, SPIRITUALIZATION, INDIVIDUALIZATION, AND HOLISTIZATION/ PERSOMIZATION

The formation of this sphere of the person begins, as was highlighted above, from **the formation of personal ontos**, from the permanentization of some profound, fundamental constitutional-ontological structure of the person, from the establishment of some formations with great ontological-psychological consistency as the soul and the ontological ego, the soul as experiential "internalizing" of the other (person, value etc.), and the ego as experiential "internalizing" of the ontic and social self.

The process implies, in addition to the formation of the personal ontos as formation, as a whole, also the formation of some constitutional component formations, or very dependent on the personal ontos. Mainly it is about the hedonic ontos, the phobic ontos-formation, he projective ontos, the prosentic ontos-formation, the malsentic ontos-formation, the soul, the compathetic ontos, the affective/ social soul, the spiritual soul (mystical, intellectual, playful, aesthetical, ethical, etc.), the humane soul, the ontic subject/ ego, the projective ego and the spiritual ego, the humane ego etc.

In the complex, profound and long process of ontosfication crucial roles have the inner activity of the organism, the mind and the environment, especially the socio-human and cultural environment. So, crucial roles have the central nervous system, the sensitive jouissance, the endocrine system, the neuro-vegetative apparatus, the mechanisms of production, storage, processing and superization of the emotions, and more.

In the process of forming of the personal ontos and its sub-formation the emergence is the quality/ capacity/ property of the processes that makes possible the appearance of new entities, structures, properties etc. from the previous ones, defined as sources, factors, conditions. The emergence generates new realities and qualities. Usually the new entities are more complex and better adapted to the environmental factors.

The imergence represents the property and capacity of the process of ontosfication to forming, developing, evolving it in themselves, in itself, from nothing, of inertia, "subversively", simultaneously with the developments, evolutions, changes caused by the determined, objective identified factors (Khan, 1981).

Transmergence represents the property and capacity of the process to carry out without limitations and physical barriers of space and organization. Telegence means much the same thing, but concerns the temporal aspect of the processes of ontosfication.

Conmergence entails the transmergence, the telegence, the imergence and the promergence and represents the tendency of the processes to organize and concentrate it "thematically" in ontos-formations, ontos-structures, etc., reflecting the inherence of some functions, beyond any limitations of "logistic" or temporal order.

Sinmergence is the quality/ capacity/ property of the ontological-psychological processes which makes it possible the coexistence, simultaneously, of some ontos-personal entities in the same personal "space", the functioning and beingness of some distinct ontos-entities, structures, relationships, processes on the same material, biological, informational, spiritual support.

These properties, laws, principles characterize/ determine also **the process of formation of the soul, the process of spiritualization**.

Even if in the soul formation are important the material conditions, the HUMAN conditions are, in fact, the ones that contribute crucially to its properly construction, to construction of a harmonious personality, fulfilled, and socio-humanly effective.

Each of the three major areas of the soul - affective (social), spiritual, and humane - is the product of the interaction of the subject with specific factors, even if cannot be traced strict boundaries between them. The contingent social-personal and socio-affective factors are crucial for the formation of the affective (social) soul, the cultural conditions of learning and training the spiritual abilities and sensibility are essential for the formation of spiritual soul, while the altruistic, solidaristic, humanitarian, morale climate greatly influences the formation of the humane soul. Thus, in a purely humanistic perspective, the human-personal, the human-social factors are decisive in the formation and development of the person's soul.

The psychological-human (humane) characteristics of the individuals/ persons from the environmental onto-system, as well agreeability, soulful warmth, carefulness, empathy, spirituality, their constant presence and consistency, in human, spiritual and moral terms, the human quality of the interpersonal relationships, the community compathy, the social relationships as *humane* relationships are the constitutional determinant factors that marks, crucially, the sense of the person/ personality development, the sense of the soul development, the adaptability, the soulful welfare, the happiness.

The soul formation, establishment and beingness in the structure, the composition of personality is an objective necessity, the soul being constitutional, ancestral, genetic, and emblematic part of the being, of the human personality, mainly through its adaptive function, through the experiential-ontological internalization of the social-contextual, spiritual-cultural, and human-ancestral environmental characteristics.

The humanization of the soul, personality, and, by this, the humanization of the person as a whole, is, so, an emergent holistic integrator process more pronounced in people that, through the specific activity, should engage or work with/or for broad categories of people, such as teachers, artists, workers in social, political, cultural areas, etc.

So, the soul is formed in the general context of the constitution and functioning of the specific human organism, in the overall process of forming and developing of personality, under the influence of the environmental factors and internal action of the principles/ laws of emergence, imergence, transmergence, telegence, conmergence, etc.

In the gradual process of forming the soul passes through the following stages: of contact, of acquisition/ accumulation, of structuration, of constitution, of instituation/ establishment in the constitution of the personality, and, finally, of endemization/ ontification.

The soul formation process is not automatically, simple and linear, through the mere presence of the body in society and culture. The biological, sensorial, cognitive, affective experiences, the successes, failures and traumas marks significantly the structure, organization, architecture/ composition and orientation (hedonic, emotional, social, intellectual, spiritual, religious) of the soul.

In this respect, the strong, deep, altruistic, humane personality is described also in the context of a consistent and structurally balanced soul - this becoming a fundamental source of spiritual, moral, humane energy for the person, also for the ontogenetic process of developing the personality as a whole.

The interaction with the other real person, dear, with the nearest persons, significant group, with the near physical environment leads to the formation of the affective soul (social), and to the personal system of attachments. Reflects the personal contingent interaction, and appurtenance of the person to the group or to the particular social context.

The interaction with the world of spirit, culture, education, art, etc., leads, by the mental capacity of idealization, projectivity and symbolization, to the formation of the spiritual soul, to virtue and spirituality as personal qualities.

The interaction with the symbolic, universal, generalized, concept other, with the "status" other, by mental facilities of the generalization, idealization, projectivity and symbolization, abstractization leads to the formation of the humane soul and to the empathy, empathetic capacity of the person. Reflects the abstract interaction and affiliation of the person to society, humanity, and his human condition and nature.

The spiritual soul and the humane soul, are, therefore, the products of the personality enlightenment and of the projection capacity of the subject. In combination determine personal qualities such as kindness and humanity, human solidarity, morality, faith, aesthetic sensitivity, and humane sensitivity. Reflect the cultural, moral, spiritual, creative and ancestral quality of the individual (Stone, 1999).

Once being established, the soul works like all the other formations, but will need of affective, spiritual and humane experiences, feelings, sentiments.

The imposing of the soul as an autonomous ontological-psychological formation and personality structure is an important step because involves the installation in the ontological-psychological system of the individual, increasing the autonomy of the onto-formation. At this level begins the process of accentuated release from references, the process of accelerated autonomization, of acquiring an higher functional autonomy.

The person begins to become receptive to the values and critical in relation to the behaviors and attitudes of the other/close people. The soul begins to contribute essentially, hence, to the formation also of the other formations, integrative, like ego, character, an personality as a whole.

The transition to the phase where prevails the other's purposes is achieved at this stage too, is the moment where the other is represented as a desirous subject and less as desirable object. The other as desirous subject, with needs, concerns, goals is anchored deeply into the ontological structure of the person. They can control, by mechanisms and unconscious strategies, the personality and even the consciousness. The person accepts this situation, not necessarily intentionally or knowingly, because the other provides content for the inner life, feelings and even emotional security.

Depending on their nature, location or source one can speak of *affective (social) processes*, *spiritual processes*, *humane processes*, etc. Each of these having specific functions/ roles in determining and sustaining the person's psyco-spiritual and humane qualities, the affective (social) processes determining and sustaining the attachment, social sensitivity and interpersonal/ contingent empathy, the spiritual processes determining and sustaining the spiritual richness and virtue, the humane processes determining and sustaining the empathy/ compathy and humanity/ humanness.

In a general way, the soul, with all its areas and components, becomes the place and central source of the humane jouissance, therefore, if in the case of the body, senses, instinct's jouissance we talk about libido and pleasure, in the case of soul's jouissance we talk about eudaimonia and happiness, and, in the case of the humane soul's eudaimonia, of happiness through the other, or altruistic happiness, and, further, of an altruistic soulful energy.

A crucial process of the great process, general, of personalization is the one **of individualization and of formation the ego**. The formation of the ego and the individualization are a necessity, together with the processes of culturalization and humanization, with which it completes and interacts, even if, at least in the psychoanalytic perspective, they are somewhat opposite; the processes of culturalization and humanization are guided by the other's interests, the common good, while the individualization process is guided by the personal-endemic motivational resorts, by the individual intrinsic jouissance, by impulse and unconscious, by the self.

However, the formation of the ego and the individualization of the process of personalization does not mean a simple counterbalance or manifestation of the biological, instinctual forces of the self and the ontic subject, but also means a personal marking of the humanizing processes; moreover, also those formations, resorts, forces that we represent as belonging to individuality are re-dimensioned and enriched through the incorporation of the spiritual, cultural, moral and human acquisitions.

Like the other processes, the process of ego formation and individualization respects, covers, pass through the six principals stages, like all the other formations and personal spheres, respectively, of contact and acquisition/ accumulation, structuration/ centralisation and constitution/ holistization, of establishing/ networking, and ontification/ fulfillment.

All these formations and processes will integrate and function, unitary and coherent, in conditions of normality, in what in the book we call ontological-psychological personality, in the processes of holistization/ persomization.

How we have seen, the process of personality formation entails the inherent tendencies of persomization and holistization of the general ontogenetic process of personalization, constitution of the person, in the context of gradually imposing of the promergent holistic factors of process, against those dismergent, entropic, endemic, fragmental.

The formation of personality is conditioned/ determined mainly by two processes: the development, growth, general personal development, which imposes the automatic establishment of certain structures with integrative function, and the process of conmergent organization of the ontological-psychological formations.

Very important it is the nature, orientation, the dominant dimension, the content of the soul. If it is dominant a soul's jouissance that includes the other's happiness in this case we can speak of an altruistic, humane soul, and a personality and behavior oriented to the other's well-being, institution, establishing the *humane personality* – core, crucial concept in humanistic personology, especially in the humanistic-ontological theory of the person.

The formation of the humane personality is essentially conditioned of the formation of the human soul, but also of the humane ego and the humane ego, The humane ego being, alongside spiritual soul and humane soul, one of the most important reservoir and treasure of spirituality and humanism in the process of personality formation and development, in the process of persomization and holistization.

The formation and establishment of the humane ego contributes, leads, finally, also to the establishment of the personal system of beliefs and assumed personal convictions, of the moral conducts, of the need for knowledge the human phenomenon, also contributes, leads to the formation and establishment of the moral/ humane sentiments, end determines the appearance of the need for social harmony, human solidarity, helpfulness.

What is very certain is that in any conditions the personality formation is carried out with the data that disposes the subject starting from some premises, required minimum conditions - the body, the mind, the environment - even very briefly represented. Consequently, any creature who tells him human being traverses the process of formation of the personality through ontogenetical gradually integration and superization. But the differences between individuals can be extremely high.

Of course, when talking about the process of forming and establishing of the human personality, as a separate and autonomous entity and force into the composition the person, we consider, alongside the structural-axiological dimension also and the ontological-psychological component. The dialectical and unique combination of the two causes so an individualization and a basis for formation of a unique personality structure, placing the individual in a typology or another.

After it has been established, ontologically and psychologically, the personality will pass through other processes of redimensionings, this time not at level of self/ ego but of person, by the feedbacks and influences that it exercises the sphere of person, involved itself in complex processes of formation and adaptation.

THE FORMATION OF THE PERSONAL-SOCIAL SPHERE – THE SOCIALIZATION AND AUTONOMIZATION OF THE PERSON

The process is conditioned mainly by the formation of the (social) conscience, character, and competences/ habitudes, and the process of social autonomization through profession, own family, and community life, etc.

One of the most important purposes of the process of formation of the conscious and, through this, of the person autonomization, being to bring, through reflection and mental processing, on the hand, the spheres of the social life, of the environment in which is formed and cohabits the subject, in the mental sphere, connecting it, organically, at the structural, axiological and functional features of the community, and, on the other hand, to reflect, still there, the subject's interests, instituting, so, a noetical forum of synthesis, as well as confrontation, a resort of dependence, as well as of free will, of autonomy of the person, of detachment by awareness both of the objective determinations of the self, as well as of the environment where it lives.

The ontological-humanistic perspective, the theoretical-axiological basis of which we approach this work, promotes the model of a humanistic conscious, therefore prioritizes and promotes the role and importance of some socio-cultural and contextual-moral factors such as the systems of moral and humane values, the socio-moral/ humane relationships of attachment, empathy/ compathy, the cultural and spiritual quality of interpersonal relationships, addressed at singular mode, but also in community context.

As we highlighted in the section where was presented the process of forming the conscience, through the construction of this psychological-personal formation takes place not only a simple formation of a new entity, but also takes place a complex, deep and global process of autonomization of the person, of the process of personalization, the person becomes aware of their own situation, condition and its ontogenetic processes, as well as of autonomization - in relation to itself and in relation to the environmental factors.

After the construction of this great formation and crossing the great phases, process, of forming personality, and of properly personalization, one can speak of person, in the complex, ancestral, social and human meaning of the word, therefore, with meaning of human, of social being, but also of being in itself, with characteristics of unicity, of being.

Unicity that is given both by the genetic inherited biological characteristics, result of the phylogenetic evolution, as well as by the environmental characteristics of the ontogenetic process. Important role having also some factors which are related to the subjective-metaphysical indeterminism, to the free will, the learning trial-error mechanism, to the world of ego, of will, with the abyssal world of the spirit and subjectivity, to the interior energy and resorts of great depthness and complexity, that determines to consider the ontological process of forming of the person as unpredictable and never ended, and the person as never perfect, identical with the themselves or with the social role that it meets.

All this leads us to consider that, at any age, the person is an opened bio-psycho-social system, fragile, influential, flexible, dynamic, in formation, change, progress and regress, with frequent changes of the internal hierarchical, economic, structural, axiological reports.

THE FORMATION OF THE PERSON AS A WHOLE

The personalization implies, as we have seen, the formation of new spheres and levels but also holistic restructurings, redimensionings, retrievable at the level of all the formations, after the "completion" of the socialization process (social maturation). that could be "located", in our opinion, somewhere after the age of 40 years.

The person, later, after completing the two major sub-processes, will be, largely, a new construction, not only the overlapping, the coexistence of the two major sub-spheres. Thus, we may speak, also, about **a third process**, of formation of the person as awhole, where the two sub-processes will merge, unify, leading to what will be ultimately a certain human individual, a PERSON.

CHAPTER 5

MATURE, FULLY FUNCTIONING AND HUMANE PERSON/PERSONALITY -- THE TARGET OF THE ONTOGENETIC PROCESS OF FORMATION AND DEVELOPMENT. A HUMANISTIC-ONTOLOGICAL MODEL OF THE PERSON & PERSONALITY

5.1. INTRODUCTORY ASPECTS 120

5.2. MATURE, FULLY FUNCTIONING AND HUMANE PERSON/PERSONALITY -- THE TARGET OF THE ONTOGENETIC PROCESS OF FORMATION AND DEVELOPMENT 121

5.2.1. MATURE PERSON 121

5.2.2. FULLY FUNCTIONING PERSON 122

5.3. HUMANE PERSONALITY AND HUMANE PERSON 124

5.3.1. HUMANE PERSONALITY 124

5.3.2. HUMANE PERSON 125

5.4. A HUMANISTIC-ONTOLOGICAL MODEL
OF THE PERSON & PERSONALITY 126

5.4.1. THE ONTOLOGICAL-PSYCHOLOGICAL SPHERE – THE NEED 127

5.4.2. THE SOCIAL-PERSONAL/ PSYCHOLOGICAL-SOCIAL SPHERE THE NEED 128

5.4.3.. THE PERSON AS A WHOLE 129

5.1. INTRODUCTORY ASPECTS

In the humanistic-ontological paradigm, which we use, largely, in this paper, the completion and the fulfillment of the process of personalization does not lead only to the mere adaptation and mechanical social integration of the person but concerns, especially, the establishment of, what can be named, *the mature person*, and *the fully functioning person*, as the main target of the ontogenetic process of formation and development with characteristics such as:

- Personal and human development;

- High degree of awareness, of self-knowledge and self-esteem (Maslow, 2011);

- High socio-emotional development, high control of the emotions;

- Emotional intelligence (Erikson, 1998);

- Realism and balance, powerful will, resistance to failure and frustrations;

- Moral development, professional development;

- Personal and social autonomy, mature personality, adaptability (Rogers, 1980);

- Interpersonal development (Erikson, 1998);

- Live with integrity;

- Responsibility;

- Flexibilility and openness to learning and to new experiences, etc.

5.2. MATURE, FULLY FUNCTIONING AND HUMANE PERSON/PERSONALITY -- THE TARGET OF THE ONTOGENETIC PROCESS OF FORMATION AND DEVELOPMENT

> ## Core Fragment
>
> *Finally, involving the two main orientations, existential-positive and spiritual-humane, a mature person and a fully functioning person may be described as a result of his/her developing at a higher level, the most high, the most close to the condition of human being as an autonomous social and rational existence, with its characteristical attributes - personal development, adaptability and efficiency, but also as personality structured through soul, self, conscience, character, motivation, skills, etc. so that determines conducts oriented towards the wellbeing of the generalized other, towards the common good, to humanity, and dominant traits such as empathy, altruism, generosity, humanness, etc.*

5.2.1. MATURE PERSON

In literature, the **Mature Person** is defined, inter alia, as an individual who is able to live life with principles and wisdom, to lead life with high emotional intelligence that aids them to stay calm and think clearly during difficult moments, to keep a harmonious and win-win attitude towards other people, to keep an autonomous mindset, to live life making conscious decisions, etc. (Maslow, 2011)

Personal development is for the person a crucial condition of its maturity, which, in the scientific literature, is associated or identified with a number of other concepts such as psychic development, growth, adaptation, social development etc. It is a crucial category of the humanist-positive/ existential approach in psychology and personology highlighting also aspects as high degree of awareness, high capacity of maximization and capitalization of the internal potential of development, self-actualization, optimization, personal and social efficiency, positive attitude, optimism, active thinking, high ability to overcoming the crisis, etc. By learning and mastering the right principles and attitudes, a mature person can overcome many challenges of the current, day-to-day life (Erikson, 1998).

An important characteristic of a mature person is also the degree of personality development in terms of cohesion, consistency, adaptability and resilience. A mature person, a professional dedicated to the common good, the good of mankind, incorporates, in sublime manner, both spiritual/ humane competencies of role-status and also concrete humane behaviors and activities, thus ensuring, besides a consistent internal spiritual/ humane personal functionality, a high external humane personal functionality. Qualities such as altruism, empathy, optimism, perseverance, idealism, faith, balance, positive thinking, moral power, pure consciousness, self-control, tolerance, soulfulness, cheerfulness, creativity, desirelessness, devotion, endurance, virtuous energy, enthusiasm and more are defining characteristics both of a humane and morale, but by result, of a mature and autonomous person.

Finally, the mature person, in current life and profession, is revealed and expressed mostly in/ by its behavior and activity, and, as a social being, in/ by its ability/ capacity of socio-human and professional adaptation and integration – aspects closely linked to the concept of Fully Functioning Person.

5.2.2. FULLY FUNCTIONING PERSON

Fully Functioning Person - term introduced by the american psychologist Carl Rogers, referring to a person who lives an ideal and good life (defined as a process and not as a state of being). Other terms and ideas used by Rogers to define mature person are:

- Awareness of all experience;
- Freshness of appreciation for all experience;
- Trust in one's own behavior and feeling;
- Freedom of choice, without inhibition;

- Creativity and spontaneity;
- Continual need to grow, to strive to maximize one's potential, etc. (Rogers, 1998).

Also, the author and promoter of the person-centered approach in psychotherapy, education, social work and other practical domains (1951), considers that the fully functioning person is one who is in touch with his or her deepest and innermost feelings and desires, unconditional positive regard playing an essential role in becoming a fully functioning person. A fully-functioning person is therefore an individual who is continually working toward becoming self-actualized. Other aspect highlighted by Rogers is that the fully functioning person is one who has embraced the existential living, an individual who is able to live fully in *the moment*, here and now, experiencing a sense of inner freedom and embracing creativity and challenges.

In our humanistic-ontological approach, the concepts of mature person and fully functioning person are closely linked to concepts and ideas as humane and spiritual development, humane conscience, humane character, soul, humane ego, humane personality, reveled by categories as altruism, empathy, spirituality, happiness, aesthetic sensibility, kindness, humanity, etc.

Finally, involving, so, the two main orientations, existential-positive and spiritual-humane, a mature person and a fully functioning person may be described as a result of his/her developing at a higher level, the most high, the most close to the condition of human being as an autonomous social and rational existence, with its characteristical attributes - personal development, adaptability and efficiency, but also as personality structured through soul, self, conscience, character, motivation, skills, etc. so that determines conducts oriented towards the wellbeing of the generalized other, towards the common good, to humanity, and dominant traits such as empathy, altruism, generosity, humanness, etc.

5.3. HUMANE PERSONALITY AND HUMANE PERSON

Core Fragment

Very important is the "weight" that has one or other of the soul's spheres in its architecture, in the beingness and functioning of the soul as a whole, as extended part of the personal ontos, but as well of the person as awhole. For example, the more pronounced development of the affective (social/ personal) soul will profile a personal structure oriented predominantly to the jouissance/ good of the dear, close people, the development more pronounced of the spiritual soul will orient the personal assembly towards a development, as the case, of artistic, mystical, scientific type, while a great development of the humane soul will imprint to the person's personality and behavior features such as altruism, empathy, humanism, etc.

5.3.1. HUMANE PERSONALITY

We use, conventionally, the syntagm *humane personality* both for referring to a set of personality's formations, such as soul (affective, spiritual, humane), humane ego, humane consciousness, humane character, and others - structural onto-psychological and intellectual sources of the person's humane and spiritual qualities, as well as to the humanistic orientation, quality, the overall humane valence, dimension of the global personality, meaning kindness, goodness, altruism, personality opened to the overall manhood jouissance, increased sensitivity to the other's suffering/ tragedy - itself, but also emergent resource of empowerment, wellbeing and happiness for the people from ambience; both being foundations and explanations of the person/ professional's humane and spiritual qualities, of his humane, altruistic, prosocial behavior in the humanistic social and human practices.

Therefore, the complex and complete meaning of the concept *humane personality* includes the both approaches, determining superior valences (qualities/ resources) of the person/ personality/ conduct, such as spirituality, virtue, humanity, authentic happiness, etc.

Essentially, the humane personality is revealed by two key features, namely:

1. Personality developed at a higher level, the most high, the most close to the condition of human being as autonomous cultural, rational, spiritual existence, with its characteristic attributes - morality, virtue, sociality, spirituality, personal development, adaptability and socio-human efficiency, and

2. Personality structured through soul, ego, conscience, character, motivation, skills, etc. so that determines conducts oriented towards the wellbeing of the generalized other, towards the common good, humanity, and dominant traits such as empathy, altruism, generosity, kindness, etc.

The humane and spiritual qualities, traits, or resources, such as empathy, virtue, spirituality, happiness, humanity, and more, are expressions of some personal constructs of a maximum complexity, generated by the existence of a mega-system that exceeds both the ontological and psychological spheres, involving the person as a whole, represented in the ancestral and socio-cultural context (Beaumont & Cobb Jr., 2012) - dimensions projected mostly in what, in the paper, we call humane personality.

A crucial idea in humanistic personology is the fact that the humane and spiritual personality and development, and the strong/ developed personality and development are complementary, interdependent, and cannot be conceived only together.

5.3.2. HUMANE PERSON

Principally, when we are speaking of humane person, we consider mainly *its* global humane and spiritual structure/ orientation, resources and traits/ features.

Therefore, regarding the *humane* (humanistic) configuration/ structure/ orientation of the person the humanist-ontological paradigm highlights, with poignancy, the determining role of some psychological-ontological spheres, formations such as the soul, with its the three large spheres (affective, spiritual, and humane), the humane ego, the humane conscience and the humane character, profiling, as we have seen, the dimension, pan-sphere, called, in the book and project, *humane personality.*

Very important is the "weight" that has one or other of the soul's spheres in its architecture, in the beingness and functioning of the soul as a whole, as extended part of the personal ontos, but as well of the person as awhole. For example, the more pronounced development of the affective (social/ personal) soul will profile a personal structure oriented predominantly to the jouissance/ good of the dear, close people, the development more pronounced of the spiritual soul will orient the personal assembly towards a development, as the case, of artistic, mystical, scientific type, while a great development of the humane soul will imprint to the person's personality and behavior features such as altruism, empathy, humanism, etc.

Of course, seeking to highlight what it would mean the humane configuration/ structure/ orientation of the person, we should to approach the holistic perspective, where to remark the importance of some configurations of system or global type, the crystallization and ontification of some internal hierarchies, reported but to the environmental factors, with whom are in a permanent feed-back and feed-before; the humane configuration, orientation of the person profilating itself, therefore, only through the dialectical conjugation of the two universes: the personality and the environment (Arnet, 2011; Rifkin, 2009).

5.4. A HUMANISTIC-ONTOLOGICAL MODEL OF THE PERSON & PERSONALITY

Core Fragment

The person, after the ontogenetical construction of its constitutional formations as the personal ontos, the soul, the ego, the conscience, character, personality, etc, and after completing the two major sub-processes, and establishing the two macro-spheres - the ontological-psychological sphere and the social-personal sphere, will be, largely, a new construction, not only an ensemble/ collection of formations or the overlapping, the coexistence of the two sub-spheres. Thus, we may speak, also, about a third process, and a third sphere, a mega-, pan-sphere, where all the formations, the two sub-processes and spheres will merge, unify, leading to what will be, ultimately, a certain human individual, a social human being, a personality, a PERSON.

5.4.1. THE ONTOLOGICAL-PSYCHOLOGICAL SPHERE

The ontological-psychological sphere includes mostly:

- The personal ontos -
    - ➤ The hedonic ontos,
    - ➤ The phobic ontos-formation,
    - ➤ The projective ontos,
    - ➤ The prosentic ontos-formation,
    - ➤ The malsentic ontos-formation;

- The soul -
    - ➤ The compathetic ontos,
    - ➤ The affective/social/interpersonal soul,
    - ➤ The spiritual soul,
    - ➤ The humane soul;

- The ego -
    - ➤ The self and the ontic subject/ego,
    - ➤ The onto-projective and the spiritual ego,
    - ➤ The social ego, and the humane ego.

Of course, both, the structure/ composition of the ontological psychological sphere, but also of the social-personal sphere, with which we operate in the book, there are descriptive constructions with theoretical-epistemological assumed purpose, actually the personal assembly operating as a unitary whole/ system, being almost impossible to pinpoint structures and formations that to be or to work distinctly, or strictly framed in some spheres, assemblies, etc.

So, three great ontological-psychological formations are essential: the personal ontos, the soul, and the ego.

1. The personal ontos could be considered *the being* of the person.

2. The soul can be represented as the formation which represents/ reflects, psychological-ontologically, the other's interest and

feelings in the person's internal jouissance, economy and functioning.

3. The ego represents/ reflects, psychological-ontologically, the inner's interest and feelings in the subject's internal jouissance, economy and functioning.

5.4.2. THE SOCIAL-PERSONAL/ PSYCHOLOGICAL-SOCIAL SPHERE -

In our opinion, what in our theory is call, the social-personal/ psychological-social sphere of the person includes mostly:

- The social ego and the humane ego;

- The conscience -

  ➢ The comscience,

  ➢ The culture,

  ➢ The humane conscience;

- The character, and

- The system of the socio-human aptitudes, skills, competencies, habitudes, conducts.

So, regarding the structure/ composition of the social-personal sphere of the person, four great formations, sub-spheres, sub-structures are essential: the social/ humane ego, the conscience, the character, and the system of the socio-human aptitudes, competencies, skills, qualities, habitudes, conducts.

1. The social/ humane ego – represents the projection of the (social/ human) other's image and jouissance in the subject' cognition and jouissance; synthesis of subjective formations constitutionally oriented to the outside, where are many of the resources and means by which the subject can fulfill it both psychologically but also socially, the social ego having a great link with the person's role-status.

2. The conscience could be considered *the reflexive-intellectual-axiological "being"* of the person; the reflection of the (social/ human) other in the ego's cognition and thinking; ensemble of

epistemological-reflexive-axiological formations constitutionally oriented to the outside.

3. The character can be represented as the personal macro-structure which reflects, psychologically-attitudinally, the other's interest and feelings in the person's internal jouissance, economy, thinking, functioning, and behavior, being, so, in a large interpretation, a product of the interaction between ego and conscience.

4. The socio-human aptitudes, skills, competencies, habitudes, conducts represent the system of relational-behavioral instruments of the person, the praxeological-technical/ instrumental relation with the (social) environment/ other.

Just like at the ontological-psychological sphere level, at the social/ personal sphere level the social/ humane ego, the conscience, the character, the socio-human aptitudes, competencies, skills, abilities, qualities, habitudes, exist and operate together and interdependently, forming, in the great frame of the personal ensemble, a structural-functional unity; also, these can be represented as an operationalization of the ontological-psychological sphere, of its elements, of the personal ontos, of the soul, of the ego, at the level of person, in relation with the (social) environment.

The main role, function, aim of the personal-social sphere is to ensure, to confer the psychological-axiological and psychological-praxeological tools for the person in relation with the (social) environment, to be, to exist in outside, in the natural, human and socio-cultural world, to maintain and ensure the link with the world of people, values, institutions, rules, with the communities where the person lives, coexists.

5.4.3. *THE PERSON AS A WHOLE*

The person, after the ontogenetical construction of its constitutional formations as the personal ontos, the soul, the ego, the conscience, character, personality, etc, and after completing the two major sub-processes, and establishing the two macro-spheres - the ontological-psychological sphere and the social-personal sphere, will be, largely, a new construction, not only an ensemble/ collection of formations or the overlapping, the coexistence of the two sub-spheres.

Thus, we may speak, also, about a third process, and a third sphere, a mega-, pan-sphere, where all the formations, the two sub-processes and spheres will merge, unify, leading to what will be, ultimately, a certain human individual, a social human being, a personality, a PERSON.

So, the person as a whole exists and acts, at maturity, through each formations, through the two great sub-spheres but also as a unitary sphere and system (Maslow, 2011), as a whole and as a distinct element in ontological and relational-social plan. Nevertheless, this construction is dynamic, evolutive, alive and always remain under the influence of the variable internal and external, subjective and objective factors. In this sense, the person as a whole, the mature person, may be also represented through the Hegelian consecrated triad *general-particular-individual*.

CHAPTER 6

THE PROCESS OF FORMATION OF THE ONTOLOGICAL-PSYCHOLOGICAL SPHERE OF THE PERSON

6.1. INTRODUCTORY ASPECTS 132

6.2. THE ONTOLOGICAL-PSYCHOLOGICAL SPHERE
OF THE PERSON 135

6.2.1. THE PERSONAL ONTOS 137

6.2.2. THE SOUL 164

6.2.3. THE EGO/SELF 159

6.3. THE FORMATION OF THE PERSONAL ONTOS 161

6.4. THE FORMATION OF THE SOUL 166

6.5. THE FORMATION OF THE EGO 175

6.1. INTRODUCTORY ASPECTS

Crucial there are in the process of formation and structuration of the person's ontological-psychological sphere the unique subjective experiences of the subject, the feelings, the emotions or the ontological ego and the free will, the psychological-spiritual factors/ formation (especially the soul – affective, spiritual, humane), the self-generative internal dynamics, through culturalization and humanization, through emergence and superization, through spiritual/ human generalization/ abstraction of the psychological-compathetic (socio-humane) subjective experience.

In the spirit of the emergent systems theory (which involves, among others, the chaos theory and the complex systems theory) regarding the formation of the personality a whole, of the human being, but also of the ontological-psychological sphere we speak about characteristics, properties, processes, principles such as onto-formatization, persomization and promergence, emergence and imergence, transmergence and telegence, conmergence and sinmergence, and about ontological stages of evolution, development, establishment of the personal ontological-psychological formations, of the person as a whole, such as of contact, of acquisition/ accumulation, of structuration/ centralization, of constitution/ holistization, of establishing/ networking, of ontification/ fulfillment.

In the light of the emergent systems theory's principles the processes of formation of the person/ personality, in humanistic personology – the ontological-humanistic perspective, make possible the appearance of new entities, structures, properties, etc. from the previous ones, defined as sources, factors, premises, (pre-)conditions, the processes being based mainly on the dynamic, transmergent, telegent, imergent, conmergent and sinmergent interaction of the existing entities, on its intrinsic law-like developmental and transformative properties, manifested in the context of the specific environmental processes and phenomena, as well as of the systems which the subject belongs.

According to the emergent systems theory the resulting entities incorporate features of the *source-entities* but are presented yet as new existences, with them own features and ways of relating, adapted also to an environmental context, in turn, usually reformed.

The processes take place, largely, without limitations and physical barriers of space and organization, transcending the structures, the organizations, and the entities already constituted, attracting and involving them in the processes of forming, constituting and establishing of the new formations, without altering them.

In humanistic personology, the ontological-humanistic perspective on the process of forming of the person/ personality the degree of freedom/ action is very large, the number of combinations and the facilities of structuration and formatization being almost unlimited; one of the most important explanation is given by the fact that in the emergent and complex systems the processes have the extraordinary quality to permit the transcendence and the multiplication to infinit to the informational/ spiritual entities, taking place without time limitations and barriers, by the fact/ explanation that in the emergent and complex systems the processes have the tendency to organize and concentrate them "thematically" in formations, persoms, structures, spheres etc., reflecting the inherence, the objective necessity of some functions, beyond any limitations of "logistic" or temporal order, by the fact that the entities coexist, simultaneously, in the same personal "space", the functioning and beingness of some distinct entities, structures, relationships, processes on/ through the same material, biological, informational, spiritual support, framework.

At any moment a number of formations, dimensions or processes are in growing, advancement, forming, are promergent, and others are in degradation decline, involution (Bickhard, 2012), are dismergent; both the formation and the beingness/ functioning of every formation, person, sphere, of the personality and the person as a whole being crucially determined by the predominance and the intensity of the promergence, of the promergent processes, the humane and spiritual experiences representing the main "substance", motivational sources/ resources and positive factors of promergence, of the promergent/ functional processes.

The humane and spiritual experiences and the promergent processes are involved in complex, emergent, dynamic mechanisms and entities, every formation, persom, personality, the person as a whole being so a product of the ontogenetical incorporation, union, synthesis, of the conmergent, emergent, transmergent unitary organization of the sub-entities/ formations, structures, energies, mechanisms, of the processes of organization in new structures, formative entities, formations, persoms, usually upper structurally and axiologically.

Finally, as result of the global process of personalization, of the processes of ontosfication, spiritualization, individualization, persomization/ holistisation, autonomization, the person, as a whole, incorporates, unifies, synthesizes, emergently, conmergently, transmergently in a unitary organization the formations, energies, mechanisms, the processes, structures and constructions on the global/ maximal level, forming a holistic entity, with unique characteristics, qualities and conducts; in humanistic personology, the ontological-humanistic perspective on the person, very important being its humanistic/ humane and spiritual dimensions/ valences/ contents.

All, as we see, therefore, begins, personologically, in ontogenesis, with the process of formation of ontological-psychological sphere, and especially of the personal ontos, with the complex and miraculous process of ontosfication.

6.2. THE ONTOLOGICAL-PSYCHOLOGICAL SPHERE OF THE PERSON

Core Fragment

Despite appearances, the ontological-psychological sphere of the person is not a simple extension. product or emanation of the existence and functioning of the body; it exists in the general context of the personal structure, economy and functioning under the influence/ determination of the environmental factors, in the conditions of the internal action of the emergence, transmergence, telegence, sinmergence, conmergence, imergence principles/ laws/ properties; it could be represented also as a distemporalized space and, relatively, protected of the action of the laws so-called objective (mechanical), the biological and psychological elements and structures can be easily translated noetically, spiritually or sympathetically, and vice-versa, the possibilities of transformation and combination becoming practically limitless. The ontological-psychological sphere is the place, the framework, the source, the environment, the premise of forming and beingness of some of the most important formations and constitutional spheres of the person, especially of the soul and the ego; the soul, as experiential "internalizing" of the other (person, value etc.), and the ego as experiential "internalization" of the ontic and social self, also of its constitutional sub-formations such as the hedonic ontos, the phobic ontos-formation, the projective ontos, the prosentic ontos-formation, and the malsentic ontos-formation.

The ontological-psychological sphere includes mostly:

- The personal ontos -
  - The hedonic ontos,
  - The phobic ontos-formation,
  - The projective ontos,
  - The prosentic ontos-formation,
  - The malsentic ontos-formation;

- The soul -

> - The compathetic ontos,

> - The affective/social/interpersonal soul,

> - The spiritual soul,

> - The humane soul;

- The ego -

  > - The self and the ontic subject/ego,

  > - The onto-projective and the spiritual ego,

  > - The social ego, and the humane ego.

Of course, both, the structure/ composition of the ontological psychological sphere, but also of the social-personal sphere, with which we operate in the book, there are descriptive constructions with theoretical-epistemological assumed purpose, actually the personal assembly operating as a unitary whole/ system, being almost impossible to pinpoint structures and formations that to be or to work distinctly, or strictly framed in some spheres, assemblies, etc.

So, three great ontological-psychological formations are essential: the personal ontos, the soul, and the ego.

4. The personal ontos could be considered *the being* of the person.

5. The soul can be represented as the formation which represents/ reflects, psychological-ontologically, the other's interest and feelings in the person's internal jouissance, economy and functioning.

6. The ego represents/ reflects, psychological-ontologically, the inner's interest and feelings in the subject's internal jouissance, economy and functioning.

We believe that these great ontological-psychological formations - the personal ontos, the soul, and the ego - exist and operate together. Sure, ontologically the personal ontos, with its principal sub-formations, the hedonic ontos, the phobic ontos-formation, the projective ontos, the prosentic ontos-formation, the malsentic ontos-formation, is more important and representative, psychologically the ego, with its principal sub-formations, the self and the ontic subject/ ego, the onto-projective and the spiritual ego, the humane ego, is more important and representative, while, the soul, with its principal sub-formations, the compathetic ontos, the affective/ social/ interpersonal soul, the spiritual soul, the humane soul, is situated at the confluence of the two, being the core and representative formation for the ontological-psychological sphere of the person.

As we have seen above the main role, function, aim of the ontological-psychological sphere is to ensure, to confer the fundamental, constitutional, ontological support of the person, to be, to exist in itself, inside, in its own bio-psychic and spiritual world, to maintain and ensure the link with the biological, ancestral and metaphysical worlds of the person, even if through socialization, culturalization, humanization the ontological-psychological sphere acquires a great opening, orientation to the exterior, values, rules, institutions, organizations, people, to the concrete, actual (socio-cultural) environment where the person lives, coexists.

So, despite appearances, the ontological-psychological sphere of the person is not a simple extension. product or emanation of the existence and functioning of the body; it exists in the general context of the personal structure, economy and functioning under the influence/ determination of the environmental factors, in the conditions of the internal action of the emergence, transmergence, telegence, sinmergence, conmergence, imergence principles/ laws/ properties; it could be represented also as a distemporalized space and, relatively, protected of the action of the laws so-called *objective* (mechanical), the biological and psychological elements and structures can be easily translated noetically, spiritually or sympathetically, and vice-versa, the possibilities of transformation and combination becoming practically limitless.

6.2.1. THE PERSONAL ONTOS

SHORT PRESENTATION

In the simplest expressing, the personal ontos could be considered *the being* of the person.

The concept includes and incorporates, inter alia, elements from the psychoanalytic theory of the unconscious (Freud, 1990; Yung, 1981), from the humanistic theory of self and ego (Maslow, 2011; Frankl, 1967), and from the philosophical-ontological (Hegelian, Heideggerian, etc.) theories of being (*in itself*) (Hegel, 1977; Heidegger, 1962) - the psychological-ontological paradigm favors the interest for the real, experiential, unique, particular, specific feelings, emotions and internal existence of the person, imposing an idiographic-empirical/ emergentical approach to its internal live, dynamics, structure and existence.

As it has been shown, ontology has consecrated, among others, the paradigmatic ontological triad: *being-existent-existence.* In ontological perspective **the being** (being in itself) of an entity represents the essence, the original content, the ontological-metaphysical foundation of the entities, of the existent and of the existence, **the existent/ existing** (being for itself) represents the organization, the concrete form, unique, part of a context, the exposed side of the being, acquiring the characteristics of form of the concrete environment where it exists, while **the existence**, or **the beingness/ functioning** (being outside-itself), represents the processual, contingent, situational-contextual side, exposed to time, dynamic, experiential, the feeling and the thinking (Maritain, 1956; Hegel, 1977). Therefore, related to this triad, the personal ontos is an important part of the person's *being.*

The personal ontos, comprises, in its broad and comprehensive acceptation/ sphere, in our opinion, mainly, the ontos-formations which we will present below, respectively

- ➢ the hedonic ontos,

- ➢ the phobic ontos-formation,

- ➢ the projective ontos,

- ➢ the prosentic ontos-formation, and

- ➢ the malsentic ontos-formation,

but also

- ➢ the soul, and

- ➢ the ego/ self.

The soul and the ego will be presented, due to the importance and very great weight, but also because of the fact that they have great degrees of autonomy, separated, in distinct sections, later.

As personal-constitutional formation, the personal ontos is not a simple product, an emanation, a result of the manifestation and development of the body, as we might represent it, but it is established in the general context of the personal development, under the influence of the environmental factors, of the person's formations, and with the internal action of the principles of emergence, transmergence, telegence, sinmergence, conmergence and imergence, traversing, in emblematic mode for all the other formations and spheres of the person, the six standard ontogenetic stages, namely of contact, accumulation, structuring, formation, establishment and ontification.

According to these principles, and after completing these steps, the ontic-psychological sphere of the person becomes a distemporalizat space and, relatively, protected of the action of so-called objective (mechanical) laws, the biological elements can be easily translated noetically or sympathetically, and vice versa, the possibilities and combinations becoming practically limitless.

This ontic-metaphysical medium cannot be located, nor technically delimited, because it is not an existent and do not exists, it is, however, the sphere of the being - space in which it is established the indetermination, and it is, ultimately, the metaphysical source of the intentionality and liberty.

We speak of the ontic core, the general ontos. Here, we must state that the personal ontos is a prime foundation, principle, element of the person which gives ontological "substance" to the person. The sensation and the internal bio-psychological living are not content of the personal ontos, nor forms of manifestation, but the specific internal environment of existence, source, "feed".

So, the personal ontos is not an independent, self-sufficient entity but it is anchored in real, in the person's manifestations - biological, psychological, socio-cultural. Their specific does not have great significance for the ontos, which through transmergente mechanisms assimilates, in undifferentiated way, their content.

The personal ontos is the place, the framework, the source, the environment, the premise of forming and beingness of some of the most important formations and constitutional spheres of the person, especially of the soul and the ego; the soul, as experiential "internalizing" of the other (person, value etc.), and the ego as experiential "internalization" of the ontic and social self, also of its constitutional sub-formations such as the hedonic ontos, the phobic ontos-formation, the projective ontos, the prosentic ontos-formation, and the malsentic ontos-formation.

THE HEDONIC ONTOS AND THE PHOBIC ONTOS-FORMATION

THE HEDONIC ONTOS

The hedonic ontos is for the personal psychological-ontological sphere of the person what it is the libido, the pleasure and the sensitive jouissance for organism (Freud, 1990; Jung, 1981). It develops from them, superizing them and integrating them in a *superior* construction of psychological-spiritual, human and cultural type.

The starting point in understanding the genesis and function of the hedonic ontos is represented, still, by the concept of *need* (Maslow, 1970), or impulse (Freud, 1990).

The meaning of the concept *hedonic ontos* it is not, therefore, reducible nor to the one of motivation, of excitation, or tension, nor to the one of libido or eros, it regards the fundamental general state of eudaimonical onto-dynamic existence of the person, and includes so also the hedonic organizations from the upper formations level.

In this case we can talk about a hedonic ontos, built in the subjective imaginary areas, which may enter in a reconstructive interaction with the basal organic and psychic ontos. The possibilities of eudaimonical reporting to the object grow indefinitely, it establishes the *projective ontinces*, taking the place of the desire, as expression of the spiritual motivational freedom of the subject, of the capacity of choice and generalization (categorization, symbolization), and of hedonical superization.

THE PHOBIC ONTOS-FORMATION

The disaggregation, decentration, denaturation, alienation are permanent dangers which threatens the stability of the subject (Jung, 1981), because "the organs" where it establishes the subject, as a contingent living being, have the property to allow unlimited energetic and structural dynamics and interactions, and it is the subject's task to secure himself in relation of those processes which may harms it.

The essential function of the phobic formation is to determine personal organizations and behavioral patterns to avoid the alienation, the failure. Its role is not limited at the situational signification and the current reaction at potential traumatic stimuli, but, being a key component of the personal ontos, it becomes a foundation of the ontogenetical general organization of the person in order of a better integration, adaptation to the environment and the fulfillment of personal destiny. Therefore the phobic formation acts as an internal critic agent, a regulator of the processes of personal organization and structuration (Stefaroi, 2008, p.78).

THE PROJECTIVE ONTOS

Through this syntagma we intend to designate a set of formations, processes and ontic assemblies of a more special nature and etiology, which, in a global, holistic transmergental representation, we might call it *the projective "being" of the person.*

The nature more special of this ontic assembly is given both by the great diversity, expanse, complexity and depth, as well as (perhaps especially) by the ideatic, semantic and projective content of it.

The onto-projective formation not emerges directly from the basic needs and psychological foundations of the person, like the hedonic ontos, the phobic formation, or the ontical subject, this magic ontological-psychological formation arising, at random, from the particular dynamics of the relationship with the socio-human and cultural environment, reflecting, in a transformative/ projective way, its features. The objects, people, situations are not assimilation in their physical-sensorial objectuality but through the social/ cultural meanings, onto-projective idealized and subjectivated (Jung, 1981b; Freud, 1990).

After being constituted the onto-projective formations operates like some mechanisms in the subject and the other's service, through the projection of the endemic needs, the individual desires and values, but also in the service of the other (environment, values, persons,) which "projects", "injects" the vectors of control in the person's formations, especially through education/ culture. In this way the individual's behaviors are doubled, guided; the individual is placed in a position to make difficult choices, compromises.

The onto-projective formations are, in fact, targets, hedonic-projective ideals, desires, aspirations which guides the conscious and unconscious searches/ choices for the ontogenetical-personal growth, training and development (Laing, 1969).

These tend to curdle, holistically, in what we might call the project (pattern) of the personal forming and development, i.e. the ideal of the good and personal happiness, the idealized image of the good and of the individual happiness.

There are some processes that are interested in understanding the process of building of the projective ontos. One of them is the idealization. This is a logical process of essentialization, abstractization and selection of some features. It is also a projection guide of the process.

The construction of the projective ontos is done on two levels. The one is the comassation of the primary and secondary formations, some of them, of course, another concerns the whole, unitary organization, as a unique formation, as a being, as a function.

The "synthesis" of the pre-formation is not done accidentally, is the expression of some trends and force, actions of an existential vectors, homologous of endemic formations: the hedonic ontos, the phobic formation, endemic/ ontic subject etc.

It can't know exactly how many formations will remain and will establish, autonomous, in the projective ontos framework. Their number can be unlimited, however, impossible to control. We believe, with certainty, one can speak of the following:

- the spiritual soul,

- the happiness (prosentic) formation,

- the depressive (malsentic) formation, and

- the onto-projective ego.

This onto-formation is a critical part of the architecture of the human personality. It is built and establishes as effect of the internalization and organization of the subjective noetic, self-projective or spiritual (mystical, playful, epistemic, aesthetic, moral etc.) experiences. It is built on bio-psychological personality, affective soul and mind foundation, and in the context of the formation of other personal onto-formations, (the endemic ontos, the affective ontos), which it inherit chronologically (although the formation and institution process and simultaneous or interactive).

The most obvious subjective-projective or onto-projective feature is, however, the fact that the human individual is born biologically, but must be born socio-humanly once more, which requires a project.

Therefore, it must assimilate symbols, meanings, values. But, the man is not a computer witch stores information. He lives, grows, is existential built, that is why, so-called assimilation, is in fact a projection. The objects, people, situations are not assimilated in their physical-sensorial objectuality, but by the social/ cultural signification, onto-projective sujectivated.

So, the subject is inserted in a noetical, axiological, cultural world, axiological, which can not survive as whole man unless it is part of a field, the world of relationships, structures, assemblies, socio-cultural formations very high complexity. Only their projection in onto-personal formation and building of personality ensure the survival. The individuals unable to make this process are excluded or it excludes himself.

In the ontological order of the person/ personality the projectivity gives the defining note as human being through the ontification of the generalized/ idealized other "pattern" of the human being), the values, ideas, knowledge, ideals, hopes.

In fact, it's an interior ontic universe, which summarizes, through double onto-projection, the subjective and the objective, the body and the environment, the inside and the outside, the feeling and the thinking.

These formations operate, experiential and emergent, by complex mechanisms of feed-back and feed-before, through the onto-projective personal referents. The projective personal referents may be the desirable social status, the personal welfare, the desirable body image, the desirable profession, the required level of intelligence and knowledge, the aspirated physical and spiritual pleasures, the aesthetic, moral, axiological aspirations, etc. (for the social services, especially those dealing with children, some of them are actually educational and welfare objectives).

The positive perspectives in favor of its meeting install positive emotions and states, comforting feelings, happiness. Instead, the low perspective of identifying with this hypostasis determines uncomfortable neuro-vegetative react and depression. The predominance of positive onto-projective feelings will lead to the establishment of a strong onto-formation of happiness and a visionary personality, tilting the balance in the positive side. So, through fixings the projective-personal balance in a favorable inclination will orient the personality to the future, will give it a positive sense, pleasant, efficient, active, dynamic, adaptable.

Projectivity, visionary and idealism are indispensable qualities of the professionals in education, social work, therapy and management, because represents one of the most important onto-psychological source of the empathy, but, also, because the professions from these domains are teleological by their nature and mission.

The humanistic professional do not make only simple services, instruction, care etc., do not concerns only the customer survival, but aims the humane development and education, humane rehabilitation in perspective, according to a humane "project"; by building, so, a new *modus vivendi* and a new architecture of the personality.

Without vision, without idealization, without projectivity his personality remains contingent, flat, obtuse (Langan, 2009). The humanistic goals will remain only on the paper. All that aims to build at the professional level must to exist in his personality, in its onto-ideational/ projective interior universe.

The customer's education, rehabilitation, development and happiness can be best achieved by operating on the projective onto-referents of the onto-projective sphere. But these must be, primarily, present at the practitioner's personality level. Therefore, in education and training of the professionals is important to put great emphasis on the training and to the eudemonic/ axiological onto-referents, perceived with roles of anchors, ideals, human values.

The process leads at forming of a vigorous professional personality, human, active, positive, autonomous, oriented to self-achievement but also to the other's humane development and wellbeing. Also, the process develops psychic functions like the will, motivation, imagination, intelligence (including the emotional intelligence). Projectivity, vision are both the professional qualities and the main resources and means of achieving the objectives of practice. These are, also, inherent dimensions of the personality and human condition, but must be cultivated and educated.

THE PROSENTIC ONTOS-FORMATION AND THE MALSENTIC ONTOS-FORMATION

THE PROSENTIC (HAPPINESS) ONTOS-FORMATION

The prosentic ontos-formation entails the soul, but is formed, mainly, within the subjective-eudaimonical and onto-projective "space" of the person/ personality; gradually integrating itself within the personality's structure, also in the psychological-personal assembly.

In essence, its formation/ constitution is conditioned by the secondary projective accumulations and synthesis that maintain the (projective) good of the subject. The psychological-eudaimonical experiences, representations, ideas are assimilated/ taken from the inner personal lives, but also from the culture, science, community (Benner, 2011).

One of the most important functions of the prosentic ontos-formation being that to ensure the positive, creative, active orientation to the future and action, to tone and balance the internal forces through eudaimonical jouissance, to ensure projective opening in order to maintain and support psychologically-energetically, onto-subjectively, the person.

The role and importance of the prosentic formation, or the happiness formation, how we could also tell it, in formation, development and functioning of the personality and person, in determining of some personality traits such as agreeableness, optimism, charisma, sociability, altruism, empathy is very important because this positivates the jouissance, the interior subjective-experiential general condition, causes the person to feel fulfilled or overflow of interior good to externalize it and contaminate the socio-human environment, affecting in good also the other; the others, perhaps more unhappy, unfulfilled, because it offers eudaimonical energy to the general process of development, superization and humanization of the personality and behavior (Stefaroi, 2014).

THE MALSENTIC ONTOS-FORMATION

In this case the onto-projective formatization will be determined by the negative, dismergent, morbid, destructive, anti-existential, dysfunctional, painful projective representations and feelings

The malsentic ontos-formation has, as fundamental function, therefore, the ontos-subjective projective securization of the internal projective/ aspirational life/ jouissance of the person (Bergson, 2007), but also the signalization of the possible dismergent stimuli and factors.

The specific activity of this formation requires the rejection of the discomfortable representations and experiences, but their presence and relevance cannot be existentially annihilated, therefore they will regroup in uncontrollable areas by the voluntary instances of the subject.

Its hyper-development can lead to acute depressions and excessively anxious, morbid, aggressive, individualistic, restrictive constructions of personality, affecting, negatively, the formation, the development of the person as a whole, its superization, humanization, its functioning, adaptation and happiness (Stefaroi, 2009b).

6.2.2. THE SOUL

SHORT PRESENTATION

The meaning of the concept of **soul** that we use in this paper is not identic, in sense and scope, nor with the one consecrated in the ancient philosophy, especially by Aristotle (Aristotle, Robinson, 1999), and frequently used also today, of *psychic*, nor with the one religious, mystical, of *spirit/ ghost/ sacred*, even if it do not exclude them, but refers to *an ontological-psychological sphere/ formation, or a set of psychological-ontological formations, ontogenetically, existentially and experientially formed and established, in the context of some objective premises and factors such as the human body, sensations, feelings, needs, the subjective and social experiences, the natural and cultural contexts, and, especially, of some socio-human/ humane and cultural factors such as the characteristics of the close and/or dear persons, the continuity and consistency of the personal/psychological-social interactions, of the particular human relationships of attachment, communication, coexistence, love, of the cultural and moral values and practices from the community where grows and lives the subject.* In other words, the main source of formation of the person's soul is THE MAN/ HUMAN, with all the biological, psychological, social and cultural-historical systems that involves it.

Therefore, in our view, the soul is not something metaphysical, though, probably, it has also such dimensions or interferences, but a very deep and complex spiritual/psychological-objective entity/ instance/ formation of the individual human being, alongside the body, personality, self/ego, conscience, character or intellect, representing, in this context, what one might call *the place, the source, or recipient/ resort of the feelings, of the social and spiritual emotions, particularly* **human** (Stefaroi, 2009b).

Depending on their nature, location or source one can speak of sub-spheres such as *affective (social) soul, spiritual soul, humane soul,* etc.

Each of these soul's spheres having specific functions/ roles in determining the person's psyco-spiritual and humane qualities and conducts:

> the affective (social) soul determining *the attachment, social sensitivity and interpersonal/ contingent empathy,*

> the spiritual soul *determining the spiritual traits, resouces, richness and virtue,* and

> the humane soul determining *the humane traits, resources and conducts, the empathy/ compathy and humanity.*

Of course, all in the global context of the personality development and functioning, especially of the humane personality.

Ontological-structurally, the soul, as sphere, content, cumulates/ unites / synthesizes, psychological-ontologically, the subjective-sensorial experiences with those intellectual and socio-affective, generating superior miraculous unique emergent and imergent psychical-spiritual phenomena as passion, love, faith, altruism, empathy, happiness, virtue - characteristic only of the human being (Benner, 2011).

Therefore, all of these must to have a "place" in the sphere of the person as a whole, of the personality, from where to come, to originate, to be produced by something, and that something is, thus, primarily, the soul, the human soul.

Thus, by the formation of the soul each person assimilates, internalizes, transmergently and experientially, subjectively, potentially, the whole human, personal/ psychological, social, cultural experience of humanity (community), the ancestral matrix of human being (Aristotle & Lawson-Tancred, 1987), of the generalized other, acquiring, just so, the supreme quality of MAN, HUMAN, the psychological-ontological belonging to the HUMAN community, with the well known existential characteristics that differentiate it to the other modes of existence, facilitating, indirectly, mediated, also, the access to the experience (pain, happiness, etc.) of the other, concrete or generalized, generating inexhaustible psychological resources for social adaptation and helping others through the qualities that they imprint to personality and behavior such as empathy, spirituality, virtue, happiness and eudaimonical-altruistic energy/ motivation, humanity, agreeableness, optimism, enthusiasm, sociability, altruism, etc. (Stefaroi, 2014).

THE COMPATHETIC ONTOS

The easiest representation of the concept *compathetic ontos* is the one of ontological-psychological place, almost metaphysical, but also almost biological, where the human soul is formed. The soul will structure himself through its main spheres in the affective (social/ personal) soul, the spiritual soul, and the humane soul, but the question is which is the ontological-psychological support/ framework, its internal psychological-ontological foundation and source? One of these is, thus, the compathetic ontos.

Mainly, the compathetic ontos is, as an important part of the personal ontos, phenomenologically-processually speaking, an inner world, deeply vegetative, of emotions, feelings, sentiments relative to the exterior, the other (including the self, as other – in psychoanalytical terms, Freud, 1990), world, values, an extra-ego. To this end the ontological-psychological sphere of the subject, will experience an extensive process of alterization, spiritualization, humanization, which debuts still with the installation of an *alter-subject*, a *pseudo-subject*.

For a long time, the alter-subject it is constituted outside of the endemic subject, determining two processes, somewhat parallel. These phenomena are possible due to the properties regarding the bio-psycho-spiritual development and organization of the perso-formations, proposed by us, respectively, mainly, the sinmergence and transmergence principles, which implies that the same structures and mechanisms that uses the endemic subject can be used also by the pseudo/alter-subject, even if the processes takes place simultaneously and in the same place.

The double or multiple "subjectivitation" should not be seen as an abnormality; it is, on the one hand, the expression of their non-maturation but also a necessity, and, secondly, because the alter/pseudo-subject will represent the pivot around to whom will take place the structuring of the soul.

This compathetic ontos, thus established, is composed of an infinite transmergent, telegent, emergent, imergent hodgepodge of emotions, feelings, sentiments, passions, positive and negative, on biological, psychological, spiritual background (Benner, 2011), an infinity transmergent, telegent, emergent, imergent woven of structures, systems, configurations, formations, entailing all the ontological-psychological and psychological-functional spheres and levels of the personality/ person.

This is the inner psychological-ontological universe from which emerge, is formed, established the soul, with his the main three spheres:

- the affective (social, interpersonal) soul,

- the spiritual (mystical, playful, aesthetic, epistemic, ethical etc.) soul, and

- the humane/ transpersonal soul.

THE AFFECTIVE/ SOCIAL/ INTER-PERSONAL SOUL

In an elementary interpretation the affective/ social/ interpersonal soul may be considered the objectual-affective (personal/social) psychological-ontological sphere/ component/ dimension of the human personality.

One of the most important function/ role of the affective soul is to determine the socio-affective qualities, of generator, producer of emotions, feelings and attachments related to the concrete and significant other (Bowlby, 1999). These can be positive or negative (Stone, 1999). Those negative have also the role of signaling the disturbances in the other's existence, beingness or jouissance, determining reactions, structures, skills and behaviors to restore the other's well-being.

In this sense, the main source of the formation of the person's affective (social) soul is the concrete PERSON/ HUMAN, with all psychological and social aspects that involves it.

In the processes of formation and functioning the affective soul cumulates/ unites/ synthesizes, psychological-ontologically, the subjective contingent experiences with those socio-personal, generating superior miraculous, unique emergent psychical phenomena, especially the attachment and love for the determined other.

By forming of the affective (social, interpersonal) soul each person assimilates, internalizes, transmergently and experiential-subjective, the psycho-sensorial, psycho-eudaimonical, psychological, social experience of the concrete other, acquiring, just so, the psychological-ontological quality of member of a (small) community, social group, social relationship, family (Benner, 2011).

The process of forming of the affective (social) soul, i.e. the personalization/ socialization of the soul, is an emergent holistic integrator phenomenon more pronounced in people involved in socio-affective relationships, in families, small groups, being formed in the general context of the constituting and functioning of the specific human organism, in the overall process of forming and developing the personality, under the influence of the environmental factors and internal action of the principles/ laws of emergence, imergence, transmergence, telegence, conmergence, etc.

Through forming and ontification of the affective soul the other as desirable subject, with needs, concerns, goals is deeply anchored into the ontological structure of person, even in the social ego; this can controls, by mechanisms and strategies, often involuntary and unconscious, the subject's personality and behavior, even the will and conscience.

The subject accepts this situation, not necessarily intentionally or knowingly, because the other provide content for the inner life, feelings and even emotional security. Each person is also an experiential „amount" of persons and existential and virtual entities.

From the perspective of affective soul is essential the presence, security and happiness of the dear, closer other. It is not a totally disinterested altruism. Person defined as a virtually assimilation of the other's jouissance is enriched itself, because without the other this lose the opportunity to be socialized and soulfully accomplished. The process determines, also, the inter-personal capacity of attachment, empathy, altruism, love, etc.

After the formation/ constitution and incorporation to the affective soul in the constitutional structure and content of the individual's personality follows his long beingness and functioning as relatively autonomous onto-formation; processes which take place in the context of the contingent and unforeseeable social-personal, socio-affective conditions and factors where the person lives, being established very close links, congruencies, interactions, inter-determinations, compathies between the affective soul and the concrete environmental (social) system, especially with the nearest persons, with their souls; their beingness and functioning being made in inter-connection, inter-determination, mutual influence and compathetical congruence.

THE SPIRITUAL SOUL

In an elementary interpretation the spiritual soul may be considered the spiritual psychological-ontological sphere/ component/ dimension of the human personality.

Through the spiritual soul, this miraculous onto-formation of the human personality, the subject accedes to culture, ancestrality, virtue, and history, practically assimilates, experiential-ontologically and ontogenetically, the evolution/ universe of the human spirituality and community through the contact with the concrete cultural environment, bearer of universal meanings, with the values, the ancestral, generalized/ spiritual human experience (Wommack, 2010; Bean, 2013).

After the establishment in the person/ personality's constitution determines the spiritual sensitivity/ development, the authentic happiness, virtue and superization of the personality and behavior; it is, so, crucial factor in the formation of the human personality, including of the professionals from the social and human practices and services.

This onto-personal formation, crucial in the architecture of human personality, is formed and established as a result of the "internalization" and organization of the noetic, ego-projective or spiritual experiences/ feelings (mystical, playful, epistemic, aesthetic, moral, etc.). In this sphere will be installed, what we might call, the spiritual-projective *being* of the person.

It is constituted on the bio-psychological foundation of the personality, of the affective soul, mind, and in the context of establishing of the other personal onto-formations, which chronologically succeeding them (even if the formation and establishing processes are simultaneous or interactive).

Depending on the types of feelings, on the subjective experiences involved, of the cultural characteristics of the environment, but also by many other factors, will forms:

- the mystical soul;

- the playful soul;

- the aesthetic soul;

- the gnostic soul;

- the moral soul, etc. (Stefaroi, 2009a).

THE MYSTIC SOUL

This onto-formation is constitutes in closely related with the phobic and malsentic (depressed) formation, the hypothesis of death, with the "non-being", with the supernatural, the superior love, with the saint as model and aspiration, with the heaven, with the fantastic/ transcedental happiness, with the absolute, the infinite, the God, etc.

The mystic sphere, component, dimension, valence of the person/ personality is not an option, is a foundation of the personal constitution, and is materialized in the setting of certain specific onto-formations (Stefaroi, 2009a, p.22).

The mystical soul is set on the opposite side of the endemic. Both poles are still *beings*, these have autonomous existences, needs and produce specific personal motivation and desires.

The persons' mystical motivation/ desires require:

- mystical experiences;

- the need of sacred;

- trances, revelations, sublime feelings;

- asceticism, faith, love, heroism, etc.

So, the mystical soul's formations and processes are somewhat in opposition with the contingent formations and processes of the consciousness, reason and behavior.

Are deep ancestral "implants" in unconscious, landmarks of the individual's beliefs and convictions (Benner, 2011), but also sources of the emotional instability, fanaticism and paranoia (in pathological view).

In some cases, the mystical soul unites, by the sacred spirit, the body, mind, the self, environment, culture and projective/ transmergent/ telegent capacity of the onto-personality, inevitable for the personal/ personality's genesis/ development (Bean, 2013). The focalization of these energies and processes is creative of high spirit. Its content is the higher/ sublime emotion (sentiment, passion) - profound, almost revealed, impossible of analyzed and described scientifically.

THE GNOSTIC SOUL, PLAYFUL SOUL, AESTHETIC SOUL, ETHICAL SOUL

The establishment of the spiritual soul generates also aesthetic, playful, gnostic, ethical needs. They are the expression of certain spiritual onto-projective formations like the gnostic soul, playful soul, esthetic soul, ethical/ moral soul, etc.

The *gnostic soul* has many similarities and connections with the noetic onto-formation. What differentiates them is that the noetic onto-formation is an organization of ideas in itself, an itself objective world, logical, intrinsic, cognitive, self-sufficient, while the gnostic soul is subjective and emotional impregnated, and determines the higher need of the subject to search gnosis that produce satisfaction. While for the noetic onto-formation the fundamental need is for the truth, for the gnostic soul prevailing the subject's spiritual need for the knowledge itself.

Between the two poles, mystic and gnostic soul, are located *the playful* and *the aesthetic soul*. The playful soul is expression of the ontological-ancestral need of the person of liberty, entertainment, of irony against the limits of existence. The personality will reflected, in its own dimension, this spirit - requirement of social, cultural, moral action, but and of creativity.

The environment and source of the playful soul is a different world than the real one, is set with its elements and laws, but placed in an ontological order inherently questionable. The playful soul illuminates and streamlines the internal communication channels and with the environment, gives to the individual comfort and authentic existence, spirituality.

From the playful soul is feeds, in great measure, also the process of formation of the *aesthetic soul*. In fact is very difficult to achieve a clear distinction between the two onto-formations.

However, the aesthetic soul, also the ethical soul, are related/ reported to the established historical-cultural values, imposed by society, but subjectively assimilated by the person (Doherty, 1996).

It is, so, very important, beyond the social, cultural, historical matters, the ontological-individual organization as *soul* of these values. Yet, it can be said that by imposing of the values, as social/ transpersonal commandments, the soul becomes more regularized, axiologically, leading to a higher organization and representation in the structure of personality, also in the socio-human behavior (Stefaroi, 2013).

THE HUMANE/ TRANSPERSONAL SOUL

In an elementary interpretation the humane/ transpersonal soul, in our view, may be considered the general humane-altruistic and pan-human/ transpersonal psychological-ontological sphere/ component/ dimension of the human personality.

The establishment and ontification of the humane and transpersonal soul may be considered the terminal stage of the complex process of formation and ontification of the soul, as essential sub-process in the overall process of formation of the *humane* personality, of the personality as a whole, also of the person's psychological-ontological structures, in general.

Brings together, emergently and transmergently, at a higher level, more complex, deeper and synthetic, the onto-formations from the affective (social) soul and spiritual soul levels, generating the extraordinary ability, ancestral, unique, of the person to feel, live and think as a human being, as an ancestral being, as an exemplar human being, but also as a *humane* being, by their ability to resonate, empathize, compathize with the human and spiritual experience of the other persons, even if they are not part of the inner circle of acquaintances, relatives, colleagues etc.

Through the formation and establishment of the humane soul the personality as a whole is reformed and is defined by solidarist-humanistic/ transpersonal qualities/ virtues and behavioral traits such as empathy, agreeableness, tolerance, humanity, human sensitivity etc. - qualities related, therefore, not only to the contingent social sphere of the subject, but to all that is human, universal-human, trans-, pan-human, anywhere and anytime.

The establishment of the humane soul is made, also, with the transmergent and emergent actions of some instances and spheres from the intellectual and moral levels, which, moreover, by feedback, determines their reformation, contributing together to the establishment of the character and of the pro-social, pro-human behavior.

Thus, by the prosocial/ humane/ transpersonal valences imprinted to personality and behavior, the humane soul becomes a crucial factor for adaptation and social integration of the person in social groups, communities, environments, other than those based mainly on attachment and knowing each other (Aristotle & Lawson-Tancred, 1987).

In this respect, the problems of adaptation, communication, or of integration of the disadvantaged persons into alternative social groups can also be interpreted as a result of the underdevelopment, disorders, injuries or weaknesses of the humane soul.

The process of formation of the humane soul, as autonomous structure and instance of personality, achieves its ontogenetical target usually in the adulthood when the person becomes sensitive to the situation of the wider community, society, humanity as a whole; the humane soul having, in this sense, a crucial role in the formation to the humanistic beliefs and convictions, solidaristic, humanitarian, also a very important role in determining the character orientation, the attitudes towards themselves, towards work, people, values, society etc.

The constitution of the humane soul, as yet a distinct personal onto-formation than the affective/ social soul and spiritual soul, as an integrated and unified formation, is conditioned/ determined mainly of two processes:

1. the general personal evolution, growth, development, which requires the automatic creation of certain morale, prosocial formations with integrative functions, and

2. the process of organization, synthesization to the multitude of the affective and spiritual formations oriented towards the

interest of the generalized other, towards common, human values and interests, towards humanity.

Of course, the basic factors of the humane and transpersonal ontification of personality are the social environment based on solidarity and empathy/ compathy, the cultural education oriented to people and values, the intellectual and of valorization capacity, the need for superior development and organization of the personality, the need for security, and, not least, the ontogenetical natural tendency of decentring of the self, of overall humanization of the personality and behavior, of socio-human integration and adaptation in groups and communities more and more complex on the course of growing.

The *humanization* of the soul and personality is an emergent holistic and integrator process more pronounced in people such as teachers, social workers, artists etc., professional and volunteers involved in specific activities for broad categories of people (McLaren, 2010).

The nature of the humane soul is probably mostly psychological-spiritual, but as a system, structure and composition is a unitary bio-psycho-cultural complex, conmergent and transmergent, which means that it is much more than a summation of the humane, altruistic feelings and passions, it is a "being", an existence also in themselves in the personality sphere.

We can speak about a genesis of this sphere, about a structure, composition, organization, content, nature and so on, but the most interesting thing in view of the theme regarding the humane qualities of the professional in social work, is its prosocial, moral, compathetical, altruistic dimension, valence, capacity, quality.

Nor the functioning, nor the genesis, nor the existence of the humane soul would not be possible without a strong cultural, anthropo-social, pan-human dimensioning. Therefore, the humane soul is established and operates by two complementary cardinal processes:

- oriented to himself, of humanization and universalization of the self, ego self- personality, and

- of cultural, anthropo-social setting, oriented towards other people, to world, society, values.

This second dimension will be the key driver for formation of the humane personality, prosocial behavior and empathy/ compathy as cardinal psychological-spiritual/ humane resources, traits, qualities of the person (Lukacs, 1978), including of the professional in the humanistic social practices and services.

In the humanistic social and therapeutic practice perspective is more than obvious the need for prioritization the development of this sphere of the professional's personality; key humane qualities and conducts in the professional's activity of evaluation and intervention with the beneficiaries, such as empathy/ compathy, agreeability, tolerance, and more, are generated, largely, by the existence and manifestation of the humane soul; of course on the background and in the context of the global spiritual development, of the overall personal, human and psychosocial development (Benner, 2011).

The humane and spiritual qualities, traits, or resources, such as empathy, virtue, spirituality, happiness, humanity, and more, are expressions of some personal constructs of a maximum complexity, generated by the existence of a mega-system that exceeds both the ontological and psychological spheres, involving the person as a whole, represented in the ancestral and socio-cultural context - dimensions projected mostly in what, in the paper, we call *humane personality*.

Thus, the humane and spiritual qualities are not mere expressions of the emotional and spiritual development, of the affective soul, of the spiritual and humane spheres, but rather expressions of the general cultural development, of the existence of certain skills or inclinations, of the character development, or of the eudemonic-spiritual and eudaimonic-prosocial spheres, and, not least, of the development of personality as a whole, through its humane/ humanistic orientation/ dimension, as a personality developed at a higher level, closer to the condition of human being of the person, as cultural, rational, spiritual and autonomous existence with its characteristic attributes - morality, virtue sociality, spirituality, personal development, adaptability and socio-human efficiency, as well as personality structured, through the soul, ego, conscience, character, motivation, skills, etc., so that determines conducts oriented to the welfare of the other, of the generalized other, of the community, humanity, also dominant traits, qualities such as empathy, altruism, generosity, kindness, etc.

Ultimately, the model of personality of the professional in the humanistic social practices, capable of generating qualities such as empathy, virtue, spirituality, happiness, humanity, altruism, is the humane personality that combines the global personality developed to a higher level with the personality so structured that determines effective professional conduct both in the objectives of personal empowerment and social integration, also in the ones of diminishing the client's suffering, or of happiness.

However, in our opinion, the central role in determining the humane and spiritual qualities of the professional is played by the soul, with the three main areas, **the affective (social) soul, the spiritual soul, and the humane soul.** Each of these having, so, as was shown in the paper, specific functions/ roles in determining the person/ professional's spiritual and humane qualities - the affective (social) soul determining the attachment, social sensitivity and interpersonal/ contingent empathy, the spiritual soul determining the spiritual richness and virtue, and the humane soul determining empathy/ compathy and humanity/ humanness; of course, therefore, in the global context of personality, especially of humane personality.

The main explanation of the humanistic, spiritual, altruistic virtues of the soul comes from the fact that this, as sphere, content, cumulates/ unites/ synthesizes, psychological-ontologically, the subjective experiences with those intellectual and socio-affective, generating superior, miraculous, emergent behaviors, strongly oriented to the other's jouissance.

By formation in a humanistic way of the professional's soul this assimilates, internalizes, transmergently and experiential-subjective, potentially, the whole human, personal/ psychological, social, cultural experience of the humanity (community), the ancestral matrix of the human being, of the generalized other, acquiring the psychological-ontological belonging to the human community (Lukacs, 1978), with the well known existential characteristics that differentiate it by other modes of existence, facilitating, indirectly, mediated, also, the access to the experience (pain, happiness, etc.) of the other/ client, generating inexhaustible psychological resources for helping other people through the qualities they imprint to personality and behavior, such as empathetic and compathetic ability/ capacity, spirituality and virtue, or contributing to the potentiation/ expression of some qualities and resources such as happiness and eudemonic-altruistic energy/ motivation, humanity, agreeableness, optimism, enthusiasm, and more - indispensable qualities and virtues of the professional in the humanistic social practices and services.

6.2.3. THE EGO/SELF

THE SELF AND THE ONTIC SUBJECT/ EGO

Within the humanistic-ontological paradigm of the person **the self** can be represented as the main ontical foundation of the ego - approached in its large representation (Maslow, .2011; Bickhard, 2012). Yet, the self explains the dismergence, the entropy, the "installation", unconsciously, of the other, the altruism, supporting a functioning frame, paradoxically, somehow opposed to the subject, even if this (the self) precedes, supports and conditionates him.

The existence of **the ontic subject/ ego** responds to the need of permanent security, of positive hedonic state, of balance, of beingness. Paradoxically, the subject is a product of the lack, but which seeks to suppress it, what make us to define the subject rather as a resort, mechanism, instrument than a "being", independent formation.

Still, the establishment of the ontic subject/ ego represents, in this light, a victory of the being and beingness against nothingness, ensuring the opening and browsing of the ontogenetical processes of formation the person, the personal ensemble, through sub-processes such as of ontosfication, spiritualization, humanization, culturalization, properly personalization (socialization), etc.

THE PROJECTIVE EGO AND THE SPIRITUAL EGO

The crucial function of **the onto-projective ego** it is to conserve the specific personal existence, the uniqueness, originality of the person, to represents at higher, intellectual, projective, teleonomic level the authentic needs and goals of the subject.

The establishment of the onto-projective self determines, consequently, the vector of the personal initiative and action to move from the basical ontological-psychological sphere, from the instinct, from the self to the superior mental sphere of the person.

The spiritual ego meets very important roles in the configuration of the motivational and axiological system of the person, in forming of some higher mental faculties such as the will or the conscience.

At the spiritual ego level is concentrated enormous energies, forces and information which, specifically assimilated and integrated, become important resources of cultural development and social adaptation (Bickhard, 2012).

Also, in this miraculous onto-projective sphere of the person take place important processes of ontic-informational synthesis generators of spirit, freedom, authentic happiness, need of knowledge, sensitivity, empathy, creativity, imprinting to the individual personality trans-personality, universality, human-spiritual specificity and unicity, because this incorporates essentialized, specifically and selective, all the spirituality and human historical experience.

THE SOCIAL EGO AND THE HUMANE EGO

In a simple interpretation the **social ego** represents the projection of the social other's image and jouissance in the subject's cognition and jouissance.

It can also to be represented as a synthesis of ontological-subjective formations constitutionally oriented to the social environment, community, society, values, where there are many of the resources and means by which the subject can fulfill it both psychologically but especially socially. The social ego has a great link with the person's social role-statuses and competencies (Burkitt, 1991).

The humane ego is, alongside the spiritual soul and humane soul, one of the most important reservoir and treasure of spirituality and humanism of the persons/ professional's personality.

This onto-formation is an important "piece" in the psychological-personal complex gear, important generator of spiritual-humane resources necessary to professionals from the social services.

The formation and establishment of the humane ego contributes, leads, finally, also to:

- the establishment of the personal system of beliefs and assumed personal convictions, of the moral conducts, of the need for knowledge the human phenomenon;

- the formation and establishment of the moral/ humane sentiments;

- the appearance of the need for social harmony, human solidarity, helpfulness.

In the internal economy and structure of the personality the humane ego meets both ontological and instrumental functions. This introjection of the other's values enriches the entire personality (Stets, Carter, 2011).

Essentially, the ontological-noetic content of the humane ego is supported by perceptual-attitudinal patterns like:

- *I'm man;*
- *l belong to humanity;*
- *the common good is also my good;*
- *I'm a good man;*
- *I'm selfless, generous;*
- *I am perceived as an altruistic citizen;*
- *I have dominant traits and conducts such as tolerance, compassion, humanness, altruism;*
- *I am happy through the happiness of the others;*
- *I like to help, to be useful,* etc.

6.3. THE FORMATION OF THE PERSONAL ONTOS

Core Fragment

In the complex and profound process of personal ontosfication the role of the mind is, along the inner activity and jouissance of the organism, very important, especially the role of memory, thinking and imagination, intellect and intelligence, but, in extension, also, of some emergent upper structures as the noetic ontos or consciousness. These operate with more advanced tools, more developed and more personalized, conditioning, crucially, through feedback, the process of ontosfication. A crucial role in process has the environment, especially the socio-human and cultural conditions where lives, cohabits, currently, the subject. In humanistic personology, even if in the child rearing are important the material conditions, the HUMAN conditions are, in fact, those that contribute crucially to the formation of the personal ontos, to the process of ontosfication, of forming a harmonious personality, fulfilled and, socio-humanly, effective. The experiential contingent social-personal and socio-affective factors are, also, crucial for the formation of the personal ontos.

If the *ontification*, as we have seen, is a stage, the final stage to whom must reach any formation, persom, etc., the **ontosfication** is the distinct process that leads to the formation, constitution, establishment and *ontification* of the personal ontos, defined, in our paradigm, as *the being* of the person.

In this sense, in the most straightforward sense, we define the process of ontosfication of the person mainly as the ontogenetic path, evolution, that leads to the formation of the personal ontos, as psychological-personal macro-formation, as well as at the process of transformation of the (occasional) experiences in stable/ constitutional personal-psychological formations, in structures, in "beings" with (according also to Kierkegaard,1981) the attributes of "admission of presence" and "steadiness".

The process leads, therefore, to the formation of the personal ontos, to the permanentization of some profound, fundamental constitutional-ontological structure of the person, to the establishment of some formations with great ontological-psychological consistency as the soul and the ontological ego; the soul, as experiential "internalization" of the other (person, value etc.), and the ego, as experiential "internalization" of the ontic/ subjective jouissance and of the social self.

The process implies, in addition to the formation of the personal ontos as formation, as a whole, also the formation of some constitutional component formations, or very dependent of the personal ontos. Mainly, is about:

- the hedonic ontos;

- the phobic ontos-formation;

- the projective ontos;

- the prosentic ontos-formation;

- the malsentic ontos-formation;

- the soul

  ➢ the compathetic ontos,

  ➢ the affective/social soul,

  ➢ the spiritual soul (mystical, intellectual, playful, aesthetical, ethical, etc.),

  ➢ the humane soul;

- the ego
  - ➢ the self and the ontic subject/ego,
  - ➢ the projective ego and the spiritual ego,
  - ➢ the humane ego, etc.

In the complex, profound and long process of ontosfication crucial role have the inner activity of the organism, the mind and the environment, especially the socio-human and cultural environment (Brakel, 2013).

But, in the humanistic genetic formation of the personal ontos the body is not represented as a simple recipient, support, skeleton or pedestal on which is constructed the ontological-psychological sphere of the person, and nor as a simple tool, servo-mechanism of interpersonal communication, but contribute, participate dynamically, dialectically, to its processual and dialectical formation, the more so the organism, meaning as the internal biological organization and dynamics of the body, enters fundamentally, functionally, processually and endemically in the process of personal ontosfication.

There are, consequently, arguments to considers the body determinative, constitutional component/ factor of the formation, structure, beingness and functioning of the personal ontos - reason why we attach it crucial importance both, so, regarding the ontogenetic process of its formation, also regarding the everyday life or the beingness of the person.

In the general process of formation of the person ontos crucial roles have the central nervous system, the sensitive jouissance, the endocrine system, the neuro-vegetative apparatus, the mechanisms of production, storage, processing and superization of the emotions, and more. The formation of the personal ontos not being, therefore, conceivable without their contribution.

In the complex and profound process of personal ontosfication the role of the mind is, along the inner activity and jouissance of the organism, very important, especially the role of memory, thinking and imagination, intellect and intelligence, but, in extension, also, of some emergent upper structures as the noetic ontos or consciousness. These operate with more advanced tools, more developed and more personalized, conditioning, crucially, through feedback, the process of ontosfication. As shown above, a crucial role in process has the environment, especially the socio-human and cultural conditions where lives, cohabits, currently, the subject (Noica, 1994).

In humanistic personology, even if in the child rearing are important the material conditions, the HUMAN conditions are, in fact, those that contribute crucially to the formation of the personal ontos, to the process of ontosfication, of forming a harmonious personality, fulfilled and, socio-humanly, effective (Cusick, 2011). The contingent social-personal and socio-affective factors are, also, crucial for the formation of the ontological-psychological sphere of the person.

In the complex, profound, process of ontosfication are, crucially, implied principles, laws, characteristics properties of process like as the promergence and the dismergence, emergence and imergence, transmergence and telegence, conmergence and sinmergence. The promergence and the dismergence are opposite ontological-procesual properties, and reflect the objective tendencies of the process of ontosfication of conservation and development, as opossition to entropy, degradation, because at any moment a number of ontos-formations, dimensions or processes are in growing, advancement, forming, are promergent, and others are in degradation decline, involution, are dismergent.

In the process of forming of the personal ontos and its sub-formations the emergence is the quality/ capacity/ property of the processes that makes possible the appearance of new entities, structures, properties etc. from the previous ones, defined as sources, factors, conditions. The emergence generates new ontological-psychological realities and qualities. Usually the new ontological-psychological entities are more complex and better adapted to the environmental factors.

The imergence is the property and capacity of the process of ontosfication to forming, developing, evolving it in itself, from nothing, of inertia, "subversively", simultaneously with the developments, evolutions, changes caused by the inner, determined, objective identified factors.

Transmergence represents the property and capacity of the process to carry out without limitations and physical barriers of space and organization. Telegence means much the same thing, but concerns the temporal and projective aspects of the processes of ontosfication.

Conmergence entails the transmergence, the telegence, the imergence and the promergence and represents the tendency of the processes to organize and concentrate it "thematically" in ontos-formations, ontos-structures, etc., reflecting the inherence of some functions, beyond any limitations of "logistic" or temporal order. Sinmergence is the quality/ capacity/ property of the ontological-psychological processes which makes it possible the coexistence, simultaneously, of some ontos-personal entities in the same personal "space", the functioning and beingness of some distinct ontos-entities, structures, relationships, processes on the same material, biological, informational, spiritual support.

The process of ontosfication, of forming its constitutional components, respects, covers, pass through the six principals stages, like all the other formations and personal spheres, respectively, of contact and acquisition/ accumulation, structuration/ centralization and constitution/ formation/ holistization, of establishing/ networking and ontification/ fulfillment.

In the phase of contact occurs the primary junction between the main elements which will come in the constitution of the probable future personal ontos. One such element can be considered also the core function, the being of the person. After the stage of contact follows a period of ontological-psychological acquisitions and accumulations intrinsic to the incipient links and connections which have already been formed. These represent "the seeds" of the future ontos-formations.

The process of structuring/ centralization and internal organization of the personal ontos, as the third preparatory stage, have very important role in laying the foundations of the personal ontos. The transition to the stage of constitution/ holistization, as ontos-formation, is essentially conditioned also of the appearance of a new "nature". It is about also of the ancestral leap from the biological to human, from the material or biological formations to the spiritual, human ontos-formations.

At the stage of establishing/ networking the personal ontos is, internally well organized, permanentizated in the personal assembly and plays the role according to the function which had formed, especially the role of *being*, establishing stable connections with the formations and with the environmental spheres, becoming part of a superior system.

If the phase of formation/ constituation/ holistization is defined through ontos-formatization and internal functioning, the phase of establishment is defined by consolidation, function and role within the personal assembly, the final stage, the ontification, means the completion of the process of ontosfication and identification with goal, of forming the person's being.

To the process of forming of the person's being participate many inner, biological, sensorial, psychological, spiritual energy, mechanisms, resorts (Brakel, 2013). In this sense, all onto-personal energy probably conditionates, largely, the promergence, the processual formation of the personal ontos. There may be an ontic-psychological mechanism of production of the energy required for the complex and dialectical process of ontosfication, of transformation the emotions, subjective experiences into energy of personal ontosfication, assimilated in ontos-formations. Then, by the internal ontic mechanisms/ processes, of the formations, of release of other forms of energy, as propeller source for ontosfication. This energy acts as a synthesizer in the process of personal ontosfication (the construction of the personal ontos). At the base of the processes stand innumerable mechanisms, montages, motivational sources and resorts, internal ontos-formative loops that "works" in infinite combinations.

6.4. THE FORMATION OF THE SOUL

Core Fragment

The interaction with the other real person, dear, with the nearest persons, significant group, with the near physical environment leads to the formation of the affective (social) soul, and to the personal system of attachments. Reflects the personal contingent interaction, and appurtenance of the person to the group or to the particular social context. The interaction with the world of spirit, culture, education, art, etc., leads, by the mental capacity of idealization, projectivity and symbolization, to the formation of the spiritual soul, to virtue and spirituality as personal qualities. The interaction with the symbolic, universal, generalized, concept other, with the "status" other, by mental facilities of the generalization, idealization, projectivity and symbolization, abstractization leads to the formation of the humane soul and to the empathy, empathetic capacity of the person. Reflects the abstract interaction and affiliation of the person to society, humanity, and his human condition and nature.

From the humanistic perspective, even if in the child rearing are important the economic, material conditions the socio-personal, the human/ humane, and the cultural conditions are, in fact, those that contribute crucially to the formation of the soul, of its constitutional components and dimensions - affective, spiritual and humane, those that have the determinative contribution in the psychological-ontogenetical process of spiritualization, those that contribute, consequently, to the formation - ontological-psychologically and socio-humanly - of a harmonious and developed personality/ person (Moore, 1994).

Each of the three major areas of the soul, affective (social), spiritual, and humane, is the product of the interaction of the subject with specific factors, even if cannot be traced strict boundaries between them. The contingent social-personal and socio-affective factors are crucial for the formation of the affective (social) soul, the cultural conditions of learning and training of the spiritual abilities and sensibility are essential for the formation of the spiritual soul, while the altruistic, solidaristic, humanitarian, morale climate greatly influences the formation of the humane soul.

Thus, in a purely humanistic perspective, the human personal, the human-social factors are decisive in the formation and development of the person's soul.

The psychological-human (humane) characteristics of the individuals/ persons from the environmental onto-system, as well agreeability, soulful warmth, carefulness, empathy, spirituality, their constant presence and consistency, in human, spiritual and moral terms, the human quality of the interpersonal relationships, the community compathy, the social relationships as *humane* relationships are the constitutional determinant factors that mark, crucially, the sense of the personality development, the sense of the soul development, the human adaptability, the soulful welfare, the authentic happiness.

Regarding the soul's formation, establishment and beingness in the structure, composition of the humane personality, of the human personality as a whole, alongside organism, conscience, ego, etc, the question it is if its existence is necessary, if the human personality, the person could not exist, function, inside and outside, without a soul, and thus, if the conclusion is that its existence is necessary (Moore,

1994), then why, and which is its sense, role, which is the contribution of its beingness in the structure, the beingness and functioning of the global human personality, in itself also in the environmental context ?

We believe that the soul formation, establishment and beingness in the structure, the composition of the human personality is an objective necessity; the soul being constitutional, ancestral, genetic, and emblematic part of the being, of the human personality, mainly through its adaptive function, through the experiential-ontological-psychological internalization of the social-contextual, spiritual-cultural, and human-ancestral environmental characteristics.

We see thus, the importance of the soul's formation and beingness is undoubted, moreover, in addition to its adaptive role, very important being, too, the internal functional and existential role - the soul of everyone being source of jouissance and psychological-behavioral energy, of existential sense, of happiness and personal fulfillment (Stone, 1999).

The formation of the soul and the process of spiritualization of the person are conditioned/ determined mainly by two processes:

> the development, growth, general spiritual development of the person, which impose the automatic establishment of certain soulful, spiritual formations with integrative function, and

> the ontogenetic process of conmergent organizations, syntheses of the multitude emotional and spiritual formations oriented towards the interest of the generalized other, to common, human values and interests.

The humanization of the soul and personality is, so, an emergent holistic integrator process more pronounced in people that, through the specific activity, engage or work with/or for broad categories of people, such as teachers, artists, workers in social, political, cultural areas, etc. (Khan, 1981).

Summarizing, the soul is formed in the general context of the constitution and functioning of the specific human organism, in the overall process of forming and developing the personality, under the influence of the environmental factors and internal action of the principles/ laws of emergence, imergence, transmergence, telegence, conmergence, etc.

According to these the soul's "sphere" becomes a distemporalized "space", partially released by the actions of the, so-called, objective (physical) laws, the physical, chemical, biological elements involved can be easily translated, noeticaly, sympathetically, and spiritually, and vice-versa, the possibilities and combinations becoming, practically, unlimited.

In the gradual process of forming the soul passes, in our opinion, up to the constituting, through the following stages: of contact, of acquisition/ accumulation and of structuring. After the constituting follows the instituting in the constitution of the personality, and, finally, follows his endemization/ ontification, i.e. the definitive enrollment in the psychological-ontological constitution of the person/ personality (Stefaroi, 2009b, p. 14).

The soul formation process is not automatically, simple and linear, through the mere presence of the body in society and culture. The biological, sensorial, cognitive, affective experiences, the successes, failures and traumas marks significantly the structure, organization, architecture/ composition and orientation (hedonic, emotional, social, intellectual, spiritual, religious) of the soul.

In this respect, the strong, deep, altruistic, humane personality is described also in the context of a consistent and structurally balanced soul - this becoming a fundamental source of spiritual, moral, humane energy for the person, also for the ontogenetic process of developing the personality as a whole.

Paradoxically maybe, the process of construction of the soul has not, as "pivot", the self, the subject, how we are tempted to say, but the other. This is not necessarily an other-person but an other perceived as all out of the intrinsic order of the endemic subject.

The other can be, however, also the self and ideal ego, desirable ego, the body, the social ego, the social representations of the ourselves, but perceived as an other, through the cognitive capacity and process of objectualization. Process which leads also to the formation of the ego, especially the social ego. The soul, itself, being, in this respect, an alter-ego into own personality/ being.

In this interpretation the most important other is the ego, but follows the people who are imposed in the subject's experiences by presence and importance (they provide food, security, prestige, self-esteem, love etc.). To this end, the formation of the soul comply the structure and existence of the other.

The interaction with the other real person, dear, with the nearest persons, significant group, with the near physical environment leads to the formation of the affective (social) soul, and to the personal system of attachments. Reflects the personal contingent interaction, and appurtenance of the person to the group or to the particular social context.

The interaction with the world of spirit, culture, education, art, etc., leads, by the mental capacity of idealization, projectivity and symbolization, to the formation of the spiritual soul, to virtue and spirituality as personal qualities.

The interaction with the symbolic, universal, generalized, concept other, with the "status" other, by mental facilities of the generalization, idealization, projectivity and symbolization, abstractization leads to the formation of the humane soul and to the empathy, empathetic capacity of the person. Reflects the abstract interaction and affiliation of the person to society, humanity, and his human condition and nature.

Spiritual soul and humane soul are, therefore, the products of the personality enlightenment and of the projection capacity of the subject. In combination determines personal qualities such as kindness and humanity, human solidarity, morality, faith, aesthetic sensitivity, and humane sensitivity. Reflects the cultural, moral, spiritual, creative and ancestral quality of the individual (Stone, 1999).

The concrete process of the soul's formation is prefigured by the formation of some occasional affective, spiritual, humane micro-formations, centered, mainly, on determined "objects". Once established, these operate as relatively autonomous formations, but they are conditioned by determined relationships. Persist as long as these objects (persons, value, ideas, models) will be imposed through the presence or importance for the subject.

So, the other person, thing, habitat, situation, value, community, ideas is not regardless for the subject. Other (environment) is means of existence and vital, material and spiritual, resources, source of good, welfare, satisfaction, security, fulfillment and happiness, or, on the contrary, is hostile, aggressive, a source of stress and negative emotions. In many cases it may be also irrespective, insignificant, without influence on the formation and beingness of the soul (Khan, 1981).

Some of them, especially people, concrete human being, gain a crucial existential meaning, as the mother, or, where appropriate, other person from the person's genuine micro-environment. These individuals act as socio-human/ personal "pivot" in the process of building the soul.

Yet, not the simple objectual presence of these causes the formation of the soul. The main sources of the internal onto-personal formation, of formation/ beingness of the soul are the feelings and subjective experiences in relation with the humans.

The soul, thus established as an autonomous onto-formation, tends to become a being in itself, ontological core, the person's being. Primarily through the internalization of the representations and of the empathized enjoyment of the other. The other becoming a constitutional part of the person's existence, beingness, and, inevitably, the other is assimilated and internalized by the subject's activism and her internal enjoyment.

Of course, the three spheres or levels of the soul form, after the establishment, a bio-psycho-ontological unit, and we do not make mistakes if we consider the soul as a fundamental existential entity of the person, her ontological-spiritual nature, even if the soul's formation and beingness are dependent on the organic-psychic existence and process. Once being established, the soul works like all the other formations, but will need of affective, spiritual and humane experiences, feelings, sentiments.

The imposing of the soul as an autonomous ontological-psychological formation and personality structure is an important step because involves the installation in the ontological-psychological system of the individual, increasing the autonomy of the onto-formation. At this level begins the process of accentuated release from references, the process of accelerated autonomization, of acquiring an higher functional autonomy. The person begins to become receptive to the values and critical in relation to the behaviors and attitudes of the other/close people. The soul begins to contribute essentially, hence, to the formation also of the other formations, integrative, like ego, character, an personality as a whole.

The transition to the phase where prevails the other's purposes is achieved at this stage too, is the moment where the other is represented as a desirous subject and less as desirable object. The other as desirous subject, with needs, concerns, goals is anchored deeply into the ontological structure of the person. They can controls, by mechanisms and unconscious strategies, the personality and even the consciousness. The person accepts this situation, not necessarily intentionally or knowingly, because the other provides content for the inner life, feelings and even emotional security.

Each person is also an experiential amount of persons and entities (Brakel, 2013). Only through communication, mind, language, through community coexistence, and by the unifying contribution of the personality as a whole, is defined, more or less, as a unified entity. The unification is, so, made by means of the intelligence, consciousness, ego and personality, but how these no pass, usually, the state of constituting remains to conclude that the common note of the internal persons's individual existence is mainly determined by the emotional interaction between the subject and the other, despite the established labels such as "Man is a rational being."

From the soul's perspective is essential so the presence, security and happiness of the dear, closer other. Is not a totally disinterested altruism. Person defined as a virtually assimilation/ internalization of the other enjoyment is enriched itself, because without the other it loses the opportunity to be enjoyed and humanized. At the birth, "the being", the enjoyment is in the other, the body itself is not enough for personalization/ humanization. This is the way whereby the humans access to social experience, culture, history, assimilating the all community experience, by contact with each other, with the environment, with values.

The process determines the capacity of attachment, empathy, altruism, inner well-being, social adjustment. It is extremely complex because it is made on many levels - physical, cognitive, emotional, volitional, axiological, spiritual, behavioral etc. (Cusick, 2011; Frankl, 1967).

After the long, complex, deep and multidimensional process of formation, with the phases of contact, acquisition/ accumulation and structuring, after the constituting and incorporation of the soul in the constitutional structure and content of the individual's personality follows his long beingness and functioning as relatively autonomous onto-formation; processes which take place in the context of the contingent and unforeseeable social-personal, socio-affective, cultural, spiritual, socio-moral conditions and factors where the person lives, being yet established very close links, congruencies, interactions, inter-determinations, compathies between the soul and the environmental system, especially with the nearest persons, with their souls; their beingness and functioning being made in inter-connection, inter-determination, mutual influence and compathetical congruence.

Even if the beingness and functioning of soul is not something metaphysical, probably, has also such dimensions and processes.

Depending on their nature, location or source one can speak of *affective (social) processes, spiritual processes, humane processes*, etc. Each of these having specific functions/ roles in determining and sustaining the person's psyco-spiritual and humane qualities:

- the affective (social) processes determining and sustaining the attachment, social sensitivity and interpersonal/ contingent empathy;

- the spiritual processes determining and sustaining the spiritual richness and virtue;

- the humane processes determining and sustaining the empathy/ compathy and humanity/ humanness.

A crucial issue regarding the soul's beingness and functioning, is, what we call, the soul's needs/ motivation, jouissance and energy, as core sources for the person's qualities such as enthusiasm, energy, optimism, happiness etc. To this end, when we speak about the soul's motivational-energetical sphere we involve concepts, ideas and syntagms as:

- *soul's needs;*

- *soul's jouissance;*

- *soul's accomplishment;*

- *soul's energy;*

- *soul's altruism;*

- *soul's consistency;*

- *soul's spirituality;*

- *happiness, enthusiasm, optimism, love, attachment, empathy, selfless, etc.*

The soul's needs/ motivation, jouissance and energy have, also, an important role in determining the general motivational-eudaimonical system of the personality, his spiritual, altruistic, moral, prosocial orientation. In this sense, is very important the nature, orientation, the dominant dimension, the content of soul. If it is dominant a soul's jouissance that includes the other's happiness in this case we can speak of a altruistic, humane soul, and a personality and behavior oriented to the other's well-being.

Further, one can speak of two motivational-humane systems of the person's soul oriented towards the good, welfare of the other:

1. soul's mobiles, needs, trends, interests, intentions, aspirations, ideals directly oriented towards the good of the other, sustaining the altruistic attitude and behavior of aid, support, care of the people in need, and

2. the soul's system of mobiles, needs, trends, emotions, interests, intentions, aspirations, ideals that acts indirectly, axiological and energetical, as factors of guidance, spiritualization and humanization of the person's humane personality, humane behavior, generating the moral will and virtue, virtuous personality, charisma, humane authority - axiological-energetical sources in the person's action and conduct, of human, personal and eudemonical development and improvement of the other, through moral and spiritual virtue, transfer and compathy, of empowerment, emancipation, fulfillment of the persons in difficulty or socio- humanely, morally, eudaimonically degraded.

In this second case we speak of a spiritual soul's jouisance, that determines a strong spiritual setting and orientation of the personality and behavior. It is mainly a jouissance of the spiritual soul, of the higher consciousness, moral ego and character, and, in the first case, about a jouissance mainly of the humane soul, but also of the affective (social) soul, and to other formations, higher, humanized instances of the personality.

In a general way, the soul, with all its areas and components, is the place and central source of the humane and spiritual jouissance (Brakel, 2013), therefore, if in the case of the body, senses, instinct's jouissance we talk about libido and pleasure, in the case of soul's jouissance we talk about eudaimonia and happiness, and, in the case of the humane soul's eudaimonia, of happiness through the other, or altruistic happiness, and, further, of an altruistic soulful energy.

The organization of the soul's energetic jouissance follows, largely, the other's organization and existence jouissance. The social-eudaimonical interaction with the other real, close, dear person, with the reference group, with the nearest physical environment, leads to the formation of the energetic jouissance of the affective soul, the cultural-eudaimonical interaction with the spiritual world leads to the formation of the energetic jouissance of the spiritual soul, and the moral-eudaimonical interaction with the generalized, symbolic other, value-person leads to the formation of the energetic jouissance of the humane soul.

The most important conclusion of this section is that, one of the crucial function/ role of the soul's jouissance, beingness and functioning it is of generator, producer of feelings and passions. These can be positive or negative. Those negative have also the role of signaling the disturbances in the other's existence, beingness or jouissance, which can be a person, value, community, etc., and determining reactions, structures, skills and behaviors to restore the normality - function absolutely necessary also of the professional's soul's jouissance, beingness and functioning in the humanistic social practices and services, in education, therapy, theatre, social work etc. (Stefaroi, 2013).

6.5. THE FORMATION OF THE EGO

Core Fragment

The formation of the ego, and the individualization of the process of personalization does not mean a simple counterbalance or manifestation of the biological, instinctual forces of the self and of the ontic subject, but also means a personal marking of the humanizing processes; moreover, also those formations, resorts, forces that we represent as belonging to individuality are re-dimensioned and enriched through the incorporation of the spiritual, cultural, moral and human acquisitions

It is difficult to operate with limits, thresholds, steps, unique, unitary age periods relating to the time when is installed as dominant the process of individualization, or to the time when the ego is formed and established with its defining attributes (Freud, 1990).

However, the formation of the ego and the individualization are a necessity, together with the processes of culturalization and humanization, with which it completes and interacts, even if, at least in the psychoanalytic perspective, they are somewhat opposite; the processes of culturalization and humanization are guided by the other's interests, the common good, while the individualization process is guided by the personal-endemic motivational resorts, by the individual intrinsic jouissance, by impulse, needs and unconscious, by the self.

However, the formation of the ego and the individualization of the process of personalization does not mean a simple counterbalance or manifestation of the biological, instinctual forces of the self and the ontic subject, but also means a personal marking of the humanizing processes; moreover, also those formations, resorts, forces that we represent as belonging to individuality are re-dimensioned and enriched through the incorporation of the spiritual, cultural, moral and human acquisitions (Brody & Axelrad, 1970).

In the complex, profound, process of formation of the ego and of individualization they have crucial role the principles, laws, characteristics properties of process like as the promergence and the dismergence, emergence and imergence, transmergence and telegence, conmergence and sinmergence. The promergence and the dismergence are opposite ontological-procesual properties, and reflect the objective tendencies of the process of individualization of conservation and development, as opossition to entropy, degradation, because at any moment a number of ego-ontosformations, dimensions or processes are in growing, advancement, forming, are promergent, and others are in degradation decline, involution, are dismergent.

In the process of forming of the personal ego/ self and its sub-formation the emergence is the quality/ capacity/ property of the processes that makes possible the appearance of new entities, structures, properties etc. from the previous ones, defined as sources, factors, conditions (Frankl, 1967). The emergence generates new realities and qualities. Usually the new entities are more complex and better adapted to the environmental factors. The imergence represents the property and capacity of the process of ontosfication to forming, developing, evolving it in themselves, in itself, from nothing, of inertia, "subversively", simultaneously with the developments, evolutions, changes caused by the determined, objective identified factors. Transmergence represents the property and capacity of the process to carry out without limitations and physical barriers of space and organization. Telegence means much the same thing, but concerns the temporal aspect of the processes of ontosfication.

Conmergence entails the transmergence, the telegence, the imergence and the promergence and represents the tendency of the processes to organize and concentrate it "thematically" in ego-ontosformations, ego-ontos-structures, etc., reflecting the inherence of some functions, beyond any limitations of "logistic" or temporal order. Sinmergence is the quality/ capacity/ property of the individualizing processes which makes it possible the coexistence, simultaneously, of some ego-ontos-personal entities in the same personal "space", the functioning and beingness of some distinct ego-ontos-entities, structures, relationships, processes on the same material, biological, informational, spiritual support.

The process of ego formation and individualization respects, covers, passes through the six principals stages, like all the other formations and personal spheres, respectively, of contact and acquisition/ accumulation, structuration/ centralisation and constitution/ holistization, of establishing/ networking, and ontification/ fulfillment.

The
HUMANISTIC
PERSONOLOGY
Project

CHAPTER 7

THE ONTOGENETIC PROCESS OF FORMATION OF THE PSHYCHOLOGICAL-SOCIAL/ RELATIONAL SPHERE OF THE PERSON

7.1. INTRODUCTORY ASPECTS 180

7.2. THE PSYCHOLOGICAL-SOCIAL/RELATIONAL SPHERE 181

7.2.1. CONSCIENCE 183

7.2.2. CHARACTER 185

7.2.3 THE SOCIO-HUMAN/ HUMANE SKILLS, COMPETENCIES, HABITUDES AND CONDUCTS 187

7.3. THE FORMATION OF THE (SOCIAL) CONSCIENCE 188

7.4. THE FORMATION OF CHARACTER 190

7.5. THE FORMATION OF THE SOCIO-HUMAN/ HUMANE SKILLS, COMPETENCIES, HABITUDES AND CONDUCTS 192

7.1. INTRODUCTORY ASPECTS

In the ontogenetic process of formation of the pshychological-social/ relational sphere of the person participate, dialectically, inter alia, the personal ontos, the soul, the mind/ intellect and the conscience, especially through comscience, determining, in the context of action of the ambiental social-moral and cultural-ethical factors, ample phenomena of ethical-socialization, culturalization, and humanization, essential for the processes of psychological-ethical structuring and holistic organization of the personality, and the person as a whole, of ethical superization of the feelings and behaviors, of the internal ethical constitution relating to the ancestral anthropo-generical human-psychological model, of the internal personal-psychological representation of the contemporary ethical model of person, specific psychological-moral configuration, characteristical for the community where the person grows, lives. Still, even if in the process of formation of the pshychological-social/ relational sphere of the person are important the formal-institutional and format-cultural and ethical conditions the concrete experiential and ideothetical-phenomenological moral-human and socio-cultural conditions contribute crucially to its structuration and orientation.

7.2. THE PSYCHOLOGICAL-SOCIAL/RELATIONAL SPHERE

Core Fragment

The soul itself, as resort and constitutional source of the spiritual and humane qualities of the person, cannot be expressed in conduct/ behavior than by means of some holistic and relational structures and spheres of the character and personality such as the humane character. The humane (prosocial, moral) character is a holistic personality structure through which are formed and crystallized the personal features relating to the common good and jouissance, to all people, where these personal features are stated as constant personal qualities of conduct. Regarding the role of the humane character, its formation and establishment as structural formation of personality will lead, with the contribution of the humane conscience, to the metamorphosis of the person's humane and spiritual resources in humanistic, prosocial, altruistic attitudes and conducts.

In our opinion, what in our theory is call, the social-personal/ psychological-social sphere of the person includes mostly:

- The social ego and the humane ego;
- The conscience -
    - The comscience,
    - The culture,
    - The humane conscience;
- The character, and
- The system of the socio-human aptitudes, skills, competencies, habitudes, conducts.

So, regarding the structure/ composition of the social-personal sphere of the person, four great formations, sub-spheres, sub-structures are essential: the social/ humane ego, the conscience, the character, and the system of the socio-human aptitudes, competencies, skills, qualities, habitudes, conducts.

5. The social/ humane ego – represents the projection of the (social/ human) other's image and jouissance in the subject' cognition and jouissance; synthesis of subjective formations constitutionally oriented to the outside, where are many of the resources and means by which the subject can fulfill it both psychologically but also socially, the social ego having a great link with the person's role-status.

6. The conscience could be considered *the reflexive-intellectual-axiological "being"* of the person; the reflectation of the (social/ human) other in the ego's cognition and thinking; ensemble of epistemological-reflexive-axiological formations constitutionally oriented to the outside.

7. The character can be represented as the personal macro-structure which reflects, psychologically-attitudinally, the other's interest and feelings in the person's internal jouissance, economy, thinking, functioning, and behavior, being, so, in a large interpretation, a product of the interaction between ego and conscience.

8. The socio-human aptitudes, skills, competencies, habitudes, conducts represent the system of relational-behavioral instruments of the person, the praxeological-technical/ instrumental relation with the (social) environment/ other.

Just like at the ontological-psychological sphere level, at the social/ personal sphere level the social/ humane ego, the conscience, the character, the socio-human aptitudes, competencies, skills, abilities, qualities, habitudes, exist and operate together and interdependently, forming, in the great frame of the personal ensemble, a structural-functional unity; also, these can be represented as an operationalization of the ontological-psychological sphere, of its elements, of the personal ontos, of the soul, of the ego, at the level of person, in relation with the (social) environment.

The main role, function, aim of the personal-social sphere is to ensure, to confer the psychological-axiological and psychological-praxeological tools for the person in relation with the (social) environment, to be, to exist in outside, in the natural, human and socio-cultural world, to maintain and ensure the link with the world of people, values, institutions, rules, with the communities where the person lives, coexists.

So, the social-personal sphere can be represented also as a link between the ontological-psychological world of the person, its authentic/ irreducible existence, and the socio-human environment where there is its "food", means, resources and resorts of existence, survival, love, happiness, fulfillment, etc.

7.2.1. CONSCIENCE

COMSCIENCE

In the broad sphere of the conscience (as whole) is formed and operates a very important component, sub-structure in the establishment, functioning and, especially, in its pro-social, morale, humane orientation.

It is about *the comscience* - term experimentally used by us in order to refer to a sub-formation that incorporates, synthetically, emergently, conmergently and transmergently, at the conscience level, the common systems of knowledge, values, ideas, beliefs of a community, social category, society, mankind. It is something similar with the *basic personality* (Mead, 2001) at the overall personality level.

Comscience conditionates the jump from animal to human and it is, in essence, the epistemic reflection, in the structure and ontogenesis of the person, of the symbolic, cultural and social environmental characteristics where the person coexists.

CULTURE

In the humanistic personology theory and philosophy (axiology), the humanistic-ontological paradigm, the person, in addition to the fact that it is "a man with a big soul", it is also an educated, informed, erudite, wise and especially creative being, the soulful/ spiritual/ humane welfare and the culture cannot be conceived than together.

In areas such as psychotherapy, education or social work the importance of these qualities is highlighted of the truth that only a person with high humane and spiritual qualities coupled with those "cultural" is able to resonate and to represent in its complexity the client/ student as cultural complex, deep, spiritual, creative, moral being (Canda & Furman, 2009); which, beyond the simplifying sociological or psychological modelations, it is itself a spiritual and moral world, with unpredictable dynamics, for whose knowledge is required to appeal to much inventiveness, to information from all areas, from the aesthetic culture, sociology, psychology, anthropology, philosophy, etc.

THE HUMANE CONSCIENCE

In a very simple interpretation, but very suggestive, the humane conscience, which includes moral conscience, is an intellectual-axiological psychological universe, a superior moral instance that signals the subject the fact that something is good or bad in the condition, existence or jouissance of the generalized other.

As against the ego, which is a formation primarily ontological, or the character, which is mainly a holistic-structural construction, the conscience, including humane conscience, is a construction predominantly intellectual-cultural and moral.

It is, therefore, the psychological-personal place where are debated and constructed:

- the value systems of the individuals;

- the conceptions toward the himself, world, people, work, society etc.

- the place of the person's humanist ideals and beliefs (Habermas & Lenhardt, 2001).

Of course, speaking of *humane* conscience we keep in mind, also, the prosocial, humanistic, solidaristic orientation of the person's general consciousness, its humanistic global dimension, valence, oriented, by means of the systems of values, concepts, beliefs, attitudes, judgments, reflections, to the good of the other, of the generalized other, not only to the good of the significant other, dear, relative, etc., oriented to the common good, to humanity as a whole (Castiello, 1936).

7.2.2. CHARACTER

The character is a crucial part of the psychological-social sphere of the person. In humanistic perspective the socio-personal, the human/ humane, and the cultural/ moral factors are, in fact, those that determine the specific constitution and the formation/ establishment of this constitutional part of the personality and of the person as a whole (Mason, 1989; Maslow, 1970). As was presented in the book, the process of formation of character entails the inherent tendencies of moral/ ethical holistization of the general ontogenetic process of personalization, of constituting of the personality, in the context of the gradual imposing of the promergent moral/ ethical holistic factors of process, implying the incorporation, union, synthesis, the conmergent, emergent, transmergent unitary organization, of the formations, energy, mechanisms, of the psychological-personal ethical processes, in structures and constructions at the level of persom/ personality, stable holistic psychological-ethical entities, characteristical for the person as a whole.

As autonomous formation, structure, and as an important persom, the character is a holistic and representative construction through which are formed and crystallized the emblematic and durable features of the person and personality, especially in relation to the dominant rules of the community/ society, to the common good, to the people, where these personal psychological-characterial features are stated as constant qualities of behavior in different situations of activity and socio-human interaction, cohabitation.

Even if in the structure and functioning of the character are important the formal-institutional and format-cultural factors, the concrete and ideothetical moral-human and socio-cultural factors contribute crucially to the character structuration and orientation (Kellerman, 2012; Mason, 1989).

THE STRONG CHARACTER

The humanistic-existential and positive approach in psychology and personology, originated in existential and positive (phenomenological) philosophy, focuses specifically on character features as *strong character* or *characterial development* (Snyder & Lopez, 2006), highlighting traits and qualities such as high control, activism, accountability, free will, social adaptability, assertiveness, resilience.

Essentially, the *strong/ developed character* is closely determined by the level of development of the strong/ developed personality, but also of the personality as a whole, which imply, inter alia, high degree of awareness, of self-knowledge, of self-esteem (Maslow, 2011), personal and social efficiency (Rogers, 1977, 1980), high socio-emotional development, high control of emotions, emotional intelligence (Erikson, 1998), realism and balance (Frankl, 1967), powerful will, resistance to failure and frustrations, hope, orientation to future. positive attitude, optimism, active thinking (Seligman, 2002), professional development (Erikson, 1998), personal and social autonomy, interpersonal development (Erikson, 1998), mature personality, adaptability (Rogers, 1980; Maslow, 1993).

Thus, the strong personality and the strong character are complementary, interdependent, and cannot be conceived in another way than together.

THE HUMANE (MORAL) CHARACTER

The soul itself, as resort and constitutional source of the spiritual and humane qualities of the person, cannot be expressed in conduct/ behavior than by means of some holistic and relational structures and spheres of the character and personality such as the *humane character.*

The humane (prosocial/moral) character is a holistic personality structure through which are formed and crystallized the personal features relating to the common good and jouissance, to all people, where these personal features are stated as constant personal qualities of conduct (Miller, 2013, Gill, 2000).

Regarding the role of the humane character, its formation and establishment as structural formation of personality will lead, with the contribution of the humane conscience, to the metamorphosis of the person's humane and spiritual resources in humanistic, prosocial, altruistic attitudes and conducts.

Only through the formation and establishment of the humane character is emphasized and highlighted the humanistic valence of the global personality and conduct, is set and manifest the humane personality as a structure expressly oriented towards the generalized other's jouissance, humane personality that, by means of the system of prosocial/ humane skills, abilities and habitudes, is reflected in the person's conduct and presence as a resource of jouissance for the well-being and socio-human fulfillment of the other, for the recovery, rehabilitation or mitigation of the customer's suffering - in the case of the professional's activity in activities such as therapy or social work.

7.2.3. *THE SOCIO-HUMAN/ HUMANE SKILLS, COMPETENCIES, HABITUDES AND CONDUCTS*

In this section we refer particularly to those human/ humane competencies, skills, abilities situated, mainly, in, what we call, conventionally, the social, relational, interpersonal sphere of the person.

The workers from areas such as education, social work, psychotherapy, etc., are not only humans with big soul, but, also, well developed in terms of socio-humane skills and abilities - between the spiritual sphere and the one intellectual instituting a very productive zone of abilities such as emotional intelligence, spiritual intelligence, empathetic communication, etc.

Only a person with these intellectual and spiritual qualities is able to represent the human being in its complexity, its socio-human reality, in suffering and difficulty situation, which beyond the simplifying sociological or psychological modeling, are some worlds itself, with unpredictable dynamics, for whose modeling it is necessary to appeal at knowledge and information from all the scientific and philosophical areas. The sociology, psychology, anthropology, theology, philosophy, ethics, aesthetics must represent, to this end, permanent preoccupations of knowledge and sources to whom to appeal for modeling, as faithfully it is possible, a problem situation, or to understand a person, a human being situated in existential impasse, personal failure or suffering.

7.3. THE FORMATION OF THE (SOCIAL) CONSCIENCE

Core Fragment

As is well known, very important in the process of conscience forming are the culture, religion, morals, and education. In process these bring simultaneously spiritual, ontological and axiological input, mainly through their systems of values, beliefs and ideals. Through the formation of the (social) conscience takes place not only simple constructions of a news psychological-personal and behavioral formations, but also takes place complex, deep and global processes of "conscientization" and adaptation of the person, of the process of personalization, the person becomes socio-humanly able, and aware of its own situation, condition and of its ontogenetic processes, as well as of autonomization - in relation to itself and in relation to the environmental factors.

One of the most important goals of the process of formation of the (social) conscience, and, through these, of the personal autonomization, is to bring, through reflection and mental processing, on the one hand, these spheres of the social life, of the environment in which is formed and cohabits the subject, in the mental and behavioral spheres, connecting the person, organically, to the structural, axiological and functional features of the community, and, on the other hand, to reflect, still there, the subject's interests, instituting, so, a noetical and attitudinal system of synthesis, as well as of confrontations, a resort of dependence, as well as of free will, of autonomy of the person, of detachment by awareness and behavioral autonomization both in relation to the objective determinations of the self, as well as to the environment where the person lives (Green, 2001).

The ontological-humanistic perspective, the theoretical-axiological basis of which we approach this work, promotes the model of a humanistic conscious, therefore prioritizes and promotes the role and importance of some socio-cultural and contextual-moral factors such as the systems of moral and humane values, the socio-moral/ humane relationships of attachment, empathy/ compathy, the cultural and spiritual quality of interpersonal relationships, addressed at singular mode, but also in community context.

So, the community, in general, the family, in special, is important factor in the formation and beingness of the conscious, especially through their human and personal compathetical dimensions. In this perspective each member of a community is a product of a unique interaction, depending on the personality of the others, place, time, cultural niche, hazard. Each person is actually part of a particular compathetical system. It is, in turn, part of a comprehensive system. The most common compathetical system and most consistent is the family. The compathetic consistency is given by the fact that the individual's personalities are composed of common experiences, by the fact that in each individual personality exists, through empathy and projection, the others. It is established a mutual existential dependence. This empathetic community works, through the organizational culture, also as a system of symbols or values that are rooted in the individual's personality or activism. These symbols and values it is imposed as link and unity resort between the two parties. Their existence and operation gives the sense of belonging, familiar, known, give comfort, safety and happiness.

Between the empathetic community and individuals which it constitutes it is established a ontological balance, an existential and functional optimum, in which is satisfied, in principle, an a harmonious and non-confrontational way, both personal and collective necessities. The empathetic community and compathy can also have also a negative influences, may be an area of non-value, of conflict, hostility or social exclusion. Likewise, the empathetic community can have a coherent organization and functioning but founded on non-value, on antisocial attitudes, or may be poorly organized, dysfunctional, immature. In both cases, members are exposed to personal under-development, marginalization and social/ moral maladjustment. All of these are reflected, inherently, in the person's (social) conscience, in the process of its formation (Davis, 2012).

As is well known, very important in the process of conscience forming are the culture, religion, morals, and education. In process these bring simultaneously spiritual, ontological and axiological input, mainly through their systems of values, beliefs and ideals. Thus, the culture offers both an axiological model, but represents also an inexhaustible reservoir of spiritual and epistemological resources. Religion, morals and education, too, both through the psychological dimensions and contents (beliefs, convictions attitudes, knowledge etc.), and through the one social (rituals, ethics rules, etc.) can be considered important spiritual and ethical factors/ sources in the ontogenetic setting of the conscience (Russell, 1991; Green, 2001).

Through the formation of the (social) conscience takes place not only simple constructions of a news psychological-personal and behavioral formations, but also takes place complex, deep and global processes of *"conscientization"* and adaptation of the person, of the process of personalization, the person becomes socio-humanly able, and aware of its own situation, condition and of its ontogenetic processes, as well as of autonomization - in relation to itself and in relation to the environmental factors.

7.4. THE FORMATION OF CHARACTER

Core Fragment

In the process of formation of character participate, dialectically, inter alia, the personal ontos, the soul, the mind/ intellect and the conscience, especially through comscience, determining, in the context of action of the ambiental social-moral and cultural-ethical factors, ample phenomena of ethical-socialization, culturalization, and humanization, essential for the processes of psychological-ethical structuring and holistic organization of the personality, and the person as a whole, of ethical superization of the feelings and behaviors, of the internal ethical constitution relating to the ancestral anthropo-generical human-psychological model, of the internal personal-psychological representation of the contemporary ethical model of person, specific psychological-moral configuration, characteristic for the community members where the person grows, lives.

A crucial sub-process of the process of personalization, of formation the person and personality, as import part of the social sphere of the person, is the one of formation of *the character*. In humanistic perspective the socio-personal, the human/ humane, and the cultural conditions are, in fact, those that contribute crucially to the process of its formation (Mason, 1989).

The process of formation of character entails the inherent tendencies of moral/ ethical holistization of the general ontogenetic process of personalization, of constituting of the personality, in the context of the gradual imposing of the promergent moral/ ethical holistic factors of process.

The "moralization" of personality is the genetic psychological-social and cultural-ethical process which implies the incorporation, union, synthesis, the conmergent, emergent, transmergent unitary organization, of the formations, energy, mechanisms, of the psychological-personal ethical processes, in structures and constructions at the level of personality, stable holistic psychological-ethical entities, characteristical for the person as a whole.

In the process of formation of character participate, dialectically, inter alia, the personal ontos, the soul, the mind/ intellect and the conscience, especially through comscience, determining, in the context of action of the ambiental social-moral and cultural-ethical factors, ample phenomena of ethical-socialization, culturalization, and humanization, essential for the processes of psychological-ethical structuring and holistic organization of the personality, and the person as a whole, of ethical superization of the feelings and behaviors, of the internal ethical constitution relating to the ancestral anthropo-generical human-psychological model, of the internal personal-psychological representation of the contemporary ethical model of person, specific psychological-moral configuration, characteristic for the community members where the person grows, lives.

Even if in the process of formation of character are important the formal-institutional and format-cultural conditions the concrete and ideothetical moral-human and socio-cultural conditions contribute crucially to the character structuration and orientation, through its specific, particular, personal formation (Kellerman, 2012; Mason, 1989).

7.5. THE FORMATION OF THE SOCIO-HUMAN/ HUMANE SKILLS, COMPETENCIES, HABITUDES AND CONDUCTS

Core Fragment

The ontological-humanistic perspective, the theoretical-axiological basis of which we approach in this work, promotes the model of a humanistic competencies, skills and conducts that prioritizes the role and importance of some socio-cultural and contextual-moral factors such as the systems of moral and humane values, the socio-moral/ humane relationships of attachment, empathy/ compathy, the cultural and spiritual quality of interpersonal relationships, addressed at singular mode, but also in community context, the community, the family, in special, being, therefore, an important formative factor.

The socio-human/ humane skills, competencies, habitudes and conducts are, almost all, products of the enculturation, education, of the modelations by examples or practices of humanist/ spiritual type such as the habit of helping disadvantaged people, of educating children by personal example, of leading communities respecting the principles of personal dignity and their concrete needs.

Of course, the consistency of these humane competencies, skills, abilities is higher if the exercise of these practices, of humanist type, comes just from the small childhood.

We are talking so about skills and sensibilities of spiritual or empathetic/ compathetic type, about competencies of deep interpersonal relationation, about communication skills formed, established not only through the verbal-logic language but also through the one corporal, gestural, etc., and also of the mental, intellectual, emotional, volitional skills to maintain the humane behavior of the person (Castiello, 1936: Habermas & Lenhardt, 2001).

One of the most important goals of the process of formation of the (social) competencies, and, through these, of the personal autonomization, is to bring, through reflection and practice/

experience, the elements of environment in which is formed and cohabits the subject, in the behavioral spheres, connecting the person, organically, to the structural, axiological and functional features of the community where the person lives (Green, 2001).

The ontological-humanistic perspective, the theoretical-axiological basis of which we approach in this work, promotes the model of a humanistic competencies, skills and conducts that prioritizes the role and importance of some socio-cultural and contextual-moral factors such as the systems of moral and humane values, the socio-moral/ humane relationships of attachment, empathy/ compathy, the cultural and spiritual quality of interpersonal relationships, addressed at singular mode, but also in community context, the community, the family, in special, being, therefore, an important formative factor.

Through the formation of the (social/ humane) conscience, of the humane caracter and competencies takes place not only some simple constructions of new psychological-personal and behavioral formations, but also takes place complex, deep and global processes of adaptation of the person, of the process of personalization, as well as of autonomization - in relation to itself and in relation to the environmental factors (Green, 2001; Russell, 1991).

The
HUMANISTIC
PERSONOLOGY
Project

CHAPTER 8

THE FORMATION OF THE PERSON

AS A WHOLE

8.1. INTRODUCTORY ASPECTS 196

8.2. THE PERSON AS A WHOLE 197

8.3. THE FORMATION OF PERSONALITY AND THE PERSOMIZATION/ HOLISTIZATION OF THE PERSON 202

8.4. STAGES IN THE HOLISTIC/ GLOBAL PROCESS OF FORMATION OF THE PERSON AS A WHOLE 209

8.1. INTRODUCTORY ASPECTS

The person, after the ontogenetical construction of its constitutional formations as the personal ontos, the soul, the ego, the conscience, character, personality, etc, and after completing the two major sub-processes, and establishing the two macro-spheres - the ontological-psychological sphere and the social-personal sphere, will be, largely, a new construction, not only an ensemble/ collection of formations or the overlapping, the coexistence of the two sub-spheres.

Thus, we may speak, also, about a third process, and a third sphere, a mega-, pan-sphere, where all the formations, the two sub-processes and spheres will merge, unify, leading to what will be, ultimately, a certain human individual, a social human being, a personality, a PERSON.

So, the person as a whole exists and acts, at maturity, through each formations, through the two great sub-spheres but also as a unitary sphere and system (Maslow, 2011), as a whole and as a distinct element in ontological and relational-social plan. Nevertheless, this construction is dynamic, evolutive, alive and always remain under the influence of the variable internal and external, subjective and objective factors.

8.2. THE PERSON AS A WHOLE

Core Fragment

From a humanistic-ontological perspective, a mature person, a human dedicated to the common good, the good of mankind, incorporates, in sublime manner, both spiritual/ humane competencies of role-status and also concrete humane behaviors and activities, thus ensuring, besides a consistent internal spiritual/ humane personal functionality, an high external humane personal functionality. Qualities such as altruism, empathy, optimism, perseverance, idealism, faith, balance, positive thinking, moral power, pure consciousness, self-control, tolerance, soulfulness, cheerfulness, creativity, desirelessness, devotion, endurance, virtuous energy, enthusiasm and more are defining characteristics both of a humane, but by result, of a mature and autonomous person.

In this sense, the person as a whole, the mature person, may be also represented through the Hegelian consecrated triad *general-particular-individual*.

Therefore, the person's *universal* is revealed by the constitutional, fundamental, frame structure, configuration and composition, by the genetical-ancestral quality of human being, man, human, species, common aspects for all people, from anywhere and anytime, and is generated by the organic constitution and by the trans-historical and trans-cultural characteristics of *human* existence, the *particular*, is evidenced mostly of and through the way of formation and development of the soul and of the (social) consciousness, and it is conditioned by the particular, concrete characteristics of the living environment, education, work, by time, space, culture, economy, ontogenetically assimilated by the psychological-personal formations, while the *individual*, structurally, is strongly linked to the personal ontos, to the ego, the self-consciousness, inner motivations and interests, being largely generated by the subjective experiences, by feelings and events. Other characteristics of the individual are the uniqueness, singularity and non-recurrence. The individual is as well the one which marks, ultimately, the globality, the totality, but also the unicity of the person.

Another formula which can be used to represent the person as a whole, this time in humanistic-ontological paradigm, it is the triad *being-existent-existence*. As it was also shown in the book, in ontological perspective, **the being** (being in itself) of an entity represents the essence, the original content, the invariable, the ontological-metaphysical foundation of the entities, of the existent and of the existence, **the existent/ existing** (being for itself) represents the organization, the concrete form, unique, part of a context, the exposed side of the being, acquiring the characteristics of form of the concrete environment where it exists, while **the existence**, or **the beingness/ functioning** (being outside), represents the processual, contingent, situational-contextual side, exposed to time, dynamic, experiential, the feeling and the thinking. In agreement with the metaphysical-ontological paradigm outlined above we will consider that ***the ontological-psychological sphere*** (the personal ontos, the soul, the ego) represents *the being* of the person, ***the psychological-social sphere*** (the conscience, character, the skills) represents *the existent/ existing*, while ***the experiential-behavioral sphere*** (the functioning, the beingness, the current life/ activity/ experience of the person, its jouissance, feelings, concrete processual thinking) represents *the existence*.

With a certain approximation, we can so associate the *universal* with the *essence*, the ***particular*** with the ***existent/ existing***, and the **individual** with the **existence**, the two triads and their elements operating so simultaneously, synergistically and unitarily, but possible also in opposition, discordance or competition. Aspect which highlights the complexity, malleability and profoundness of the individual human being, of the person, of the person as a subject, ego, individuality, personhood, of the person as ideal and finality of the ontogenetical process of personalization, as well of the person surprised, existentially, at a certain time, in a given time of its evolution and existence.

If we consider especially the humanistic-ontological and spiritual perspective we will look the person as a whole through holistical-humanistic and spiritual/ moral/ cultural characteristics like the spiritual, morale and humane orientation, introversion and extroversion, individualism and altruism, and, in relation to them, the way in which in the general psychological-personal structure and architecture are positioned formations like the soul relative to the ego, how are positioned the humane ego, the humane conscience, the humane character in relation to inferior formations and instances, or expressly focused to itself, the humanist-ontological paradigm of the person highlighting, with poignancy, the determining role of some psychological-ontological spheres, formations such as the soul, with its the three large spheres (affective, spiritual, humane), the humane ego, the humane conscience and the humane character, very important being therefore the "weight" that has one or other of the soul's spheres in its architecture, in the beingness and functioning of the soul as a whole, as extended part of the personal ontos, but as well of the person as a whole.

Another important characteristic which is envisaged when it is analyzed, structurally, compositionally and architecturally, the person as a whole is its degree of development in terms of cohesion, consistency, adaptability and resilience (Murray, 2007) - closely related to the concept of personal development (category of the humanist-positive/ existential orientation/ approach from the social and human sciences) - identified with a number of other concepts such as psychic development, growth, adaptation, social development, high degree of awareness, self-knowledge, self-esteem, psychological-emotionally well-being, satisfaction, happiness, hedonism, socio-emotional development, control of emotions, emotional intelligence, realism and balance, powerful will, resistance to failure and frustrations, positive attitude, optimism, active thinking, professional development, personal and social autonomy, interpersonal development, mature personality, adaptability, etc.

From a humanistic-ontological perspective, a mature person, a human dedicated to the common good, the good of mankind, incorporates, in sublime manner, both spiritual/ humane competencies of role-status and also concrete humane behaviors and activities, thus ensuring, besides a consistent internal spiritual/ humane personal functionality, an high external humane personal functionality. Qualities such as altruism, empathy, optimism, perseverance, idealism, faith, balance, positive thinking, moral power, pure consciousness, self-control, tolerance, soulfulness, cheerfulness, creativity, desirelessness, devotion, endurance, virtuous energy, enthusiasm and more are defining characteristics both of a humane, but by result, of a mature and autonomous person.

The studies and researches in the fields involving working with people conclude that the professionalism in these fields is strongly conditioned by the level of general personal and human development, including the degree of spirituality, virtue, moral will and "aesthetic" charisma of the person/ professional who provide social services. The practitioners with high developed humane personality spirituality, as holistic traits of personality, the spiritual sensibility and virtue will be imposed as main factors of organization and holistic adjustment of the humanistic professional behavior, becoming a crucial attribute of the prosocial action/ activity and effective professional practice. Humanity, as holistic and synthetic humane quality of the person, of the professional, is closely determined by the level of development of the humane soul, humane conscience, humane character, humane ego, humane personality as a all, in the context of a high development of the global personality. The professional's humane soul engages at a higher level, more complex, deeper and synthetic, the onto-formations from the professional's affective (social) soul and spiritual soul levels, generating the extraordinary ability of this to feel, live and think as a human being, as an ancestral being, as an exemplar humane being, but also as a *humane* being, by their ability to resonate, empathize, compathize with the human and spiritual experience of the other persons, of the client. Through the great development of the professional's humane soul his personality as a whole is reformed and is defined through solidarist-humanistic qualities and behavioral traits such as empathy, agreeableness, tolerance, humanity, human sensitivity etc.

In this connection, the professional's humane qualities, virtue, and humanity are expressions of some personal constructs of a maximum complexity, generated by the presence of a mega-system which involve the person as a whole. Thus, this professional's qualities are not mere expressions of the emotional and spiritual development, of the affective soul, of the spiritual and humane spheres, even if it involves and are fundamental, but also expressions of the professional's general development, existence of certain skills or inclinations, character development, eudaimonical-spiritual and eudaimonical-prosocial spheres, development of personality/ person as a whole, through its humane orientation/ dimension, as a personality, as a person.

So, the professional's humanity, as core dimension of his global personality, of its quality as person as a whole, of his humane behavior, being of very high complexity, and having many dimensions (Rogers, 1959), involves the two main orientations of the humanistic psychology regarding the personality and the person as a whole - the "humanistic-positive/ existential" orientation, which focuses on personal development and social adaptation by using the psycho-volitional and adaptive resources, and the "humanist-ontological/ spiritual" orientation, that highlights especially the spiritual content of the self, the soul and the inner-ontological personality, the aesthetic, playful, moral or religious resources.

Involving, so, the two main orientations, humanity as core feature of the person as a whole, as fundamental, core personality resources of the professional, is however a unitary, synthetic and holistic quality, bringing together both sets of traits, afferent to the concept of *humane personality.*

To this end, the professional's humane personality, as the main source of the professional's humanity/ humanness, may be described as a set of onto-formations, such as soul, humane self, humane consciousness, humane character, and others - structural onto-psychological and intellectual sources, as well as the overall humane valence, dimension of the professional's global personality, meaning kindness, goodness, altruism, personality opened to the overall manhood jouissance, increased sensitivity to the other's suffering - itself, but also emergent resource of empowerment, wellbeing and happiness for the people from ambience; both being foundations and explanations of the professional's humane qualities, to humanity as cardinal traits/ characteristic of its "person a whole". Finally, the person as a whole, in current life and profession, is revealed and expressed mostly in/ by his behavior and activity, and, as a social being, in/ by his ability/ capacity of socio-human and professional adaptation and integration (Murray, 2007; Rogers, 1959).

8.3. THE FORMATION OF PERSONALITY AND THE PERSOMIZATION/ HOLISTIZATION OF THE PERSON

Core Fragment

The purpose of the process of personalization, from this point of view, being that the person to reach to be fulfilled/ developed both in spiritual/ psychological plan as well as in social plan. The stage where, therefore, the person is fulfilled/ developed in psychological-human and psychological-ontological plan, characterized through features as balance, complacency, self-acceptance, but also with a high degree of self-control and cerebralization (wisdom). In this last stage ends the processes of homogenization, compatibilization, inter-communication between the levels and the structures so heterogeneous by nature and sense/ function, that characterizes the personal assembly, leading to (what we call) the psychological-personal izomorfization, that involves, emergently, transmergently, sinmergently, conmergently and telegently, both the personality (subject) and the (social) environment.

The process of formation of personality entails the inherent tendencies of persomization and holistization of the general ontogenetic process of personalization, of constituting of the person, in the context of the gradual imposing of the promergent holistic factors of process, against those dismergent, entropic, endemic, fragmental.

Persomization, so, is the genetic psychological-ontological process which implies the incorporation, union, synthesis, the conmergent, emergent, transmergent unitary organization, of the formations, energy, mechanisms, of the sub-personal processes, in structures and constructions at the level of personality, stable holistic entities, characteristic for the person as a whole, usually upper, structurally and axiologically, in comparison to the onto-formations, which are mainly circumstantial, contextual, fluctuate, relational.

In process participate, dialectically, inter alia, the body, the personal ontos, and conscience (comscience); these causing ample phenomena of socialization, culturalization, spiritualization and humanization, essential for the processes of structuring and holistic organization, superization of the feelings and behaviors, of the internal constitution of the ancestral anthropo-generical human-psychological model, but also of the basic personality - internal personal-psychological representation of the contemporary personal and cultural model, specific psychological configuration, characteristic for the community members in which the subject grows and lives.

Even if in the personality formation process are important the material conditions especially in the humanistic perspective, in humanistic personology, the cultural, moral and human conditions contribute crucially to the personality structuring, to formation of a harmonious character, fulfilled person (Kellerman, 2012).

The major spheres of the personality, motivational, emotional, attitudinal, volitional, etc. are the product of the interaction of the subject with specific factors, even if cannot be traced strict boundaries between them. But, in a purely humanistic perspective, the human-personal, the human-social factors are decisive in the formation and development of the personality.

The ontogenetic process of formation of personality, establishment and beingness in the structure, composition of the person as a whole, one of the question it is if its existence is necessary, if the person could not exist, function, inside and outside, without a personality, and thus, if the conclusion is that its existence is necessary, the question is why, and which is its sense, role, which is the contribution in the structure and functioning in the global structure of the person as a whole.

Indubitable, the answer is that the formation and establishment of the personality, especially of the character, in the structure, the composition of the human person is an objective necessity, personality being a constitutional, ancestral, genetic, and emblematic part of the person (Mason,1989), mainly through its adaptive function, through the social-contextual, spiritual-cultural, and human-ancestral environmental characteristics, that, structurally and substantially, it reflect, and bring, in a formative mode, in the complex architecture of the personal assembly.

The formation of personality is conditioned/ determined mainly by two processes: the development, growth, general personal development, which imposes the automatic establishment of certain structures with integrative function, and the process of conmergent organization of the ontological-psychological formations.

In the gradual process of forming personality, like the others formations, spheres etc, passes, through the following stages: of contact, of acquisition/ accumulation and of structuring, constituting, instituting, and, finally, follows his ontification, i.e. the definitive enrollment in the structure and constitution of the person. The personality formation process is not automatically, simple and linear, through the mere presence of the body in society and culture. The biological, sensorial, cognitive, affective experiences, the successes, failures and traumas marks significantly the entirely process. In this respect, the strong personality is described also in the context of a consistent and structurally balanced soul.

In this sense, is very important the nature, orientation, the dominant dimension, the content of the soul. If it is dominant a soul's jouissance that includes the other's happiness in this case we can speak of a altruistic, humane soul, and a personality and behavior oriented to the other's well-being, instituting, so, the *humane personality* – core, crucial concept in humanistic personology, especially in the humanistic-ontological theory of the person.

So, the formation of the humane personality is essentially conditioned of the formation of the human soul, but also of the humane ego and the humane ego, The humane ego being, alongside spiritual soul and humane soul, one of the most important reservoir and treasure of spirituality and humanism in the process of personality formation and development, in the process of persomization and holistization.

The formation and establishment of the humane ego contributes, leads, finally, also to the establishment of the personal system of beliefs and assumed personal convictions, of the moral conducts, of the need for knowledge the human phenomenon, also contributes, leads to the formation and establishment of the moral/ humane sentiments, end determines the appearance of the need for social harmony, human solidarity, helpfulness (Brody & Axelrad, 1970).

In the personality forming process, the humanistic personological perspective, one can speak of inborn *humane* organic predispositions, more humane temperamental types, more altruistic or more spiritual temperaments, let's say the melancholic temperament in report of the choleric temperament, without absolutization, but, in process, the humanistic orientation of the personality is given, mostly, by the conjugated actions, more or less premeditated and systematized, of the education, of the environmental socio-human and cultural factors, of the personal-human models with whom, constantly and intensely, interacts the person in formation.

Regarding the role of the humane character in the formation of personality, this will lead, with the contribution of the humane conscience, to the metamorphosis of the person's humane and spiritual resources in humanistic, prosocial, altruistic traits and qualities. Only by the formation and establishment of the humane character it is emphasized and highlighted the humanistic valence of the global personality, is set and manifest the humane personality as a structure expressly oriented towards the generalized other's jouissance.

The process of personality formation is significantly influenced by aspects of health, disability or the level and structure/ orientation of the mental and intellectual development (Kellerman, 2012).

In process, a intelligence quotient situated more below the average is a disturbing factor. Serious health problems, the infirmities, handicaps, dysfunctions, dystrophies, anomies and other abnormalities give the process specific aspects, usually with the sense of disorder, decline, underdevelopment, alteration, compensation, pathology.

What is very certain is that in any conditions the personality formation is carried out with the data that disposes the subject starting from some premises, required minimum conditions - the body, the mind, the environment - even very briefly represented. Consequently, any creature who tells him human being traverses the process of formation of the personality through ontogenetic gradually integration and superization. But the differences between individuals can be extremely high.

Of course, when talking about the process of forming and establishing of the human personality, as a separate and autonomous entity and force into the composition the person, we consider, alongside the structural-axiological dimension also and the ontological-psychological component. The dialectical and unique combination of the two causes so an individualization and a basis for formation of a unique personality structure, placing the individual in a typology or another.

The process of "typologization" accelerates together with the entrance of the personality in the process of person socialization, in the properly process of personalization - as we call it in the paper, of formation of the person as an social individual, as a social being, process that ends and fulfilling, in fact, the global process of personalization, process that will cover, as we will see more broadly later, the six standard stages of ontogenetic construction of the personal formations, in humanistic personology – the humanistic-ontological perspective on the person, namely of contact/ primary junctions, accumulation/ acquisition, structuring/ primary organization, constitution/ formation, establishing/ networking/ autonomization, and ontification / fulfillment.

So, after it has been established, ontologically and psychologically, the personality will pass through other processes of redimensionations, this time not at level of self/ ego but of person, by the feedbacks and influences that it exercises the sphere of person, involved itself in complex processes of formation and adaptation. In process, this time, the personality is involved as an entity, as a system, and less through its internal ontological-psychological elements and structures, being thus, existentially, in opposition to the new social environments in which is involved the individual at the mature age. The influence it is mostly exercised through the social conscience experiences, the social activities, and the roles and statuses as person socially accepted as such.

In the contact phase occurs, mainly, the primary interaction, junction personality-community/ social and human environment, the junction *personality – his own (new) family, personality - administrative community*, and *personality - professional organization.* At this stage the personality, as has been it established in the childhood period, is less affected in its structure, nature, direction. The stage/ process of accumulation, which represents for the person a long, sluggish, confrontational and sinuous period of acquisitions of social knowledge and experiences, begins to mark the personality, but mainly in its relational formal-behavioral sphere, where tend to impose, without much success, some systemic reconstructions. under the exterior ambiance pressure.

These constructions must organize in a uniform way, but their internal structural and functional coherence, consistency, at this stage, is very low.

In the stage/ process of personal structuring the ontological-psychological personality makes great efforts to conserve and maintain the status quo but, in the conditions of a very big socializing exposure, may occur certain tendencies of restructuring, even psychological-ontologically, with chances of success in the following steps. The social patterns, assimilated by cognitive reflection, feelings, social experiences, operate, in formative way, on the process of personal formation and development determining so an evident tendency of internal re-organization and re-structuration. A crucial structuring impact they have the roles, statuses, functions, activities which the person begins to perform, carry out in the professional organizations where it integrates gradually, in the family that founded it as a marital partner, in the local community where coexists or carries out various activities.

With the advancement in the adulthood period of life, in the general context of the social maturation and competitional personal/ social development, with the inherent formation of the humane soul, humane consciousness, in the step of establishment of the person as a whole, where important roles they meet processes and mechanisms such as the feed-back, where happens an consistent symbiosis personality-community, where realistically one can speak of person one can see, here, the first substantial changes/ adjustments in the personality traits. It can even talk about an ancestral leap from personality as bio-psychological system to personality as a social-psychological system, about a process of opening and social maturation, of exit from the tight "straps" of the body, of the ego, from egocentrism.

From an excessive focalization on itself, from the obsession of the self-fulfillment through itself it moves on the preoccupation of fulfillment by the others, through social relationships and community. These changes are the expression of some consistent restructurings and even of the imposition of a new global construct of personality where is much represented the social context, the system of values. In this stage, which corresponds to the stage of establishment in the properly process of formation of the person, the changes and the restructurings not are highlight only in the superficial spheres of the personality but entails the ontological-psychological sphere too, even the being of the person. The self, the hedonic ontos, the projective ontos, the soul, the ego, and more, they lose much from their "substance", from their instinctual, bio-psychical, subjective essence, entering in profound processes of socialization, culturalization, humanization. Already, in this phase the personality, as structure, as system and a whole, it is set up for existence and functioning of the subject acting as a person almost perfectly adapted, integrated in the professional, family, community environment.

But the defining, final characteristics/ traits of the personality it establishes only when the individual is totally, socio-humanely, integrated and functional, in the last stage of the process of properly personalization, in the stage of ontification, of fulfillment of the person, that will be discussed, in more detail, in a later subchapter, dedicated to the properly personalization, the properly formation of the person, as human and social being.

As we will see, at the end of this stage, in the organization and functioning/ beingness of the person, the environment and personality it merge, being found in structures, formations almost exclusively subordinated to the functions of the person as unitary system.

The purpose of the process of personalization, from this point of view, being that the person to reach to be fulfilled/ developed both in spiritual/ psychological plan as well as in social plan. The stage where, therefore, the person is fulfilled/ developed in psychological-human and psychological-ontological plan, characterized through features as balance, complacency, self-acceptance, but also with a high degree of self-control and cerebralization (wisdom).

In this last stage ends the processes of homogenization, compatibilization, inter-communication between the levels and the structures so heterogeneous by nature and sense/ function, that characterizes the personal assembly, leading to (what we call) the *psychological-personal izomorfization*, that involves, emergently, transmergently, sinmergently, conmergently and telegently, both the personality (subject) and the (social) environment.

It's a situation where we can speak of a psychological-social unitary structure/ constitution of personality, established not only in themselves and through themselves but also as part of a socio-human system.

This constitution of personality ensures, simultaneously, the existence, the beingness of the person both in interior in the bio-psychological and spiritual life of the subject, and also in exterior, in the professional life, in the family life (his own family), in community, society, etc.

Of course, addressing, representing personality in the humanistic personology's perspective - the humanistic ontological paradigm, what we could consider, in the paper, mature personality, developed ontological-psychologically and socially, would characterize through a series of traits linked both to the internal structure, nature, and functioning as openness, optimism, peace of soul, spirituality, happiness, patience, allocentricity, balance, calm, passion, humane energy, enthusiasm, faith, flexibility, melancholy, genuinity, idealism, culture, humanistic intelligence, intuitivity, profoundness, rationality, realism, creativity, reflectiveness, relaxation, romantism, self-criticism, self-reliance, sensitivity, sentimentalism, seriosity, stability, stoicism, resistance, wisdom, youthfulness, complexity, femininity, emotionality, impressionability, intensity, invisibility, purity, self-consciousness, unaggressivity, etc., as well as to the social-behavioral component as empathy, flexibility, friendliness, generousity, grace, helpfulness, adaptability, agreeability, amiability, carity, charisma, cheerfulness, compassion, confidence, cooperation, courage, curiousity, decency, dynamism, efficiency, elegance, honestity, honorability, humor, incorruptibility, independence, assertivity, invulnerability, loyalty, moderation, modesty, nonauthoritarism, openness, persuasivity, protectivity, prudence, respect, responsivity, responsibility, selfless, sociability, sympathy, vivacity, confidentiality, informalism, paternalism, solidarity, humanism, etc.

8.4. STAGES IN THE HOLISTIC/ GLOBAL PROCESS OF FORMATION OF THE PERSON AS A WHOLE

Core Fragment

In the humanistic-ontological paradigm, which we use in this paper, the completion and the fulfillment of the process of personalization through ontification, does not concern only the mere adaptation and mechanical social integration of the subject but concerns also issues of subjective-eudaimonical or ontological-psychological order. The goal of the process of personalization, from this point of view, is that the person to reach to be fulfilled, humanly and personally, happy, of course, primarily through social affirmation/ achievement, stage where, therefore, the person is fulfilled in psychological-human and psychological-ontological terms, characterized by balance, complacency, self-acceptance, but also by high degree of self-control (Waldrop, 1993; Erikson &, Erikson, 1998; Bickhard, 2012). After crossing these phases are accomplished so the both processes, of proper personalization, as we call it in the paper, of forming of the person as a social being, as well as the overall process of personalization, of forming as a human (personality) and social being - as a PERSON.

In this paper we use the term *process of personalization* for two separate issues, but also complementary. First, for *the general process of personalization*, of forming the person as man, as human being, that contains, as we have seen, the processes of ontosfication, of spiritualization/ humanization, of individualization, of persomization, of autonomization, and, the final one, *of properly personalization*, as we call it, of forming of the person as an individual, as person, as a social being, that completes and reaches, in fact, the global process of personalization.

This stage, process, phase of proper personalization, will traverse, in our view/ paradigm, the six standard stages of ontogenetic formation of the personal formations, that was described summary in a previous section of the book, namely

> ➢ of contact/ primary junctions,

> ➢ accumulation/ acquisition,

> ➢ structuration/ primary organization,

> ➢ formation, holistization,

> ➢ establishing/ networking/ autonomization, and

> ➢ ontification / fulfillment.

Thus, in the properly process of personalization, that begins from the moment when the subject leaves his childhood, it is established the psychological personality, and starts in life as autonomous person, the phase of **contact** imply the interaction, the primary junction personality-community/ socio-human environment; we refer especially at the junction personality-family (through marriage, etc.), personality-administrative community (vicinity, street, neighborhood, village, city, county, etc., even society), and personality-professional organization.

After the stage of contact follows a prolonged period, difficult, conflictual and sinuous of **accumulation** of knowledge and social experiences, essential premise for the optimal completion of the perso-genetic steps that follows. It is a period that takes place by sub-processes as experimentation, social learning, and "experientialization". In other words, by acquisition in cascade, largely uncritical, of new knowledge and experiences, from the position, recognized by others, formally, of person, but, in fact, more of personality, of person yet immature.

In the stage/ process of personal **structuration**, part of the effective process, "mature", of personalization, the knowledge and experiences acquired in the phase of accumulation, unorganized, punctually organized, or structured around of some poles, formations, more or less representative in the sense and goal of the process of personalization, are now holistically structured, at the level of personal assembly.

In the stage of **formation** is carried out the jump from structure to system, in the complex process of personalization of forming and establishing the person. The structuring, the organization of the knowledge and experience, processes made in the previous step, lead, inter alia, together with the personal ontogenetic *system*-atization, to the formation of the social consciousness, the social self, and other integrative perso-formations. An important role they meet processes and mechanisms such as the feed-back, feed-before, etc. In this stage occurs, including by means of these processes and mechanisms, a consistent symbiosis personality-community. It is the point from where, properly, one can speak of person.

After has made the jump from structure to system, in the complex process of constitution of the person, occurs the process of **institution**, **establishing**, the exit from the narrow straps of the body, ego, personality, self-consciousness, occurs "the exit in the world" of the person, recently constituted, its birth, the launching, affirmation, with full rights of person, in the social "jungle". At this stage the person is not a bunch of formations, of knowledge and experiences, it is not only a structure more or less organized, or only a system of formations, knowledge, experience, etc., but is an entity, an existential unit, a person, in determined socio-human context, environment, well integrated and adapted to its structural and functional particularities.

In the last stage, of **ontification**, the environment and the personality are merged, being found in structures, formations subordinated almost exclusively to the person's functions. It occurred, so, during the properly personal ontogenesis, a process of "en-beingness" (or "en-beingness-ing"), of apparition of a new existential entity, process at the end of which is established the being and starts the beingness as person.

In the humanistic-ontological paradigm, which we use in this paper, the completion and the fulfillment of the process of personalization through ontification, does not concern only the mere adaptation and mechanical social integration of the subject but concerns also issues of subjective-eudaimonical or ontological-psychological order.

The goal of the process of personalization, from this point of view, is that the person to reach to be fulfilled, humanly and personally, happy, of course, primarily through social affirmation/ achievement, stage where, therefore, the person is fulfilled in psychological-human and psychological-ontological terms, characterized by balance, complacency, self-acceptance, but also by high degree of self-control (Waldrop, 1993; Erikson &, Erikson, 1998; Bickhard, 2012). After crossing these phases are accomplished so the both processes, of proper personalization, as we call it in the paper, of forming of the person as a social being, as well as the overall process of personalization, of forming as a human (personality) and social being - as a PERSON.

CHAPTER 9

THE INTERNAL JOUISSANCE, THE BEINGNESS AND THE FUNCTIONING OF THE PERSON/ PERSONALITY

9.1. INTRODUCTORY ASPECTS 214

9.2. THE HUMANE MOTIVATIONAL SYSTEM, THE JOUISSANCE AND ENERGY OF THE PERSON/ PERSONALITY 215

9.2.1. THE HUMANE MOTIVATIONAL SYSTEM 215

9.2.2. THE HUMANE JOUISSANCE 216

9.2.3. THE HUMANE ENERGY 219

9.3 THE INTERNAL BEINGNESS AND FUNCTIONING OF THE PERSON/ PERSONALITY 220

9.3.1. THE INTERNAL BEINGNESS OF THE PERSON/ PERSONALITY 221

9.3.2. THE INTERNAL FUNCTIONING OF THE PERSON/ PERSONALITY 222

9.4. THE EXTERNAL BEINGNESS AND FUNCTIONING OF THE PERSON/ PERSONALITY 226

9.4.1. THE SOCIO-HUMANE BEHAVIOR OF THE PERSON 227

9.4.2. THE SOCIO-HUMANE ADAPTATION AND INTEGRATION OF THE PERSON 228

9.1. INTRODUCTORY ASPECTS

The ontological-personological paradigm/ approach prioritizes the role and importance of the personal ontos, in the beingness and the functioning of the person/ personality, which as it was shown, could be considered *the being* of the person, and comprises, in its broad and comprehensive acceptation/ sphere, in our opinion, mainly, ontos-formations such as the hedonic ontos, the phobic ontos-formation, the projective ontos, the prosentic ontos-formation, and the malsentic ontos-formation, but also the soul and the ego, determining especially its humane and spiritual dimensions, valences, content.

Regarding the internal psychological-ontological bengness and functioning of the person/ personality it is closely determined and linked, inter alia, to the existence, action and interaction of two ontological-psychological poles, located in the extremes of the psychological-personal assembly, respectively *the hedonic-phobic* pole and *the projective-aspirational pole*. Each of the onto-formations of the two poles, *the hedonic ontos* and *the phobic onto-formation* - from the hedonic-phobic pole, and *the projective ontos* and *the aspirational/ideal ego* - from the projective-aspirational pole, operates with autonomous functional role but very important, too, is the psychological-ontological balances, levers, mechanisms, tensions/ conflicts that form and operate by their involvement and through their interactions, as well, each pole, the hedonic-phobic pole and the projective-aspirational pole, works/ functions autonomously but is also, in the same time, part of a trans- and pan-personal mega-balance, mega-mechanism, mega-conflict/ tension with very important role/ contribution in the internal general, global functioning, beingness and dinamics of the person/ personality.

In the complex and profound phenomenon of internal beingness and functioning of the person/ personality participate many inner motivational, eudaimonical, and energetical resorts, many biological, sensorial, psychological, spiritual mechanisms. In this sense, all the onto-personal mechanisms probably conditionate, largely, the promergence and the imergence, the processual internal beingness and functioning of the person. In humanistic-ontological/spiritual perspective very important being, also, theirs *humane and spiritual dimensions, valences and orientations*.

9.2. THE HUMANE MOTIVATIONAL SYSTEM, THE JOUISSANCE AND ENERGY OF THE PERSON/ PERSONALITY

Core Fragment

In a general way, the soul, with all its areas and components, is the place and central source of the humane jouissance. Therefore, if in the case of the body, of the senses, instinct's jouissance we talk about libido and pleasure, in the case of the soul's jouissance we talk about eudaimonia and happiness, while in the case of the humane soul's eudaimonia of happiness through the other, or altruistic happiness and jouisance. There is, also, an altruistic eudaimonia of the spiritual soul, and an altruistic and spiritual eudaimonia of the self/ ego.

9.2.1. THE HUMANE MOTIVATIONAL SYSTEM

When we speak of the motivational-energetical sphere or perspective of/on person/ personality we involve concepts, ideas and syntagms as:

- Altruistic motivational system;

- Altruistic and spiritual eudaimonical system;

- Altruistic and spiritual jouissance;

- Happiness/ eudaimonical onto-formation;

- Authentic happiness;

- Spiritual and altruistic happiness;

- Altruistic and spiritual energy;

- Altruistic energy;

- Spiritual energy.

The Altruistic and Spiritual Motivational System

It is, in our view, a superior ontogenetical construction within the general motivational system and global personality, and may be represented, succinctly, as a composition of motives, needs, trends, interests, intentions, aspirations, ideals of the person that supports the realization, expressing, disinterested, altruistic, compathetical, of certain conducts, actions, facts, activities oriented towards the fulfillment of the needs, desires, aspirations of other people, that support personal behaviors suitable to facilitate the spiritual, human, social development and welfare of the generalized other, social and psychological-eudaimonical rehabilitation of the individuals/ groups in need, suffering, in crisis (Stefaroi, 2014).

In this sense, one can speak, arbitrary of course, of two motivational-humane systems of the person/ professional oriented towards the good/ welfare of the other

1. mobiles, needs, trends, interests, intentions, aspirations, ideals directly oriented towards the good of the other, sustaining the altruistic attitude and behavior of aid, support, care of the people in need, which we could tell *humane motivation of help and compassion,* and

2. the system of mobiles, needs, trends, emotions, interests, intentions, aspirations, ideals that acts indirectly, axiological and energetical, as factors of guidance, spiritualization and humanization of the person's behavior, generating the moral will and virtue, the virtuous personality, charisma, humane authority - axiological-energetical sources in the person's action and conduct, of human, personal and eudemonical development and improvement of the other, through moral and spiritual virtue, transfer and compathy, of empowerment, emancipation, fulfillment of the persons in difficulty or socio-humanly, morally, eudaimonically degraded (Adler, 1959).

9.2.2. THE HUMANE JOUISSANCE

The Altruistic and Spiritual Jouissance

The concept *altruistic and spiritual jouissance* involves at least two major meanings:

1. the jouissance related to higher, humane development of the personality, and

2. the jouissance oriented towards the good/ well-being of the other.

In the first case it is mainly about of a jouissance of the spiritual soul, of the higher consciousness, moral ego and character, while, in the second case, about a jouissance mainly of the humane soul, but also of the affective (social) soul, and to other formations, higher, humanized instances of the personality. In a general way, the soul, with all its areas and components, is the place and central source of the humane jouissance. Therefore, if in the case of the body, sense, instinct's jouissance we talk about libido and pleasure (Freud, 1990; Adler, 1959), in the case of the soul's jouissance we talk about eudaimonia and happiness, while in the case of the humane soul's eudaimonia of happiness through the other, or altruistic happiness and jouisance. There is, also, an altruistic eudaimonia of the spiritual soul, and an altruistic and spiritual eudaimonia of the self/ ego.

The Altruistic and Spiritual Happiness

Without doubt, it is hard to speak of humane personality, humane behavior, humane and spiritual qualities of the person in the conditions of a basal, elementary psychological jouissance, expressed in reactions, emotions and feelings predominantly conative, primitive, impulsive, based on the pleasure-pain hedonic-biological mechanism.

The humane personality, humane behavior, the humane, moral, spiritual qualities must have an interior psychological-eudaimonical correspondent, a jouissance to match, and the most appropriate term for this is that of *altruistic and spiritual happiness.*

Regarding the source of the altruistic and spiritual happiness one thing is clear, namely the fact that a crucial role has the jouissance of soul, of the psychological-ontological sphere of humane personality, thus representing, here, the soul as a being that feeds, develop from/ with virtue, from/ with the good/ well-being, happiness of the other, of the community, of the man in general.

At the process contributes but also what we call, in our onto-personological theory, the happiness, or eudaimonical onto-formation. It involves the soul, but is formed, predominantly, in the onto-projective "space" of the person, gradually integrating in the personality's structure (Stefaroi, 2009b).

The role and importance of the happiness onto-formation in the process of personal formation and development, in determining personality traits such as agreeableness, optimism, charisma, sociability, altruism, empathy is very important because it improves, elevates the jouissance, the interior subjective-experiential general state, causes the person to feel fulfilled or overflow of interior well, and to externalize, contaminating, affecting for better and the other, others, perhaps more unhappy, unfulfilled, because it provides eudaimonical, psychological-spiritual energy for the general process of development, superization and humanization of personality and social behavior.

Here one can talk about what was established, as philosophical, even scientific debate, the theme of *authentic happiness* (Seligman, 2002).

In our conception the authentic happiness is derived from the spiritual/ soulful and humane development, well-being and fulfillment of the person, as well as from the humane ego/ self development and fulfillment, because it is an eudaimonia of a psychological-ontological type, deeply, involving, holistically and trans-temporal, the personality as whole, is permanent, is a being, an existence, and not an emotion or pleasure of moment.

Thus, the ego will not be a contingent conative, autonomic, self-sufficient ego, subject of the organic fluctuations, of impulsivity, egotistic emotions, but an universalized, spiritualized, humanized, superized ego, the personality's eudaimonia involving, so, not only the resources of pleasure and jouissance of the self but the cultural resources of virtue and moral good of the entire humanity (Adler, 1959).

Results, from here, a happiness of the person as a *human being*, a true happiness, a interior world and a psychological-spiritual, eudaimonical welfare that exceeds the personal need of internal homeostatical jouissance, the surplus, thus, pouring in outside, in behavior, in social activities, practices, energy that reaches, so, also at the other, possible in difficulty, through the altruistic, humane behavior of the subject, through charisma, agreeableness, transfer of spirituality, virtue and happiness.

9.2.3. THE HUMANE ENERGY

Without a doubt, the main energetic source of the person's humane behavior and one of the crucial resorts of the humane and spiritual qualities is the soul: affective (social) soul, spiritual soul, and humane soul.

The explanation is simple: the soul is a being, an existence, an ontos, a spiritual/ transpersonal "organism" with a, relatively, own internal genesis and dynamics, as well as a producer and accumulator of humane and spiritual energy.

The altruistic motivation, jouissance, attitude, conscience and behavior are, energetically, supported by the soul because the soul was constituted through the transmergent internalization of the other, and the gained energy is actually a resource for the other's jouissance. The organization of the soul's energetic jouissance follows, largely, the other's organization and existence jouissance.

In this sense it can states that:

- The social-eudaimonical interaction with the other real, close, dear person, with the reference group, with the nearest physical environment, leads to the formation of the energetical jouissance of affective soul;

- The cultural-eudaimonical interaction with the spiritual/ cultural world leads to the formation of the energetical jouissance of spiritual soul;

- The moral-eudaimonical interaction with the generalized, symbolic other, value-person, through the mental facilities of generalization, idealization, symbolization and valorization leads to the formation of the energetical jouissance of the humane soul.

In the forming process of the motivational-energetic system of soul and personality are involved the instincts, emotions, cognition, will, skills, structures, automatisms. The formation, with their involvement, of some mechanisms, automatisms, montages, complexes, patterns of functioning of the jouissance and motivational system oriented towards the good and spiritual empowerment of the other represents actually the stage where it can speak about altruistic and spiritual energy, as constitutional resource and component of the motivational-energetic system of global personality.

The altruistic and spiritual motivational-energetic system is a superior ontogenetical construction within the general motivational system and overall personality, and it can be represented, succinctly, as a set of energies associated of some motives, needs, trends, interests, intentions, aspirations, ideals of the person that support the achievement, expression, disinterested, altruistic, compathetic some behaviors, actions, facts, activities oriented towards the fulfillment of needs, desires, aspirations of the other people, communities, etc. (Bergson, 2007; Adler, 1959).

In this case we can speak of energy of the humane personality - resort, factor, indispensable resource of the altruistic behavior of the person/ professional, energy that not emerge from a circumstantial decision of the individual to contribute to the present welfare or change the person in difficulty, but an energy, resource existing permanently at the whole being level (Hubbard, 2012), corresponding of an eudaimonical-spiritual welfare and motivational structure of the personality, constitutionally oriented towards the good/ well-being of the other, towards the common good/ welfare.

9.3. THE INTERNAL BEINGNESS AND FUNCTIONING OF THE PERSON/ PERSONALITY

Core Fragment

in the complex and profound phenomenon of beingnes and functioning of the person/ personality participate many inner, biological, sensorial, psychological, spiritual mechanisms, resorts. In this sense, all the onto-personal mechanisms probably conditionate, largely, the promergence and the imergence, the processual internal beingness of the person. There may be also many ontic-psychological mechanisms of production of existential sense and prontos, of transformation of the emotions, of the subjective experiences in prontos and resorts for beingness, for a high consistency and continuity of the "being". At the base of the processes standing innumerable mechanisms, montages, motivational sources and resorts, internal ontos-formative loops that "work" in infinite combinations to assure continuity, subjective existential meanings and the internal beingness of the person.

9.3.1. *THE INTERNAL BEINGNESS OF THE PERSON/ PERSONALITY*

The ontological-personological paradigm/ approach prioritizes the role and importance of the personal ontos, in the beingness of the person/ personality, which as it was shown, could be considered *the being* of the person, and comprises, in its broad and comprehensive acceptation/ sphere, in our opinion, mainly, ontos-formations such as the hedonic ontos, the phobic ontos-formation, the projective ontos, the prosentic ontos-formation, and the malsentic ontos-formation, but also the soul and the ego, determining especially its humane and spiritual dimensions, valences, content.

As we have seen, therefore, the personal ontos is not a simple product, an emanation, a result of the mere manifestation and development of the human organism, as we might simply represent it, but it is established in the general context of the personal development, under the influence of the environmental factors, of the person's formations and with the internal action of the principles of emergence, transmergence, telegence, sinmergence, conmergence and imergence, traversing, in an emblematical mode for all the other formations and spheres of the person, the six standard ontogenetic stages, namely of contact, accumulation, structuring, formation, establishment and ontification.

According to these principles, and after completing these steps, the ontic-psychological sphere of the person becomes a distemporalized space and, relatively, protected of the action of the so-called *objective* (material, mechanical) laws, the biological elements can be easily translated noetically or sympathetically, and vice versa, the possibilities and combinations becoming practically limitless (Danesh, 1994). This ontic-metaphysical medium cannot be, therefore, located, nor technically delimited, because it is not an existent and do not exists, it is, however, *the sphere of the being* - space in which it is established the indetermination, and it is, ultimately, the metaphysical source of the intentionality and liberty.

These are so the conditions and limitations where is made the internal, subjective-psychological-personal beingness of the person.

In this context, we must state that the beingness of the personal ontos is a foundation which gives ontological "substance" to the beingness of the person as a whole. The personal ontos is the place, the frame, the source, the internal environment, the premise of beingness of some of the most important formations and constitutional spheres of the person, especially of the soul and the ego, the soul as experiential "internalization" of the other (person, value etc.), and the ego, as experiential " internalization " of the ontic and social self (May, 1987), also of its constitutional sub-formations such as the hedonic ontos, the phobic ontos-formation, the projective ontos, the prosentic ontos-formation, and the malsentic ontos-formation.

In the complex and profound "phenomenon" of beingness of the person crucial role have the inner activity of the organism, the mind, but also the environment, especially the socio-human and cultural environment. To this end, the organism is not represented as a simple "place" for the internal beingness of the person, but contributes, participates dynamically, dialectically, to its internal dynamics (Hubbard, 2012; Aristotle & Lawson-Tancred, 1987). This is, consequently, arguments to consider the organism as determinative, constitutional component/ factor of the beingness and functioning of the personal ontos, and of the person as a whole - reason why we attach to it crucial importance both, so, regarding the ontogenetical process of formation, also regarding the beingness of the person.

Concluding, in the complex and profound phenomenon of beingnes and functioning of the person/ personality participate many inner, biological, sensorial, psychological, spiritual mechanisms, resorts. In this sense, all the onto-personal mechanisms probably conditionate, largely, the promergence and the imergence, the processual internal beingness of the person. There may be also many ontic-psychological mechanisms of production of *existential sense* and prontos, of transformation of the emotions, of the subjective experiences in prontos and resorts for beingness, for a high consistency and continuity of the "being". At the base of the processes standing innumerable mechanisms, montages, motivational sources and resorts, internal ontos-formative loops that "work" in infinite combinations to assure continuity, subjective existential meanings and the internal beingness of the person.

9.3.2. *THE INTERNAL FUNCTIONING OF THE PERSON/ PERSONALITY*

The internal psychological-ontological functioning of the person/ personality is closely determined and linked, inter alia, to the existence, action and interaction of two ontological-psychological poles, located in the extremes of the psychological-personal assembly, respectively *the hedonic-phobic* pole and *the projective-aspirational pole.*

Each of the onto-formations of the two poles, *the hedonic ontos* and *the phobic onto-formation* - from the hedonic-phobic pole, and *the projective ontos* and *the aspirational/ideal ego* - from the projective-aspirational pole, operates with autonomous functional role but very important, too, is the psychological-ontological balances, levers, mechanisms, tensions/ conflicts that form and operate by their involvement and through their interactions, as well, each pole, the hedonic-phobic pole and the projective-aspirational pole, works/ functions autonomously but is also, in the same time, part of a trans- and pan-personal mega-balance, mega-mechanism, mega-conflict/ tension with very important role/ contribution in the internal general, global functioning, beingness and dinamics of the person/ personality.

The hedonic ontos is, functionally, for the personal psychological-ontological sphere of the person, but also for the person as a whole, what is the libido, the pleasure and the sensitive jouissance for organism (Freud, 1990). It develops from them, superizing them and integrating them in a superior construction of psychological-spiritual, human and cultural type, with, also, functionally, a superior, integrative and representative/ expressive role.

The starting point in understanding the functioning and the role of the hedonic ontos, but also with important role in the functioning of the person as a whole, is represented by the concepts of *need, pleasure,* and *desire.* Still, the meaning of the concept *hedonic ontos* is not reducible nor to the one of motivation, of excitation, or tension, nor to the one of libido or eros, it regards the fundamental general state of eudaimonical onto-dynamic existence of the person, and includes so, also, the hedonic organizations from the upper formations level, its functioning involving therefore the personality, ego and conscience.

In this case we can speak, in "functional" meaning, about a hedonic ontos that exists and functions in the subjective imaginary areas, which may enter in a reconstructive interaction/ functioning with the basical organic and psychic ontos. The functional possibilities of eudaimonical reporting to the object grow infinitely, it establishes the *projective ontinces,* talking about the place of the desires, as expression of the spiritual motivational freedom of the subject, of the capacity of choice and generalization (categorization, symbolization), and of hedonical superization. Aspects which leads the hedonical functioning and dynamics towards superior and much expanded areas of the personal assembly, personality (Jung, 1981).

Regarding the functional role of *the phobic onto-formation* the analysis must to start from the term and concept of *fear,* and the state of *anxiety/ tension* that it determines. The disaggregation, decentration, denaturation, alienation are permanent dangers which threatens the stability of the subject, because "the organs" where it is established the subject, as a contingent living being, have the property to allow unlimited energetical and structural dynamics and interactions, and it is the subject's task to secure himself in relation to those processes which may harm it.

The essential function of the phobic formation is therefore to determine personal "organizings" and behavioral patterns to avoid the alienation, the failure. Its role is not limited to the situational signification and the current reaction to potential traumatic stimuli, but, being a key component of the personal ontos, becomes a foundation of the ontogenetical general functioning of the person in order of a better integration, adaptation to the environment and the fulfillment of personal destiny. Therefore the phobic formation functions and acts as an internal critic agent, a regulator of the processes of personal organization, structuration, and functioning.

At the opposite pole of the psychological-personal ensemble, **the projective-aspirational pole**, the contribution to the functioning of the person as a whole is carried out by many formations, instances and structure, among which the prosentic (happiness) onto-formation and the malsentic (depressive) onto-formation, but crucial roles they have, as have seen, the projective ontos and the ideal/ aspirational ego.

The projective ontos is, as has been shown in the book, a set of formations, processes and ontic assemblies of a more special nature and etiology, which, in a global, holistic transmergent representation, might be called *the projective "being" of the person.* The nature more special of this ontic assembly is given both by the great diversity, expanse, complexity and depth, as well as (perhaps especially) by its the ideatical, semantical and projective content. Its onto-projective formation/ constructioning not emerges directly from the basical needs and psychological foundations of the person, like the hedonic ontos, the phobic formation, or the ontical subject, this magic ontological-psychological formation arising, grow from the particular dynamics of the relationship with the socio-human and cultural environment, reflecting, in a transformative/ projective way, its features. The objects, people, situations are not assimilated in their physical-sensorial objectuality but through the social/ cultural meanings, onto-projectively idealized and subjectivated.

The onto-projective formations function, operate like some mechanisms in the subject and the other's service, through the projection of the endemic needs, the individual desires and values, but also in the service of the other (environment, values, persons,) which "projects", "injects" the vectors of control in the person's formations, especially through education/ culture. In this way the individual's functioning is guided both by the inner desires and tendencies and by the other/ environmental's values, requirements and restrictions (Jung, 1981; Freud, 1990). The onto-projective formations are, in fact, targets, hedonic-projective ideals, desires, aspirations which guide the conscious and unconscious searches/ choices and the internal and external functioning of the person/ personality.

These formations function, act, experientially and emergently, through complex mechanisms of feed-back and feed-before, through onto-projective personal referents. The projective personal referents may be the desirable social status, the personal welfare, the desirable body image, the desirable profession, the required level of intelligence and knowledge, the aspirated physical and spiritual pleasures, the aesthetic, moral, axiological aspirations, etc. (for the social services, especially those dealing with children, some of them are actually educational and welfare objectives).

The positive perspectives in favor of their meeting install positive emotions and states, comforting feelings, happiness. Instead, the low perspective of identifying with this hypostasis determines uncomfortable neuro-vegetative reacts and depression. The predominance of the positive onto-projective feelings will lead to the establishment of a strong onto-formation of happiness and a visionary personality, tilting the balance in the positive side. So, through fixings the projective-personal balance in a favorable inclination will orient the personality to the future, will give it a positive sense, efficient, proactive personality, in its onto-ideational/ projective interior universe.

Regarding the role of **the ideal/ aspirational ego** that is, inter alia, to move the functional jouissance and energy from the basal ontological-psychological sphere, from instinct, from the self towards the superior mental/ ideal and aspirational sphere of the person (Hubbard, 2012; Jung, 1981). At the ideal/ aspirational ego level are concentrated enormous energies, forces and information which, specifically assimilated and integrated, become important functional forces/ agents. In this miraculous sphere of the person take place important processes of ontic-informational synthesis generators of functionality, of spirit, freedom, authentic happiness, need of knowledge, sensitivity, empathy, creativity, imprinting to the individual personality trans-personality, universality, human-spiritual specificity and unicity, because this incorporates essentially, specifically and selectively, all the spirituality and human historical experience.

In the internal economy and functioning of the person the onto-projectivity and the aspiration gives the defining note of human being through the axiological-projective ontification of the generalized/ idealized other (the "pattern" of the human being), of the humanistic values, ideas, knowledge, ideals, hopes, of the human functioning. It is thus about an interior ontic-psychological universe where it is synthesized and functions, operates, though double onto-projection, the subjective and the objective, the body and the environment, the inside and the outside, the feeling and thinking relative to the general condition of ancestral human being of the person.

9.4. THE EXTERNAL BEINGNESS AND FUNCTIONING OF THE PERSON/ PERSONALITY

Core Fragment

The socio-human adaptation and integration of the person is much more than a simple social/ professional structural-functional integration into a collective, organization, community, group, it is also a compathetical integration among humans, beings with souls, emotions, feelings, sufferings, happinesses, loves, tragedies, etc. This is the concrete, human world where integrates and lives the person. That is why there are essential features of the humane personality such as empathetic capacity, spiritual well-being, personal/ humane development, selflessness, intelligence, culture, idealism, humanistic vision, or features of behavior such as agreeability, tolerance, kindness, compassion, playfulness, cheerfulness, sociability.

9.4.1. THE SOCIO-HUMANE BEHAVIOR OF THE PERSON

The socio-humane behavior of the person expresses, largely, the *humane* structure/ configuration, orientation and functionality of the personality, its *humane* personality, speaking of features (of behavior/ conduct) such as:

- altruism;
- agreeableness;
- tolerance;
- humanity;
- compassion;
- playfulness;
- joviality;
- sociability;
- irony;
- flexibility;
- extraversion;
- non-discrimination;
- human adaptability;
- respect for the life, happiness and personal values of the other;
- presence of spirit;
- resistance to social frustration;
- openness to new social/ human/ humanistic ideas and values etc. (Baumeister, Bushman, 2013; Stone, 1999).

Through these qualities the social (interpersonal) behavior of the person acquires humane-teleonomical orientation/ quality, without which it would be reduced to a mere "automaton" or it would be described like a "robot". The *humane* orientation of the behavior gives to person virtue and efficiency in activities and professions in fields as social work, education, therapy, art (theater), social management etc. (Sinnott-Armstrong, 2014).

9.4.2. THE SOCIO-HUMANE ADAPTATION AND INTEGRATION OF THE PERSON

The socio-human adaptation and integration of the person is much more than a simple social/ professional structural-functional integration into a collective, organization, community, group, it is also a compathetical integration among humans, beings with souls, emotions, feelings, sufferings, happinesses, loves, tragedies, etc.

This is the concrete, human world where integrates and lives the person. That is why there are essential features of the humane personality such as empathetic capacity, spiritual well-being, personal/ humane development, selflessness, intelligence, culture, idealism, humanistic vision, or features of behavior such as agreeability, tolerance, kindness, compassion, playfulness, cheerfulness, sociability, irony, flexibility, extraversion, non-discrimination, adaptability, respect for the life, happiness and personal values of the other, presence of spirit, resistance to frustration, and so on (Arnet, 2011; Hubbard, 2012).

The dominance of these humane qualities of the persons from a community makes as between the compathetic community and the persons that compose it to establish an ontological balance, an existential and functional optimum where it is meet, in principle, harmoniously and non-confrontational, both the personal necessities and the ones collective (Sinnott-Armstrong, 2014; Stairs, 2000).

Just this ontological balance, existential and functional optimum, the community compathy, the compathetic-ontological congruence between the person and the socio-human environment in which it lives guarantees the social and humane adaptability and integration of the person.

CHAPTER 10

THE DEVELOPMENT/ FULFILLMENT OF THE PERSON/ PERSONALITY. EDUCATION AND THERAPY/ COUNSELING

10.1. INTRODUCTORY ASPECTS 230

10.2. THE DEVELOPMENT AND FULFILLMENT OF THE PERSON/ PERSONALITY 231

10.2.1..THE DEVELOPMENT OF THE PERSON/ PERSONALITY. PERSONAL DEVELOPMENT 231

10.2.2. THE FULFILMENT OF THE PERSON/ PERSONALITY. PERSONAL ACCOMPLISHMENT 232

10.3. THE EDUCATION AND THE THERAPY/ COUNSELING OF THE PERSON/ PERSONALITY 240

10.3.1. HUMANISTIC PEDAGOGY AND EDUCATION 240

10.3.2. HUMANISTIC PSYCHOTHERAPY AND COUNSELING 258

10.1. INTRODUCTORY ASPECTS

Humanistic Genetic Personology promotes both the realization/ FULFILLMENT of the person as an INDIVIDUAL, with the atribut of free will, personal well-being and happiness, but also the realization as a HUMAN, with the atribut of humanity, as human among humans, as human who through his personal FULFILLMENT and happiness not undermines the FULFILLMENT and the happiness of the others, the common interests of the community, but, on the contrary, through his individual FULFILLMENT and happiness contributes to the FULFILLMENT and happiness of the others, to the promotion, affirmation, FULFILLMENT of certain humanistic values or higher social ideals. One can speak so of human FULFILLMENT and happiness of the person through individual human development and by assuming of certain goals and ideals congruent with those of the community in which he daily lives.

10.2. THE DEVELOPMENT AND FULFILLMENT OF THE PERSON/ PERSONALITY

Core Fragment

In this context, one can speak also about human fulfillment and happiness of the person, through individual human development and by assuming of certain goals and ideals congruent with those of the community in which it lives. The humanistic-ontological personology joins thus the efforts of displacement the focus from the quantitative approach to the one qualitative/ intensive in the motivational-eudaimonical representation of the person (including of the professional), addressed, therefore, not so instrumental or symbolic, but by attributes relative to the quality of human being such as: personal fulfillment through humane development, plenary personality, happiness through the happiness of all and the common good, professional happiness, etc.

10.2.1. THE DEVELOPMENT OF THE PERSON/ PERSONALITY. PERSONAL DEVELOPMENT

In the scientific literature, the concept *personal development* is associated or identified with a number of other concepts such as psychic/ psychological development, growth, adaptation, social development, high control, emotional intelligence, etc.

It is a crucial category of the humanist-positive/existential current/ theory from the social and human sciences, and implies, highlights, the following issues:

- High degree of awareness, self-knowledge, self-esteem (Maslow, 2011);

- High socio-emotional development, high control of the emotions, emotional intelligence (Erikson, 1998);

- Realism and balance;

- Powerful will, resistance to failure and frustrations;

- Positive attitude, optimism, active thinking (Seligman, 2002);

- Maximal capitalization of the skills and talents (Maslow, 2011);

- Professional development;

- Personal and social autonomy;

- Interpersonal development (Erikson, 1998);

- Hope, projectivity, orientation towards the future;

- Mature personality, adaptability (Rogers, 1980);

- Psychological-emotional well-being, satisfaction, happiness, hedonism (Seligman, 2002);

- Maximization and capitalization of the internal potential of development, self-actualization, optimization, personal and social efficiency (Rogers, 1980);

- High capacity of overcoming the crisis, the existential anxieties, the frustrations (Frankl, 2009).

Personal development is, in fact a process that ss taking place throughout all life, but it is associated with the maturity period and involves the formation of *the mature person* and *fully functioning person,* person who is able to live life with principles and wisdom, to lead life with high emotional intelligence that aids them to stay calm and think clearly during difficult moments, to keep a harmonious and win-win attitude towards other people, to keep an autonomous mindset, to live life making conscious decisions, etc. (Maslow, 2011).

An important characteristic of a mature and fully functioning person is also the degree of personality development in terms of cohesion, consistency, adaptability and resilience. A mature and fully functioning person, a professional dedicated to the common good, the good of mankind, incorporates, in sublime manner, both spiritual/ humane competencies of role-status and also concrete humane behaviors and activities, thus ensuring, besides a consistent internal spiritual/ humane personal functionality, a high external humane personal functionality. Qualities such as altruism, empathy, optimism, perseverance, idealism, faith, balance, positive thinking, moral power, pure consciousness, self-control, tolerance, soulfulness, cheerfulness, creativity, desirelessness, devotion, endurance, virtuous energy, enthusiasm and more are defining characteristics both of a humane and morale, but by result, of a mature and autonomous person.

In our humanistic-ontological approach, the concepts of mature person and fully functioning person are closely linked to concepts and ideas as humane and spiritual development, humane conscience, humane character, soul, humane ego, humane personality, reveled by categories as altruism, empathy, spirituality, happiness, aesthetic sensibility, kindness, humanity, etc.

Finally, involving, so, the two main orientations, existential-positive and spiritual-humane, a mature person and a fully functioning person may be described as a result of his/her developing at a higher level, the most high, the most close to the condition of human being as an autonomous social and rational existence, with its characteristical attributes - personal development, adaptability and efficiency, but also as personality structured through soul, self, conscience, character, motivation, skills, etc. so that determines conducts oriented towards the wellbeing of the generalized other, towards the common good, to humanity, and dominant traits such as empathy, altruism, generosity, humanness, etc.

10.2.2. THE FULFILLMENT OF THE PERSON/ PERSONALITY. PERSONAL AND PROFESSIONAL ACCOMPLISHMENT

In the humanistic genetic personology perspective and the humanistic-ontological paradigm of the person, of the formation of the person and personality, the FULFILLMENT (and happiness) regards both the realization/ FULFILLMENT of the person as an INDIVIDUAL, with the atribut of well-being, happiness, and the realization as a HUMAN, with the atribut of humanity, as human among humans, as human who through his personal FULFILLMENT and happiness not undermines the FULFILLMENT and the happiness of the others, the common interests of the community, but, on the contrary, through his individual FULFILLMENT and happiness contributes to the FULFILLMENT and happiness of the others, to the promotion, affirmation, FULFILLMENT of certain humanistic values or higher social ideals.

In this context, one can speak also about human FULFILLMENT and happiness of the person, through individual human development and by assuming of certain goals and ideals congruent with those of the community in which it lives (Arnet, 2011; Aristotle & Lawson-Tancred, 1987).

The humanistic-ontological personology joins thus the efforts of displacement the focus from the quantitative approach to the one qualitative/ intensive in the motivational-eudaimonical representation of the person (including of the professional), addressed, therefore, not so instrumental or symbolic, but by attributes relative to the quality of human being such as: personal FULFILLMENT through humane development, plenary personality, happiness through the happiness of all and the common good, professional happiness, etc.

Although it may seem insignificant the happiness is an essential humanistic resource of the professional, especially in the humanistic social practices.

That is the reason why happiness and the eudaimonical-altruistic energy/ motivation, as professional's qualities, resources, energies and conducts, may be considered crucial factors in the activity effectiveness and achieving the specific objectives of practice, especially in casework, in caring, education, and therapy, in the activities with children, elderly and persons with disabilities, in the activities with sick people, and others.

As was also emphasized in the paper, in the humanistic social practices between the practitioner's personality and the client's personality is established a high degree of emotional, empathetical, human, spiritual congruence.

This aspect highlights the importance of some socio-affective and eudaimonical interpersonal processes, where the conduct and interpersonal traits of the practitioner acquire therapeutic significance in both the integrative, prosocial objectives but also in those related to the psychological/ spiritual well-being of the clients (Jex and Gudanowski, 1992).

In this sense, there are a number of personal/ personality characteristics such as high level of personal FULFILLMENT, interior comfort, altruistic motivation, irony, relaxed attitude towards life, hardships and professional difficulties, i.e. the soulful/ psychological welfare and happiness, which are crucial qualities in social work practice, because they are important source of the altruistic, prosocial energy and humane/ humanitarian behavior.

Important is the curative and eudaimonical relationship between the happiness of the client and the happiness of the practitioner.

The happiness and eudemonic-humane energy of the practitioner is a crucial factor in activity effectiveness and important resource in achieving the objectives in practice (Achor, 2010), especially in the activity with children, elderly, sick persons and with disabilities.

So, because one of the most important, constitutional objective of practice in humanistic social practices is to enhancing the psychological welfare/ well being, the happiness of the beneficiaries, especially for children and the elderly, is very important to emphasize the aspect that one cannot speak about the clients' happiness and their rehabilitation in an environment where the personnel, employees, practitioners are unhappy, poor emotionally and eudaimonically.

Humanistic personology promotes, after empathy/ compathy and spiritual welfare, the happiness and the eudaimonical-altruistic energy/ motivation as core resources and crucial qualities of the professional in the specific practice, especially for the professionals who are in direct and prolonged contact with the customers (care personnel in institutions, foster parents, psychologists and others), indispensable resource of the altruistic and virtuous behavior, of the psycho-spiritual and humane qualities of the professional

This energy is able to contribute at the spiritual welfare or change to the distressed clients, permanent resource existing at the professional's personality level - resource afferent to an eudemonic-spiritual welfare and characterial structure constitutional oriented to the good of the other, to the common welfare and happiness (Arnet, 2011; Hubbard, 2012).

In the humanistic social practices we speak about a kind of professional's happiness puts into the customer's service, where the psychological-eudaimonical jouissance of the professional, reflected in the professional behavior, has a strong assistential, educational and curative role.

To this end, the professional's altruistic and spiritual jouissance involves, in the humanistic social practices, at least, two major meanings:

- the jouissance related to higher, humane development of his personality, and

- the jouissance oriented towards the good of the client.

In the first case it is mainly about a jouissance of the spiritual soul, of the higher consciousness, humane ego and character, and, in the second case, about a jouissance mainly of the humane soul, but also of the affective (social) soul, and of other prosocial formations, higher, humanized instances of the personality.

The soul, with all its areas and components, is the place and central source of the professional's humane jouissance, therefore, if in the case of the body, senses, instinct's jouissance we talk about libido and pleasure, in the case of soul's jouissance we talk about eudaimonia and happiness, and in the case of the humane soul's eudaimonia of happiness through the other, the client, or altruistic happiness of the professional.

Without a doubt, it is hard to speak of the professional's humane personality, humane behavior, humane and spiritual qualities in the conditions of a basal, elementary psychological jouissance, expressed in reactions, emotions and feelings predominantly conative, primitive, impulsive, based on the *pleasure-pain* hedonic-biological mechanism.

The professional's humane personality, humane behavior, the humane, moral, spiritual qualities of this, must have an interior psychological-eudaimonical correspondent, a jouissance to match. And so, in the humanistic social practices, we speak about *altruistic and spiritual happiness* of the professional.

Regarding the source of the professional's altruistic and spiritual happiness a crucial role has the jouissance of the professional's soul, of the psychological-ontological sphere of his humane personality, the soul represented as a "being" which feeds, develops from/with virtue, from/with the good, welfare, happiness of the client.

To the process contributes also the professional's happiness onto-formation. The role and importance of the happiness onto-formation in the process of professional's development, in determining personality traits such as agreeableness, optimism, charisma, sociability, altruism, empathy is very important because it improves, elevates the jouissance, the interior subjective-experiential general state, causing to the professional to feel fulfilled, authentically happy, or overflow of interior well, and to externalize, contaminating, affecting for better also the client, more unhappy, unfulfilled. The authentic happiness of the professional is derived from the spiritual/ soulful and human development, wellbeing and FULFILLMENT as person and profession, as well from the humane ego/ self development and FULFILLMENT, because it is an eudaimonia of a psychological-ontological type, involving, holistically and trans-temporally, the personality as an whole, is permanent, is a being, an existence, and not an emotion or pleasure of moment.

Thus, the professional's ego is not a contingent conative, autonomic, self-sufficient ego, subject of the organic fluctuations, of impulsivity, egotistic emotions, but an universalized, spiritualized, humanized, superized ego, the personality's eudaimonia of the professional involving, so, not only the resources of pleasure and jouissance of the self but the cultural resources of virtue and moral good of the entire humanity. Resulting, from here, a humane energy, a happiness of the professional as a *human being*, a true happiness, an interior world and a psychological-spiritual, eudaimonical welfare that exceeds the personal need of internal homeostasical jouissance.

The surplus, thus, pouring in outside, in the professional behavior, energy that reaches, so, also at the client, at the person in difficulty, through the altruistic, humane behavior of the practitioner, through charisma, agreeableness, transfer of spirituality, virtue and happiness.

In this sense, in the humanistic social practices, we can state that the professional's altruistic and spiritual motivational-energetic system is a superior ontogenetical construction within the general motivational system and overall personality of the professional, and it can be represented, succinctly, as *a set of energies associated to some motives, needs, trends, interests, intentions, aspirations, ideals of the professional that support the achievement, expression, disinterestedly, altruistical, compathetical, of some professional behaviors, actions, facts, activities oriented towards the FULFILLMENT of the needs, desires, aspirations of the people in need or difficulty, of the client.*

It is an energy of the professional's humane personality - resort, factor, indispensable resource of the altruistic professional behavior, energy that not emerge from a circumstantial decision of the practitioner to contribute to the present welfare or change the person in difficulty, the, client but an energy, resource existing permanently at his whole being level, corresponding of an eudaimonical-spiritual welfare and motivational structure of personality constitutionally oriented towards the good/ welfare/ well being of the other, of the client.

In this case we must speak of an altruistic and spiritual motivational system of the professional, a superior ontogenetically construction within the general motivational system and global personality, and may be represented, succinctly, as a composition of motives, needs, trends, interests, intentions, aspirations, ideals of the person that support the realization, expressing, disinterested, altruistic, compathetic, of certain conducts, actions, facts, activities oriented towards the FULFILLMENT of the needs, desires, aspirations of other people, of the clients, that support personal behaviors suitable to facilitate the spiritual, human, social development and welfare of the generalized other, the social and eudaimonical rehabilitation of the individuals groups in need, suffering, in crisis, of the clients.

In this sense, one can speak, arbitrary of course, of two motivational-humane systems of the professional oriented towards the good of the other:

1. mobiles, needs, trends, interests, intentions, aspirations, ideals of the professional directly oriented towards the good of the client, sustaining the altruistic professional behavior of aid, support, care of the people in need, of the client, which we could tell *humane motivation of the professional of help and compassion,* and

2. the system of mobiles, needs, trends, emotions, interests, intentions, aspirations, ideals of the professional that acts indirectly, axiologically and energetically, as factors of guidance, spiritualization and humanization of the professional's behavior, generating the moral will and virtue, virtuous personality, charisma, humane authority - axiological-energetical sources in the practitioner's action and conduct, of human, personal and eudemonical development and improvement of the client, through moral and spiritual virtue, transfer and compathy, of empowerment, emancipation, FULFILLMENT of the persons in difficulty, socio-human, moral, eudaimonically degraded, of the client (Rifkin, 2009).

It is, so, impossible to imagine professional efficiency, in the social practices and services, and more so in the humanistic social practices, practically in the jobs that involve working with people in need and suffering, especially in the activities that involve children, elderly and persons with disabilities, in casework, in caring, education, and therapy, without qualities of the professional such spirituality, virtue, culture, but also without qualities of the professional as happiness and eudemonical-altruistic energy/ motivation.

The literature concludes that the professionalism in working with people is strongly conditioned by the degree of happiness, enthusiasm, energy, optimism and charisma of the professional. The professional efficiency being correlated with the positive attitudes, with the degree of internal relaxation, the irony and personal happiness (Weisman, Nathanson, 1986, Bandura, 1986).

James (1981) believes that the job happiness/ satisfaction is the relationship between the individual aspirations and the achievements. At the same time, happiness is an onto-subjective psychological feature and it aprioristically guides the professional to performance.

We believe that the following professional's psychological-eudaimonical and motivational-energetical predispositions, qualities, states, personality configurations, situation stimulates the activity effectiveness and achieving the objectives in the humanistic social practices: authentic happiness, altruistic happiness; humane, altruistic motivation; eudemonic-altruistic energy; the high level of personal FULFILLMENT; interior comfort, irony, relaxed attitude towards the life, hardships and professional difficulties; soulful/ spiritual welfare; the psychological-eudaimonical welfare; the characterial structure constitutionally oriented to the good and happiness of the other, to the common welfare; the jouissance oriented towards the good and happiness of the client; positive emotions, feelings, thoughts, attitudes; the humane ego's development and FULFILLMENT; mobiles, needs, trends, interests, intentions, aspirations, ideals oriented towards the good of the client; the professional and social satisfactions; relaxation, extraversion, democratic spirit, tolerance, openness to new ideas, epistemological and methodological flexibility, agreeableness, optimism, charisma, sociability, empathy, virtue; mature personality, emotional stability, self-control, etc.

10.3. THE EDUCATION AND THE THERAPY/ CONSELING OF THE PERSON/ PERSONALITY

Core Fragment

The therapeutic process begins, so, with what we could call spiritual-humanistic and psychological-transpersonal evaluation, that seeks to identify and diagnoses mostly the structural-functional and situational impairments of the customer relating its psychological-humane and spiritual development and beingness. In the spiritual-humanistic therapy the practitioner, through his complex and spiritual/ transpersonal personality, contributes crucially to the achievement of the humanistic established objectives, mostly those relating to the spiritual wellbeing of the client, to the reduction/ relieving the sufferings and anguishes, but also to those concerning the empowerment, autonomization, the social, socio-humane integration and adaptation in the community where the client lives.

10.3.1. HUMANISTIC PEDAGOGY AND EDUCATION

Essentially, the humanistic (spiritual-humane and existential-positive) paradigm of education as process and activity brings in the forefront concepts and ideas such education through psychological-personal, spiritual and human development, through empathy, happiness, love and attachment, child/student-centered approach, self-determination, self-actualization, the power/force of the ego, personality, consciousness, strength-based education/teaching, spirituality, empowerment, personal development, personal accomplishment, holistic assessment and teaching, optimism, creativity, happiness, the child's uniqueness, focus on the particular aspects of its human coexistence, tolerance, love, etc.

In general, the humanistic approach to pedagogy and education prioritizes the role of some formative factors such as the human/humane quality of the adults' personalities, of the social, interpersonal, relationships, crucial role having in this sense the human quality of the learning community. Here we consider mainly the family and the school class, but also the communities of friends, neighbors, relatives etc. Both the family and the school class must be represented more than mere social groups, but especially like human/humane, spiritual, cultural, compathetic communities, that have essential contributions especially in the formation of social personality, core objective in humanistic education.

The humanistic perspective on the parent/teacher operates with a concept of professional personality of humane-spiritual type, which combines, dialectically, the humane and spiritual dimension with the one pragmatic. Empathy, spiritual welfare, humane and personal development and spiritual sensibility are crucial, indispensable traits of the teacher in humanistic pedagogy. These crucial interpersonal qualities and resources, involved in the educational process, have, mainly, as psychological-ontological source, its humane and spiritual personality, but also its strong personality.

The teacher/ adult's personality is important especially in the educational objectives that involve the personal and human empowerment/ development/ formation. The theories of personality (development) describe and approach the child/ student as *human being* situated in *process* of psychological, human, emotional and social development, where the adults' personalities have great contributions.

In this sense, crucial resources of education promoted by the humanistic pedagogy are empathy, happiness and love (attachment), being used as formative instruments, ways by the educators in achieving objectives as psychological-human and social-personal development, the educator-child educational relationship being in fact a framework for transfer humanity and spirituality, a subtle lane that the educator uses, intentionally and professionally, to achieve the assumed educational goals.

From a humanistic-positive position it is highlighted the importance in the educational process/ activity of some issues and resources as the strengths, the virtues, the talents of the child/ student, its positive experiences of learning, the positive relationships, happiness, the states of pleasure or flow, the positive emotions, the orientation of the learning to future, the positive expectations, appreciations, etc.

Essentially, the humanistic and positive pedagogies promote especially the formation, in the educational process, of the personality, of the person as a whole (holistic education), as person in socio-human context, putting the objectives which aim the intellectual formation in second plan, yet without disregarding them. That is the reason way in process are used operational objectives as personality formation, personality development, personality empowerment, self-realization, psychological-personal development and empowerment, the humanization and spiritualization of the child/ student.

The existential directions/ modalities/ approaches focuses on the inner capacity of self-determination and formation of the child's personality, based on free will and self-realization, while the spiritual (humane, ontological, etc.) approaches focus on the formation, through education, of the child/ student as spiritual and humane personality.

Regarding the humanistic pedagogy/ education - the humanistic-ontological paradigm of the child/ student and the educational process - it involves the humanistic pedagogy and education as were consecrated these practically and not declarative, but is not limited to these, it exceeds, completes and fulfills through the interest and focus on the child/ student and the educational process as a whole, through the interest and focusing on the ontological-spiritual aspects of the educational process, both in family as well in the school, proposing, therefore, educational objectives relating to the condition of person as a whole, focusing both on the formation of the interior psychological-ontological structures, as well as on the involvement, in the comprehensive educational process, to the interpersonal, social, cultural resorts which determines, ontogenetically, structurally, functionally and existentially, the formation of the student/ child as a person; on the one hand, developed personally, humanly and spiritually, and, on the other hand, ego-personally fulfilled and socio-humanely integrated (Castiello, 1936).

HUMANISTIC PEDAGOGY

In great measure, the humanistic paradigm of pedagogy is a replica of the humanistic paradigm of psychology, the humanistic psychological theory and methodology succeeded, gradually, to make place in the pedagogy's literature and educational practice through values, objectives and terms such as *human and personal development, happiness, self-determination, person/child-centered education, positive education* etc., also to determine even a shift of emphasis to humanistic and positive values and goals of the education as institution.

As it was established, consecrated, affirmed, in theory and practice, **humanistic pedagogy,** as science, proposes and promotes, in essence, the displacement of emphasis, in the educational process, from the teacher and method on the child/ student, and the exploitation of its psychological and spiritual resources of learning, growing, developing, creativity and self-affirmation (Hall and Hall, 1988; Vico, 1993).

In this sense, humanistic pedagogy promotes mainly the representation of the child/ student as *ego* and *personality*, the power of its consciousness and will, its freedom and responsibility to self-determination, the ontogenetical and scholar evolution/ development in accordance with its bio-psycho-social characteristics and choices (Steiner, 1996).

From the humanistic pedagogy's position, every healthy child has the capacity to self-determination, has the capacity to use its potential in human, social and spiritual terms; all depends of its internal activism and of the willingness for change or self-FULFILLMENT.

These are also some of the main resources of the humanistic pedagogy and its applications in education and teaching, which bring, therefore, in the forefront concepts and ideas such as:

> - child/ student-centered approach,
> - self-determination, self-actualization,
> - the power/ force of the ego, personality, and consciousness,
> - strength-based education/ teaching,
> - spirituality,
> - empowerment,
> - personal development,
> - personal accomplishment,
> - holistic assessment and education,
> - optimism, creativity, happiness,
> - the individual/ child uniqueness,
> - focus on the particular aspects of its human existence, tolerance, love, etc. (Steiner, 1996; Hall and Hall, 1988; Vico, 1993; Montessori, 1968).

According to Rogers, who dedicated a great attention to humanistic pedagogy and education, the child/ student's need to achieving personal FULFILLMENT is a crucial way for it psychological and scholar development.

Regarding the humanistic education, as process, activity and action, it involves the education as were consecrated these practically and not declarative, but is not limited to these, it exceeds, completes and fulfills through the interest and focus on the child/ student and the educational process as a whole, through the interest and focusing on the ontological-spiritual aspects of the educational process, both in family as well in the school, proposing, therefore, educational objectives relating to the condition as personality of the child/ student, focusing both on the formation of the interior psychological-ontological structures, as well as on the involvement, in the comprehensive educational process, to the interpersonal, social, cultural resorts which determines, ontogenetically, structurally, functionally and existentially, the formation of the student/ child as a person; on the one hand, developed personally, humanly and spiritually, and, on the other hand, ego-personally fulfilled and socio-humanely integrated (Steiner, 1972; Montessori, 1968).

Positive Pedagogy is a relatively new field of academic study, being considered either an autonomous science, either a part of the humanistic pedagogy, either an extension of the humanistic psychology. Probably all the affirmations are valid.

This pedagogical discipline investigates and proposes the formation end development of specific skills that assist the child/ student to strengthen their relationships, build positive emotions, enhance personal resilience, promote mindfulness and encourage a healthy lifestyle (Seligman & Fowler, 2011).

Essentially, this kind of pedagogy highlights the importance in the educational process/ activity of some issues and resources as the:

- strengths, virtues, talents;

- positive experiences of learning;

- positive relationships and communities;

- happiness, states of pleasure or flow;

- positive emotions;

- orientation of the learning to the future;

- positive expectations, appreciations;

- empathy (Montessori, 1968; Seligman & Fowler, 2011).

THE CHILD/STUDENT AND THE PARENT/ TEACHER

The epistemological foundation in the representation of **the child/ student**, from the humanistic pedagogy's perspective, is, in fact, its educational and projective-teleological representation as personality, ego, character, creative and spiritual being. Therefore, it is brings in the forefront of the educational strategies and processes, of the educational objectives, its *human, spiritual, personal and social formation and development*(Seligman & Fowler, 2011; Vico, 1993).

In the process of representation it is indicated to be involved also the system of the socio-humane relationships, the humane community.

Through the humane ego, humane conscience, and humane character the child/ student is formed, educates and exists as part of a humane community (network) of attachments, values, persons, humane relationships, and, in conclusion, its personality formation and development are conditioned by the personal-humane and compathetical-cultural quality of this community.

In relation to the two (humanistic) paradigms, perspectives of representation and approach to personality, one can speak of two types of values and resources of the child/ student's personality in the humanistic educational practice:

> of his *humane and spiritual personality,*

> and of his *strong, developed personality.*

The first is related to the term *humane and spiritual development/ resources* of the child/ student's personality, and the second to the term *personal-psychological development/ resources* of the child/ student's personality.

The syntagma child/ student's *humane and spiritual personality* refers mainly to the psychological-humane and spiritual content/ nature of the child/ student's personality, also to the humanistic orientation, quality, the overall humane and spiritual valence, dimension of the client's global personality.

Too, the issue relating the **parent/ teacher's personality** is of great importance, that's why it requires a comprehensive approach.

The model of representation is, therefore, opposed to the didactic-intellectualist model. The humanistic-ontological perspective on the parent/ teacher operates with a concept, of professional personality, of humane-spiritual type, which combines, dialectically, the humane and spiritual dimension with the one pragmatic (Vico, 1993).

That's why, also in the process of teacher education, is put accent on an applied spiritual-humanistic curriculum; the aim is that of training and cultivation of the complex professional humane personality, the ability to empathize with the student.

Empathy and compathy, spiritual welfare, humane development and spiritual sensibility are crucial, indispensable traits of the teacher in humanistic-ontological pedagogy. These crucial interpersonal qualities and resources, involved in the educational process, have, mainly, as psychological-ontological source, the humane and spiritual personality, but also its strong personality.

THE LEARNING COMMUNITY

In humanistic and positive pedagogy the optimal learning community is the one that assures, facilitates, stimulates, leads both to the formation of a strong personality, evidenced by features such as high capacity for self-determination, optimism, energy, free will, active consciousness, social adaptability, assertiveness, resilience, happiness, personal and social autonomy, interpersonal development, mature personality, adaptability, personal and social efficiency, socio-emotional development, control of emotions, emotional intelligence, realism and balance, powerful will, resistance to failure and frustrations, hope, orientation to future. positive attitude, optimism, active thinking, high degree of awareness, self-knowledge, self-esteem, professional development, activism, etc., as well as to the formation of the human and spiritual sphere, dimension of the child/ student's personality, characterized by qualities such as spirituality, virtue, altruism, generosity, kindness, morality, sociality, love, attachment, socio-human efficiency and adaptability, humanity/ humanness, empathy, etc.

Thus, the humanistic approach in pedagogy and education prioritizes the role of some factors such as the human quality of the adults' personalities, of the social, interpersonal, relationships, but crucial role has the human quality of the learning community. Here we consider mainly the family and the school class, but also the communities of friends, neighbors, relatives etc.

Both the family and the school class must be represented, in humanistic perspective, more than mere social groups, but especially like human, spiritual, cultural, empathetic communities, that have essential contributions especially in the formation of personality, the main objective in the humanistic education (Montessori, 1968).

Between the learning community and the individuals which it constitutes it is established a ontological-socio-human balance, an existential and functional optimum, in which is satisfied, in principle, in a harmonious and non-confrontational way, both the personal and the collective necessities.

But this learning community can also have a negative influences, may be an area of non-value, of conflict, hostility or social exclusion, or can have a coherent organization and functioning but founded on non-value, on antisocial attitudes, or may be poorly organized, dysfunctional, immature. In both cases, the members are exposed to personal, humane, spiritual and intellectual under-development. (Steiner, 1972).

The optimal educational conditions, learning community for the construction of a strong, developed, equilibrate and humane personality of the child/ studenf, both in the school class and family, but also in the communities of friends, neighbors, relatives, are the ones opposites, characterized bg qualities as positive, functional relationships, social/ human solidarity, unity, communication, cooperation, inter-empathy, humanity, altruism, responsibility. Essential being the quality of the social relationships from the learning community represented as *humane* relationships in the humanistic pedagogy.

EDUCATION AND TEACHING

Humanistic and positive pedagogies promote especially the formation, in the educational process, of the personality, of the person as a whole, putting the objectives which aim the intellectual formation in second plan, yet without disregarding them.

That is the reason way in process are used terms, ideas, values as:

- personality formation;

- personality development;

- personality empowerment;

- self-actualization;

- child/ student's intern potential;

- personality transfer and empathy;

- psychological-personal development and empowerment;

- child/ student-centered-intervention;

- existential education;

- gestalt pedagogy;

- transpersonal pedagogy;

- spiritual education

- the humanization of the child/ student;

- the spiritualization of the child/ student, etc. (Steiner, 1972; Montessori, 1968; Seligman & Fowler, 2011).

Essentially, in humanistic pedagogy are dominant two great directions/ modalities/ approaches regarding the educational goals:

- existential (positive, phenomenological, etc.), and

- spiritual (humane, ontological, etc.).

The existential directions/ modalities/ approaches focuses on the inner capacity of self-determination and formation of the child's personality, based on free will and self-realization.

The spiritual (humane, ontological, etc.) approaches focus on the formation, through education, of the child/ student as a "spiritual" and "humane" personality.

In the first case the objectives aim principally the personal development, highlighted of traits as:

- Personal and social autonomy;

- Interpersonal development;

- Mature personality, adaptability;

- Personal and social efficiency (Rogers, 1977, 1980);

- Socio-emotional development, control of emotions, emotional intelligence;

- Realism and balance;

- Powerful will, resistance to failure and frustrations;

- Hope, orientation to future. positive attitude, optimism, active thinking (Seligman, 2002);

- High degree of awareness, self-knowledge, self-esteem (Maslow, 2011);

- Professional development;

- Activism, self-determination;

- Optimism, energy, free will;

- Active consciousness;

- Social adaptability, assertiveness, resilience;

- Psychological wellbeing, happiness, etc. (Seligman & Fowler, 2011; Vico, 1993).

Regarding the spiritual (humane, ontological) formation of the child/ student, the objectives, in the educational process, aim principally the spiritual and humane development, the formation of a structure of personality dominated of traits as:

- Spirituality;

- Humanity;

- Empathy;

- Altruism;

- Generosity;

- Kindness;

- Morality;

- Virtue;

- Sociality;

- Love, attachment;

- Socio-human efficiency and adaptability, etc. (Steiner, 1972; Montessori, 1968).

Through the FULFILLMENT of the spiritual and humane objectives of education the child/ student's personality can be described both as personality developed at a higher level, the most high, the most close to the condition of human being as autonomous cultural, rational, spiritual existence, with its characteristic attributes - morality, virtue, sociality, spirituality, personal development, adaptability and socio-human efficiency, and as personality structured through the self, ego, conscience, character, motivation, skills, etc. so that determines conducts oriented towards the wellbeing of the generalized other, towards the common good, humanity, and dominant traits such as empathy, altruism, generosity, kindness, etc. (Steiner, 1972; Montessori, 1968; Seligman & Fowler, 2011).

PERSONALITY AS RESOURCE OF EDUCATION / THEACHING

Abraham Maslow imposes in humanistic psychotherapy, but perfectly applicable in humanistic education and theaching, the concept of *self-actualization*, which essentially represents a method of bringing in the process of education and of exploitation of the internal resources of the actors' personalities involved in process (children, educators, parents etc.).

In relation to the two (humanistic) paradigms, perspectives of representation and approach, one can speak of two types of resources of the person/personality in humanistic education/ theaching. It is about resources of *the strong, developed personality*, on the one hand, and of the *humane and spiritual personality*, on the other hand. The first category is related to the term *personal-psychological resources* and the second to the term *humane and spiritual resources*.

The personal-psychological resources have, as main sources, formations and instances of personality such as *the ego, the active/proactive consciousness, the will* being related to *the proactive and adaptive quality, valence, dimension of the global personality* (Campbell-Sills, Cohan, Stein, 2006; Schellhamme, 2012; Eley & co, 2013; Barrick & Mount, 1991).

In this sense, the *psychological-personal resources* of the humanistic education are closely determined by the level of development of the strong/developed personality, but also of the personality as a whole, implying:

- High degree of awareness, self-knowledge, self-esteem (Maslow, 2011);

- Personal and social efficiency (Rogers, 1977, 1980);

- Socio-emotional development, control of emotions, emotional intelligence (Erikson, 1998);

- Realism and balance (Frankl, 1967);

- Powerful will, resistance to failure and frustrations (Schellhamme, 2012);

- Hope, orientation to future. positive attitude, optimism, active thinking (Seligman, 2002);

- Professional development (Erikson, 1998);

- Personal and social autonomy (Schellhamme, 2012);

- Interpersonal development (Erikson, 1998);

- Mature personality, adaptability (Rogers, 1980, Maslow, 1993).

The humane and spiritual resources of the humanistic education and theaching have, as main sources, formations and instances of personality such as *the self, the soul, the character, the moral conscience* being related to *the psychological-humane and spiritual content/nature of personality, also to the humanistic orientation, quality, the overall humane and spiritual valence, dimension of the global personality.* The humane and spiritual resources of the person are closely determined by the level of development of the humane and spiritual personality. For example, through the great development of the theacher/parent's humane personality his behavior is defined through solidarist-humanistic qualities, such as empathy, agreeableness, tolerance, humanity, human sensitivity, altruism (Carlo et al., 1991) - core resources in working with the students in humanistic education/ theaching.

The humane and spiritual personality and development, and the strong/developed personality and development as resources are complementary, interdependent, and must to be conceived only together în the humanistic educational process.

THE (HUMANISTIC) EDUCATIONAL PROCESS

The *Humanistic* educational process brings in the forefront of evaluation and educational action concepts and ideas such as:

- holistic assessment and education;
- optimism;
- creativity;
- happiness;
- the child/ student's uniqueness;
- focus on the particular aspects of its socio-human existence;
- tolerance, love, etc.
- child/student-centered approach (Rogers, 1951;
- self-determination, self-actualization;
- the power/ force of the ego, personality, and consciousness;
- strength-based education/ teaching;
- spirituality;
- empowerment;
- psychological-personal development;
- socio-human and professional accomplishment, etc. (Rogers, 1951; Steiner, 1972; Montessori, 1968; Seligman & Fowler, 2011).

The humanistic education has, inter alia, the task, to operate/ determine those compathetical, humane improvements at the level of inter-personal relationship, group, organization, family, couple, etc. that would lead, through the humanising force that exercise the socio-human/ humane relationships and the humanistic group upon the child, to beneficial improvements in its psychological and social development/ formation.

In this sense, the humanistic education/ teaching uses the human personality as core resources and values with priority in the objectives regarding the personal-psychological development and formation, where the educator, with his humane and developed global personality and behavior, succeeds to have a greater efficiency, both in the objectives involving the psychological welfare and happiness of the child, as well as in those pursuing his formation and development.

The educational process starts with the demarche of evaluation through the representation of the child as personality. That is why it is necessary the settlement, in the front-plan of the evaluative panel, of the dysfunctional elements and deviations from a so-called normality in the psychological-personal, humane and spiritual development/ wellbeing of the child/ student, evaluated in the context of some systems of human/ social relationships more or less humane/ pro-humane or developed.

In his educational activity, through his humane/ strong personality and behavior, the educator can contributes crucially to the achievement of the humanistic established objectives, mostly those related to the psychological-emotional developed of the child, those concerning the empowerment, autonomization, the social, socio-humane integration and adaptation in the community where the child lives.

From the humanistic methodology and praxeology perspective the efficiency of the educational process is high especially when it is considered the direct psychological relationship between the educator and the child. Especially through the empathetic capacity and resources of his personality the educator acquires access to the child's personality and psychological experience, and, also, acquires an effective method/ way of psychological/ humane/ spiritual development/ empowerment.

CHILD/ STUDENT-CENTERED EDUCATION/ TEACHING

The core idea of the child/ student-centered education/ teaching is that, in the educational process must to take the child's personality, desires, feelings, attitudes, beliefs, aspirations seriously, because these can be the basis for an authentic and durable education, development, formation, by finding his inner authentic resources, in his personality and concrete (circumstantial) socio-human/ educational relationships.

Essentially, this kind of education and teaching is characterized by:

- the educator experiences an empathic understanding of the child/ student's internal sentiments, desires, aspiration, ideas etc.;

- the educator must manifest increased trust in the child/ student potential and in its capacity to grow and develop with its own resources, the role of the educator being principally to guide it;

- the educational relationship must be a relationship in which each person's perception of the other is very important;

- into the framework of the educational relationship must to exist an empathetical/ compathetical congruence (emotional, cognitive etc. between the child/ student and therapist;

- the educator must accept the child/ student unconditionally, without judgment, disapproval or approval;

- the educator helps the child/ student to believe that the therapist has an unconditional love for them;

- the educator must involve in the educational relationship his own experiences to facilitate the development, emancipation, empowerment of the child/ student. (Rogers, 1951; Steiner, 1972; Montessori, 1968; Seligman & Fowler, 2011).

From an existential-spiritual perspective the child/ student-centered education/ teaching seeks, inter alia, as evaluation, to research/ identification the existential-spiritual and existential-humane potentialities, while, in intervention, it aims to achieve the internal-ontological spiritual rebalancing/ empowerment through spiritual growth and emancipation/ development. From a gestaltist perspective the child/ student-centered education/ teaching involves principally its representation and approach as a whole, existing and learning "here and now".

EDUCATION THROUGH PSYCHOLOGICAL-PERSONAL, SPIRITUAL AND HUMAN DEVELOPMENT

Among the most important schools that promote and apply this type of humanistic and positive education should be mentioned Waldorf, Montessori, Reggio Emilia, and Neo-humanist schools.

The theories of personality (development) and (human) being in the humanistic education and teaching describe and approach the child/ student as human being situated in process of psychological, human, emotional and social development, with his personality, desires, sentiments, knowledge as core resource for growing.

The psychological-personal, human, emotional and social development is, so, one of the most important key tool of formation as person, personality, as accomplished human being and well integrated in society when will be a mature and autonomous person (Vico, 1993).

In this sense, one of the most important way of intervention in the process of emancipation, empowerment and development of the child/ student is through *spiritualization* and *humanization*, through spiritual and human/ humane development. Even if is a very complex and difficult endeavor the humanization and spiritualization of the child is described by the theoreticians of the humanistic-spiritual pedagogy as miraculous solutions for the education in perspective of formation of a complex, profound and creative personality.

The educational process begins with what a personological-humanistic-spiritual evaluation. The epistemological foundation of the evaluation in humanistic-spiritual perspective it is, actually, the representation of the child as complex and profound personality, spiritual being.

In the spiritual-humanistic education the practitioner, through his spiritual personality and behavior, contributes crucially at the achievement of the humanistic established objectives, mostly those relating to the spiritual wellbeing of the child, but also at those concerning the empowerment, autonomization, the social, socio-humane integration and adaptation in the community where the student lives.

Through spirituality and creativity, the humanistic educator works at the construction of a new (spiritual) *modus vivendi,* of some new behaviors of the student, with humanistic-spiritual tools and methods (Steiner, 1972; Montessori, 1968).

So, with methods and behaviors of humanistic-spiritual type, the educator performs changes and re-modelings of the current spiritual, social, cultural and psychosocial situation of the child, changes and improvements in the concrete situations of depersonalization and dehumanization, in the individual and collective situations of spiritual-existential impasse, spiritual-existential crisis.

Regarding the importance of spirituality and virtue, as qualities of the educator's personality in activity effectiveness and achieving the objectives, this is given by the fact that the relationship with the child is not objectual but "spiritual", and very complex, and therefore the dominant resources involved must be also of this nature (Seligman & Fowler, 2011).

EDUCATION THROUGH EMPATHY, LOVE AND ATTACHMENT

Other sources and methods of education promoted by the humanistic pedagogy are empathy, happiness and love (attachment).

Empathy is a formative instrument used by the educators in achieving objectives as psychological-human and personal education/ development. The educator-child proactive empathetic relationship is in fact a framework for transfer, a subtle lane that the educator uses, intentionally and professionally, to achieve the assumed educational goals (Rogers, 1951, Steiner, 1972).

Crucial it is the goal regarding the humanly growing and development of the child through the development of the empathetic spheres of his personality and behavior.

Also, another role of the educator is to use or create the optimal socio-human environment for the human grow and development of the child/ student in the educational process.

Regard the role of **love and attachment** as resource and method in humanistic education the humanistic theoreticians bring in attention, inter alia, the stipulations of the attachment theory that highlights the importance of affection and attachment relationships in the social/ interpersonal relationships and coexistence, especially regarding the role of *child-parent attachment*, but also of the relationships of attachment between the student and the educator in the formation of a balanced and adaptive personality of the child (Bowlby, 1999), stimulating, improving the process of learning, the formation and maturation in all the personality and behavior's areas - cognitive, emotional, social, moral, personal development, professionalization, etc. (Vico, 1993; Steiner, 1972).

Therefore, essentially, in theory and practice, humanistic pedagogy proposes and promotes, inter alia, the displacement of emphasis, in the educational process, from the intellectual resources, from the memory and memorization, and cognitive and intellectual development (as core objective and aim), to resources as empathy, happiness and love (attachment), and the *personal development* – as core objective and aim.

POSITIVE EDUCATION/ THEACHING

Positive Education and Theaching, as process, activity and action, is focuses especially on flourishing, formation and development of the child/ student through learning on multiple levels that include the biological, personal, relational, institutional, cultural, and global dimensions of life.

On of the most important aim of positive education in the psychological-personal development through the use of the psycho-eudaimonical, psycho-volitional and adaptive resources, developing, therefore, its existential, hedonic and adaptive dimension, the happiness, the freedom, responsibility and the will, the formation of traits and qualities such as general psychological wellbeing, activism, self-determination, freedom-accountability, optimism, energy, free will, self-realization, hope, active consciousness, personal development, social adaptability, assertiveness, resilience, happiness, etc. (Seligman & Fowler, 2011; Vico, 1993).

Regarding the relevance and usefulness of **happiness** as important resource and method in humanistic education the aspect is revealed by ideas, facts, aspects as:

- Happiness is a source of personal development, for formation of a strong and balanced personality, social/ professional efficiency and factor for the acquisition of the autonomous social reintegration capacity;

- The student is not only a simple consumer of educational services, it is also a cultural, spiritual, aesthetic, playful being - this has therefore and emotional, cultural, spiritual, aesthetic, playful needs and resources, which, for a full valorization, must be unconditionally satisfied (Stefaroi, 2009b).

- Every person, regardless of age, sex, nationality, race, social status, profession is entitled to a dignified life, to happiness, to personal FULFILLMENT;

- The essential indicator of the human life quality is the internal satisfaction, subjective felt, the happiness and complacency of the person (Montessori, 1968; Seligman & Fowler, 2011).

Therefore, essentially, positive pedagogy as theory and positive education as practice bring together the science of positive psychology with the best practices in teaching to encourage and support the child to psychologically flourish and personal developing, as a combination of feeling good and doing good.

10.3.2. HUMANISTIC PSYCHOTHERAPY AND COUNSELING

As ways/ methods of personal development, of empowerment, and FULFILLMENT of the person **Humanistic Psychotherapy and Counseling**, bring in the forefront of knowledge, evaluation and therapeutic action/ activity terms, concepts, values, techniques and ideas such as:

- personality psychotherapy and counseling;

- empathy as core resource of change and empowerment;

- psychological-personal development and empowerment;

- ethical responsibility;

- self-actualization;

- client's intern potential;

- person/ client-centered-intervention;

- existential psychotherapy and counseling;

- gestalt psychotherapy and counseling;

- group psychotherapy and counseling;

- transpersonal psychotherapy;

- spiritual psychotherapy and counseling;

- the humanization of the client;

- the spiritualization of the client;

- positive psychotherapy and counseling;

- morality;

- virtue;

- sociality, love, attachment, etc. (Rogers, 1959, 1977, 1980; Maslow, 1993, 2011; Frank, 1967, etc.).

In theory and practice the humanistic psychotherapy and counseling are dominant two great directions/ modalities/ approaches:

- existential (positive, phenomenological, etc.), and

- spiritual (humane, ontological, etc.).

The existential directions/ modalities/ approaches focuses on the inner capacity of the self-determination of person/ client, on free will and self-realization, where the evaluation and intervention are based too to the research and identification of the client's existential anxieties and crisis, its internal-ontological imbalances, the rehabilitation being made through personal/ human growth and emancipation/ empowerment (Horner & Kindred, 1997).

The spiritual (humane, ontological, etc.) approaches would include, comprises, certainly, the humanistic psychotherapy as enshrined it practically, and not declarative, but it is not limited to this, it exceeds, completes and fulfills through the interest and focus on the person as spirit, as a spiritual and humane personality, with curative emphasis on the ontological-psychological interior disorders and affectations, as well as on the compathetical, inter-personal, social, cultural resorts that determine, ontogenetically, structurally, functionally and existentially, the client's disorders, affectations, problems, underdevelopments, etc.

Through the humane and spiritual personality the person/ client is formed, works and exists as part of a compathetical community of attachments, values, persons, humane relationships, and, in conclusion, the "health" of its personality and behavior is conditioned by the humane quality of this community.

In this regard, the evaluation in the humanistic-ontological paradigm of the person/ client, seeks to identify and diagnose, mostly, the structural-functional and situational disorders of the client related to its humane and spiritual development and beingness as part of a compathetical relationship and/ or community.

Also, it is important to realize an inventory of the motivational system of the customer where to highlight the more pronounced deviations from the normality of the system of needs, motives and aspirations by reference to a motivational-humane and spiritual optimum (Strack, 2005).

The humanistic-spiritual therapy has, so, inter alia, this first curative/ recuperative/ ameliorative task, in the process of intervention, to operate/ determine those compathetical, humane improvements at the level of inter-personal relationship, group, organization, family, couple, etc. that would lead, through the humanizing force that exercise the socio-human/ humane relationships and the humanistic group, to beneficial improvements in the internal ontological-psychological condition/ economy/ jouissance of the person (Stolorow, 2011).

CLIENT-CENTERED THERAPY

The person-centered psychotherapy and counseling are linked especially to the name of Carl Rogers.

Through the person/ client-centered therapy/ psychotherapy, the person/ client-centered counseling, or the rogerian psychotherapy as it is also called, Rogers (1951) has the crucial merit to be worked to the foundation of the modern psychotherapy as a whole, also through the *non-directive* therapeutic-humanistic methods and values promoted in theory and practice, with large application also in education, social work and other domain of the socio-human practices and activities.

The core idea of the established client-centered therapy, promoted by Rogers and developed by followers, is that, in the therapeutic process must to take the client's accounts seriously, because he, his personality is the basis for helping and healing, by finding his inner resources, in his personality and concrete (circumstantial) socio-human relationships.

In this sense, the therapist can use the internal circumstantial experiences of the client as resources in the process of rehabilitation, empowerment, normalization.

Today, the person/ client-centered therapy is known and applied by considering the following aspects:

- the therapist must accept the client unconditionally, without judgment, disapproval or approval;

- the therapist experiences an empathic understanding of the client's internal frame of reference;

- the therapist helps the client to believe that the therapist has an unconditional love for them;

- the psychotherapist/ counselor must manifest increased trust in the client potential and in its capacity to recover, rehabilitate, grow and develop with its own resources, the role of the therapist being principally to guide it;

- the therapeutic relationship must be a relationship in which each person's perception of the other is very important;

- into the framework of the therapeutic relationship must to exist an empathetical/ compathetical congruence (emotional, cognitive etc.) between the client and therapist;

- the therapist must involve in the therapeutic relationship his own experiences to facilitate the rehabilitation, development, emancipation, empowerment of the client (Rogers, 1977).

Interpreting the person/ client-centered therapy through the humanistic persotherapy perspective, the humanistic ontological theory/ paradigm of the person/ client, is important to take the clients' spiritual and psychological-ontological experience and live seriously, because these are the basis for helping and healing, by finding their soulful/ spiritual and humane inner resources, in their humane personality and concrete human, compathetic relationships. In this end the therapist can use the internal psychological-ontological experiences of the clients as resources in the process of rehabilitation, empowerment, normalization.

EXISTENTIAL THERAPY

The existential psychotherapy and counseling focuses, especially, on aspects, objectives and approaches such as:

- the research/ identification and the solving, diminishing the client's existential anxieties/ crisis, impasses,

- self-determination of the person/ client,

- freedom and responsibility,

- free will, and

- the search and develop of the inner client's meanings of life, etc. (Deurzen and Kenward, 2005).

This kind of therapy approaches the client as a whole and as person being, existing in situation, concrete, unique existential context using a psychological-positive/ phenomenological approach that promotes the client's inner psychological-personal, volitional capacities and aspirations, but simultaneously acknowledging its limitations and weaknesses (Yalom, 1980).

In the therapeutic process of evaluation and intervention the therapist and the client must reflect together upon how the client has answered life's questions in the past, but attention will be put to searching for a new and increased awareness in the present and enabling in conclusion a new freedom and responsibility to act.

Both, the evaluation and intervention are based on a series of philosophical-existential theses, proposing the research/ identification of the existential anxieties/ crisis and internal-ontological rebalancing/ rehabilitation through personal/ human growth and emancipation/ empowerment – solutions very useful both in evaluation as well as in intervention, especially in the practice with the clients with depression and anxiety, also with problems of adaptation and social integration (Krill, 1978).

In existential therapy and counseling, but from the humanistic ontological perspective of the person/ client, the activity seeks, inter alia, as evaluation, to research/ identification the existential-spiritual and existential-humane anxieties/ crisis, while, in intervention, it aims to achieve the internal-ontological spiritual rebalancing/ rehabilitation through spiritual growth and emancipation/ empowerment – solutions very useful in the practice with clients with depression and anxiety, with problems of adaptation and social integration, but also in the practice with clients with great problems of personal and human FULFILLMENT (Deurzen and Kenward, 2005).

One of the most important goal of the existential (perso)therapy and (perso)counseling is that to determine the clients to find meanings, suports and purposes in their souls, selves, in their lives and destines.

TRANSPERSONAL AND SPIRITUAL PSYCHOTHERAPY

Transpersonal and spiritual psychotherapy seeks to explore and capitalize the profound and complex levels of the client's personality and consciousness, representing the person in general as a cumulation/ overlapping of (human and spiritual) personalities, persons and universal, ancestral or even, in some interpretations, cosmic "entities" and "values" (D.H. Lajoie & S. I. Shapiro, 1992).

In transpersonal psychotherapy are used especially terms, concepts, ideas as spiritual, transhuman and transpersonal development, spiritual and human self-development, systemic trance, spiritual crises, etc.

Regarding the specifics of this kind of therapy the authors and therapists emphasize that its goals include both traditional outcomes, such as symptom relief and behaviour change, as well as action at the transpersonal level, which may transcend psychodynamic issues.

One of the most important way of intervention in transpersonal and spiritual psychotherapy is the emancipation, empowerment and development of the client through its (re-) spiritualization and humanization, through spiritual and human/ humane empowerment and development (R. Walsh, F. Vaughan, 1993).

Even if is a very complex and difficult endeavor, the humanization, spiritualization and humane-spiritual (cosmic) integration of the person is described by the therapists, for some categories of clients, as miraculous solutions for many kinds of problems, sufferings, deviances, etc.

The therapeutic process of (re-) humanization and spiritualization starts from the observation that many of the people's disorders, sufferings, deviations and problems are caused or favored of some serious deficits of psychological-humane and spiritual development.

The therapeutic process begins, so, with what we could call spiritual-humanistic and psychological-transpersonal evaluation, that seeks to identify and diagnoses mostly the structural-functional and situational impairments of the customer relating its psychological-humane and spiritual and transpersonal development and beingness.

Therefore, the epistemological foundation of the evaluation in humanistic-spiritual and transpersonal perspective it is, actually, the representation of the client as "trans-human" personality, as spiritual, multi-dimensional, "multilayer" and transpersonal being.

That is why it is necessary the settlement, in the front-plan of the diagnostic panel, of the dysfunctional elements and deviations from a so-called normality in the transpersonal and spiritual development of the client as person and personality, with their main spheres, areas, dimensions - psychological-ontological, psychological-relational, axiological, praxeological, etc.

In the transpersonal-humanistic therapy the practitioner, through his complex and spiritual/ transpersonal personality, contributes crucially to the achievement of the humanistic established objectives, mostly those relating to the spiritual wellbeing of the client, to the reduction/ relieving the sufferings and anguishes, but also to those concerning the empowerment, autonomization, the social, socio-humane integration and adaptation in the community where the client lives.

Through his behavior, creativity and projectivity, the humanistic therapist works at the construction of a new (spiritual) *modus vivendi*, of some new (socio-human) behaviors of the customers, with humanistic-transpersonal and spiritual tools and methods.

So, with methods and behaviors of humanistic-ontological type, the therapist performs changes and re-modelings of the current psychological-spiritual, social, cultural and psychosocial situation of the client, changes and improvements in the concrete situations of depersonalization and dehumanization, in the individual and collective situations of transpersonal-existential impasses and crisis, in the client' situations of loss of the spiritual meaning in his life, and, so, to fulfill, also with the transpersonal and spiritual resources of the therapist's personality, especially through (re-) humanization and (re-) spiritualization, the constitutional objectives of the transpersonal and spiritual psychotherapy.

In this respect it is presumable that the importance of the transpersonal and spiritual qualities of the therapist to increase, the results following to highlights, especially in enhancing the activity effectiveness and achieving the objectives, where the role of these resources and qualities of the therapist to imposes almost decisive (D.H. Lajoie & S. I. Shapiro, 1992).

The researches and clinical evidences indicates that, in all the areas of the social and therapeutic practices, spirituality and humanity are some innate human capability, resource of the practitioners and clients that can be used to increase the efficiency in both the psychological-spiritual and the integrative, prosocial objectives.

In transpersonal and spiritual psychotherapy the efficiency is high especially when it is considered the direct assistential/ therapeutic relationship between the therapist and the client.

So, the therapist, with the spiritual, transpersonal capacity of his personality and behavior succeeds to have a greater efficiency, both in the objectives involving the welfare and happiness of the client, as well as in those pursuing his empowerment, autonomization, socio-human integration.

The level of development of the spiritual-empathetic capacity/ qualities of the professional, in any philosophy or theoretical orientation, form, doctrine of therapy, represents essential predictors of effectiveness and FULFILLMENT of the objectives, the more in humanistic therapy, where this quality/ resource of the professional exceeds the original psychosocial meaning, instituting so as a core value of the efficiency in practice.

The reason is that, in the humanistic therapy practice by means of the empathetic-spiritual resources of their own personality, the professional can engage most effective the resources for spiritual, eudaimonical and social rehabilitation of the customer's personality. Spiritual, eudaimonical and social rehabilitation being core objectives and efficiency indicators of this important path of therapy (R. Anderson, 2011; D.H. Lajoie & S. I. Shapiro, 1992).

Therefore, regarding the importance of spirituality and virtue, as qualities of the professional's personality in activity effectiveness and achieving the objectives, this is given by the fact that the relationship with the client is not objectual but "spiritual", and very complex, and therefore the dominant resources involved must be of this nature.

It is, so, impossible to imagine professional efficiency, in the jobs that involve working with people in need and suffering, without spirituality, virtue, culture, with the soulful welfare and happiness state that it determines. The professionalism, in working with people, being so strongly conditioned by the level of general personal and human development, including the degree of spirituality and charisma/ virtue of the person who provide social services.

At the professionals with developed spiritual personality the spiritual sensibility and virtue will be imposed as main factors of organization and holistic adjustment of the humanistic professional behavior, becoming a crucial attribute/ source of prosocial action and effective professional practice; without virtue and spirituality the professional being under the dominion of selfishness, impulsiveness, personal undeveloped, laziness, lack of involvement, inactivity, inefficient professional behavior, dominating the defensive behaviors and non-involvement (R. Anderson, 2011).

That is one of the reasons why the therapist's virtue and spirituality becomes, in transpersonal and spiritual psychotherapy, important sources of efficiency and achievement of the assumed humanistic objectives, of psychological and social change, rehabilitation and empowerment of the people in need or suffering, of the clients (R. Walsh, F. Vaughan, 1993).

POSITIVE PSYCHOTHERAPY

Essentially, the positive psychotherapy, in evaluation and intervention, starts from the premise that human beings are often, perhaps more often, drawn by the future than they are driven by the past, using in therapeutic process of intervention especially the inner psychological-eudaimonical resources of the client, but also of the psychotherapist (Seligman and Csikszentmihaly, 2000).

Regarding the aspect of efficiency in positive psychotherapy, for example in the therapeutic work with clients in suffering, especially in the activities that involve children, elderly and persons with disabilities, the studies conclude that the efficiency, the success of intervention is strongly conditioned by the degree of happiness, enthusiasm, energy, optimism and personal charisma of the therapist.

The achievement of therapeutic goals in positive psychotherapy and counseling is so, among others, correlated with the therapist and clients's positive attitudes towards the life, with the degree of internal psychological relaxation, the irony and the personal happiness (Seligman, 2002), qualities and resources that need to be identified, promoted and developed both at the client's level but also at the therapist's level.

Therefore, more broadly, the positive psychotherapy and counseling use, in assessment and intervention, terms, ideas and resources as:

- positive emotions;

- orientation of the intervention to the future;

- the use and determination of positive experiences;

- positive expectation;

- psychological wellbeing and happiness;

- the use and determination of positive relationships;

- positive institutions;

- love, attachment, appreciation, empathy;

- states of pleasure or flow;

- values, strengths, virtues, talents, etc. (Seligman and Csikszentmihalyi, 2000; Seligman, 2002).

Concluding, essentially, the core idea of positive psychotherapy and counseling is that, in practice, the therapist and counselor aim to increase the positive feelings, the happiness, the psychological wellbeing, but also the positive behaviors and relationships, to increase also the positive cognitions but also the positive expectations, as opposed to focusing on the negative thoughts and expectations, and dysfunctional behaviors and relationships.

Interpreting the positive psychotherapy through the humanistic persotherapy perspective, the humanistic ontological theory/ paradigm of the person/ client, is important to take the clients' psychological-eudaimonical experience seriously, because these are an important means for helping and healing, by finding their spiritual/humane-eudaimonical resources, in their souls, in their humane and spiritual personality.

GESTALT THERAPY AND GROUP THERAPY

As was stated in theory and especially in practice the **Gestalt Therapy** proposes/ involves the achievement of the convergence between consciousness, experience and behavior, between the person and environment, "between the figure and the background", "here and now", from a holistic philosophical perspective. So, this kind of therapy emphases the importance, for the client, of being aware of what it is *here and now*, and accepting the responsibility for his situation, in its psycho-social environment (Wheeler, 1991, p. 65).

Going forward, and interpreting the gestalt therapy in the humanistic personology – the humanistic ontological theory/ paradigm of the person/ client's perspective we say that the gestalt therapy proposes/ involves the achievement of the convergence between the client's psychological-ontological sphere, soul, humane personality, consciousness, experience and behavior, between the person's humane personality and the compathetic community, "between the figure and background", "here and now", from a holistic philosophical-ontological and humanistic perspective.

So, the gestalt therapy in humanistic personology – the humanistic ontological theory/ paradigm of the person/ client, emphases the importance, for the client, of being aware of what is its spiritual and humane situation and state *here and now*, and accepting the responsibility for his psychological-ontological, spiritual, humane situation, in its psycho-social compathetic environment.

In the **Group Therapies**, the humanistic-ontological theory/ paradigm of the person, the group is not represented as a simple bunch of persons in difficulty, but it is formed gradually as an elevated cultural, spiritual and human environment, healer compathetic/ humane community by the unimaginable force that generates the emergence/ conmergence of the spiritual, humane energies involved.

INSTEAD
OF CONCLUSIONS

**THE INTRODUCTORY SECTIONS
OF THE SUBCHAPTERS 271**

**THE INTRODUCTORY SECTIONS
OF THE CHAPTERS 287**

THE INTRODUCTORY SECTIONS OF THE SUBCHAPTERS

Humanistic genetic personology could be defined as the theoretical domain/ discipline that researches, theorizes and represents the processes of formation of the person, of the human personality, in a complex and ideothetical manner, incorporating knowledge, ideas, theories from the humanistic-existentialist and spiritual-transpersonal spheres of thought/ philosophy and culture, from humanistic genetic psychology, humanistic sociology, and other disciplines, sciences and practices of humanistic orientation/ approach, developing, consequently, a multidisciplinary, interdisciplinary, and profound humane, spiritual and existential-positive perspective on the complexe, profound and unique process of formation, ontogenetical construction of the PERSON, theories, means, methods of theHumanistic personology,Humanistic genetic psychology, Positive psychology, Transpersonal psychology, Humanistic sociology, Existential philosophy, Cultural anthropology, etc.

The humanistic paradigm/ way of representation of the person and personality prioritizes the role of the self and of the ego, of the psychological-existential/ experiential, psychological-spiritual/ transpersonal and socio-humane factors, in combination with the ones concrete social, cultural, moral, etc., representing the process of **formation** *of the person as a successive and concomitant, emergent and imergent, phenomenological and ideothetical constructions of personal onto-formations, spheres, etc., and less as a simple activation and enabling of certain existing structures, of certain universal patterns (less variable), recognizing, therefore, the self-determination, the ontogenetical autonomy, the role of the subject, or the importance of some ideographical, imergent and emergent psychological-ontological constructions as the ego, the conscience, or the soul.*

In our ontological-humanistic paradigm of formation, beingness and functioning of the person/ personality - of the human being - we will speak, therefore, about characteristics, properties, processes, principles such as onto-formatization, persomization and promergence, emergence and imergence, transmergence and telegence, conmergence and sinmergence, about stages of evolution, formation, development, establishment of the personal ontological-psychological formations, of the person as a whole, such as of contact, of acquisition/ accumulation, of structuration/ centralization, of constitution/ holistization, of establishing/ networking, of ontification/ fulfillment, and about ontological-subjective humane and spiritual experiences that represent the main "substance", motivational-energetical sources and resorts of forming of the personality/ person's formations and spheres, driven in mechanisms and assemblies from where the formations are "fed", with genetic/ formative or functional/ existential purpose - some categories of experiences being destined, with a great accuracy, to certain formations.

In humanistic personology, in the humanistic representation of the person, we operate with the hypothesis that in the consolidated structure of the person the body, as distinct bio-physical entity and as biological organism, retains the functional autonomy and it constitutes their own humoral and neuro-psychic mechanisms of internal control/ regulation and of interaction with the environment, but a substantial dimension (edge) of the organism enters, directly or indirectly, in the process of personalization. The solution of cohabitation which is find by the organism it is a concession, compromise - by which, lastly, the organism "supports" the morpho-physiological personalization, with influences and changes on the majority biological systems and phenomena, in exchange for its survival. In this way they go further and develop mutually both the organism and the person/ personality (Million, 1990).

The contingent social-personal and socio-affective factors are crucial for the formation of the ontological-psychological sphere, while the cultural, morale conditions of learning and training are essential for the formation of the social-psychological sphere. The professional climate greatly influencing the formation of the person as a whole. Thus, in a purely humanistic perspective, the human-personal, the human-social factors are decisive in the formation and development of a strong, balanced, adaptable and happiness person. The psychological-human (humane) characteristics of the persons from near environment such as agreeability, soulful warmth, carefulness, empathy, spirituality, their constant presence and consistency, in human, spiritual and moral terms, the human quality of the interpersonal relationships, the compathy, the social relationships as humane relationships are the constitutional determinant factors that marks, crucially, the sense of the personality development, the sense of the person development, the adaptability, the soulful welfare, the happiness.

Each of the two major spheres of the person - the ontological-psychological sphere and the social-personal sphere - is conditioned and is, inter alia, the product, of the existence, beingness and functioning of the mind as a whole but also of the existence, beingness and functioning of certain mind substructures, formations, processes, etc. For example, in the processes of formation, beingness and functioning of the ontological-psychological sphere of the person more important are the sensations, memory and thinking, while in the processes of formation, beingness and functioning of the social-psychological sphere more important are some emergent upper structures as the noetic ontos, intellect, culture or the conscience/ comscience.

In humanistic personology, according to our opinion, transmergence represents the property and capacity of the personal onto-subjective, bio-psychological, and noetical-spiritual processes and phenomena to carry out without limitations and physical barriers of space and organization. According to these properties/ laws/ principles the processes of formation, establishment and functioning of the onto-formations, persoms, spheres, etc. transcend the structures, the organizations, and the entities already constituted, it attract and involve them in the processes of forming, constituting and establishing of the new formations, without altering them. The degree of freedom/ action is very large, the number of combinations and the facilities of organization, structuration, "formatization" and "persomization" being almost unlimited. This property/ law is explained, in part, by the structural, generic, and genetic unity/ cohesion of the living and spiritual world, the multiplication at infinit of the informational/ spiritual systems/ entities, and through the extraordinary quality of the living, psychological, noetic and spiritual environments, systems to permit the transcendence.

The transition to the stage of formation, constitution/ holistization, as formation, persom, person, etc., is essentially conditioned, among others, by the appearance, imposing of a new "nature". It is about, for exemple, of the ancestral leap from the biological to the psychological or human nature/ level, from the material or biological formations to the spiritual, human formations. In the global processes of personalization, now is carried out the jump from structure to system, from organism + personality + environment to (=) person as a whole, as unique, individual human being. An important role they meet processes and mechanisms such as the feed-back, feed-before, etc. In this stage occurs, including by means of these processes and mechanisms, a consistent symbiosis personality-community - it is the point from where, properly, one can speak of person, of social and relatively autonomous human being.

The ontological-psychological subjective human/ humane and spiritual experiences represent the main "substance", motivational sources and resorts, driven in mechanisms and assemblies from where the formations are "feed", with genetic/ formative or functional/ existential purposes. In this sense, we believe that some categories of experiences are destined, with a great accuracy, to certain formations, persoms, spheres, structures, etc., also, we believe that one can speak of experiences with polyvalent motivational-energetic qualities/ valances/ functions, so motivational-ontological sources for more formations or assemblies, or for formation, beingness and functioning of the personality, or of the person as a whole, as individual in relation.

The promergence and the dismergence are opposite ontological-procesual properties, qualities of the processes and phenomena of formatization, persomization and personalization, of the processes of construction or development of the formations, persoms, structures, spheres, reflecting the objective-emergent tendencies of the living and spiritual systems of conservation, development, growing, or entropy, degradation, decrease. At any moment a number of formations, dimensions or processes are in trends of growing, advancement, formation, are promergent, and others are in degradation decline, involution, are dismergent.Both the formation and the beingness/ functioning of every formation, person, structure, sphere, of the personality and the person as a whole are cucially determined by the predominance and the intensity of the promergence, by the promergent processes, by the positive tendencies of conservation, development, growing, progress.

In any moment a number of formations, dimensions or processes are in growing, advancement, forming, are promergent, and others are in degradation decline, involution, are dismergent; both the formation and the beingness/ functioning of every formation, person, sphere, of the personality and the person as a whole being crucially determined by the predominance and the intensity of the promergence, of the promergent processes, the humane and spiritual experiences representing the main "substance", motivational sources/ resources and positive factors of promergence, of the promergent/ functional processes, of the process of personalization.

The unicity of the person, and of the process of personalization, is given both by the genetic inherited biological characteristics, result of the phylogenetic evolution, as well as by the environmental characteristics of the ontogenetic process, but important roles have also some factors which are related to the subjective-metaphysical indeterminism, to the free will, the learning trial-error mechanism, to the world of ego, of will, to the abyssal world of the spirit and subjectivity, to the interior energy and resorts of great depthness and complexity, that determine us to consider the ontogenetical process of formation of the person as unpredictable and never ended, and the person as never perfect, identical with himself or with the social role that it meets.

Each of the three major areas of the soul - affective (social), spiritual, and humane - is the product of the interaction of the subject with specific factors, even if cannot be traced strict boundaries between them. The contingent social-personal and socio-affective factors are crucial for the formation of the affective (social) soul, the cultural conditions of learning and training the spiritual abilities and sensibility are essential for the formation of spiritual soul, while the altruistic, solidaristic, humanitarian, morale climate greatly influences the formation of the humane soul. Thus, in a purely humanistic perspective, the human-personal, the human-social factors are decisive in the formation and development of the person's soul.

Finally, involving the two main orientations, existential-positive and spiritual-humane, a mature person and a fully functioning person may be described as a result of his/her developing at a higher level, the most high, the most close to the condition of human being as an autonomous social and rational existence, with its characteristical attributes - personal development, adaptability and efficiency, but also as personality structured through soul, self, conscience, character, motivation, skills, etc. so that determines conducts oriented towards the wellbeing of the generalized other, towards the common good, to humanity, and dominant traits such as empathy, altruism, generosity, humanness, etc.

Very important is the "weight" that has one or other of the soul's spheres in its architecture, in the beingness and functioning of the soul as a whole, as extended part of the personal ontos, but as well of the person as awhole. For example, the more pronounced development of the affective (social/ personal) soul will profile a personal structure oriented predominantly to the jouissance/ good of the dear, close people, the development more pronounced of the spiritual soul will orient the personal assembly towards a development, as the case, of artistic, mystical, scientific type, while a great development of the humane soul will imprint to the person's personality and behavior features such as altruism, empathy, humanism, etc.

The person, after the ontogenetical construction of its constitutional formations as the personal ontos, the soul, the ego, the conscience, character, personality, etc, and after completing the two major sub-processes, and establishing the two macro-spheres - the ontological-psychological sphere and the social-personal sphere, will be, largely, a new construction, not only an ensemble/ collection of formations or the overlapping, the coexistence of the two sub-spheres. Thus, we may speak, also, about a third process, and a third sphere, a mega-, pan-sphere, where all the formations, the two sub-processes and spheres will merge, unify, leading to what will be, ultimately, a certain human individual, a social human being, a personality, a PERSON.

Despite appearances, the ontological-psychological sphere of the person is not a simple extension. product or emanation of the existence and functioning of the body; it exists in the general context of the personal structure, economy and functioning under the influence/ determination of the environmental factors, in the conditions of the internal action of the emergence, transmergence, telegence, sinmergence, conmergence, imergence principles/ laws/ properties; it could be represented also as a distemporalized space and, relatively, protected of the action of the laws so-called objective (mechanical), the biological and psychological elements and structures can be easily translated noetically, spiritually or sympathetically, and vice-versa, the possibilities of transformation and combination becoming practically limitless. The ontological-psychological sphere is the place, the framework, the source, the environment, the premise of forming and beingness of some of the most important formations and constitutional spheres of the person, especially of the soul and the ego; the soul, as experiential "internalizing" of the other (person, value etc.), and the ego as experiential "internalization" of the ontic and social self, also of its constitutional sub-formations such as the hedonic ontos, the phobic ontos-formation, the projective ontos, the prosentic ontos-formation, and the malsentic ontos-formation.

In the complex and profound process of personal ontosfication. the role of the mind is, along the inner activity and jouissance of the organism, very important, especially the role of memory, thinking and imagination, intellect and intelligence, but, in extension, also, of some emergent upper structures as the noetic ontos or consciousness. These operate with more advanced tools, more developed and more personalized, conditioning, crucially, through feedback, the process of ontosfication. A crucial role in process has the environment, especially the socio-human and cultural conditions where lives, cohabits, currently, the subject. In humanistic personology, even if in the child rearing are important the material conditions, the HUMAN conditions are, in fact, those that contribute crucially to the formation of the personal ontos, to the process of ontosfication, of forming a harmonious personality, fulfilled and, socio-humanly, effective. The experiential contingent social-personal and socio-affective factors are, also, crucial for the formation of the personal ontos.

The interaction with the other real person, dear, with the nearest persons, significant group, with the near physical environment leads to the formation of the affective (social) soul, and to the personal system of attachments. Reflects the personal contingent interaction, and appurtenance of the person to the group or to the particular social context. The interaction with the world of spirit, culture, education, art, etc., leads, by the mental capacity of idealization, projectivity and symbolization, to the formation of the spiritual soul, to virtue and spirituality as personal qualities. The interaction with the symbolic, universal, generalized, concept other, with the "status" other, by mental facilities of the generalization, idealization, projectivity and symbolization, abstractization leads to the formation of the humane soul and to the empathy, empathetic capacity of the person. Reflects the abstract interaction and affiliation of the person to society, humanity, and his human condition and nature.

The formation of the ego, and the individualization of the process of personalization does not mean a simple counterbalance or manifestation of the biological, instinctual forces of the self and of the ontic subject, but also means a personal marking of the humanizing processes; moreover, also those formations, resorts, forces that we represent as belonging to individuality are re-dimensioned and enriched through the incorporation of the spiritual, cultural, moral and human acquisitions.

The soul itself, as resort and constitutional source of the spiritual and humane qualities of the person, cannot be expressed in conduct/ behavior than by means of some holistic and relational structures and spheres of the character and personality such as the humane character. The humane (prosocial, moral) character is a holistic personality structure through which are formed and crystallized the personal features relating to the common good and jouissance, to all people, where these personal features are stated as constant personal qualities of conduct. Regarding the role of the humane character, its formation and establishment as structural formation of personality will lead, with the contribution of the humane conscience, to the metamorphosis of the person's humane and spiritual resources in humanistic, prosocial, altruistic attitudes and conducts.

As is well known, very important in the process of conscience forming are the culture, religion, morals, and education. In process these bring simultaneously spiritual, ontological and axiological input, mainly through their systems of values, beliefs and ideals. Through the formation of the (social) conscience takes place not only simple constructions of a news psychological-personal and behavioral formations, but also takes place complex, deep and global processes of "conscientization" and adaptation of the person, of the process of personalization, the person becomes socio-humanly able, and aware of its own situation, condition and of its ontogenetic processes, as well as of autonomization - in relation to itself and in relation to the environmental factors.

In the process of formation of character participate, dialectically, inter alia, the personal ontos, the soul, the mind/ intellect and the conscience, especially through comscience, determining, in the context of action of the ambiental social-moral and cultural-ethical factors, ample phenomena of ethical-socialization, culturalization, and humanization, essential for the processes of psychological-ethical structuring and holistic organization of the personality, and the person as a whole, of ethical superization of the feelings and behaviors, of the internal ethical constitution relating to the ancestral anthropo-generical human-psychological model, of the internal personal-psychological representation of the contemporary ethical model of person, specific psychological-moral configuration, characteristic for the community members where the person grows, lives.

The ontological-humanistic perspective, the theoretical-axiological basis of which we approach in this work, promotes the model of a humanistic competencies, skills and conducts that prioritizes the role and importance of some socio-cultural and contextual-moral factors such as the systems of moral and humane values, the socio-moral/ humane relationships of attachment, empathy/ compathy, the cultural and spiritual quality of interpersonal relationships, addressed at singular mode, but also in community context, the community, the family, in special, being, therefore, an important formative factor.

From a humanistic-ontological perspective, a mature person, a human dedicated to the common good, the good of mankind, incorporates, in sublime manner, both spiritual/ humane competencies of role-status and also concrete humane behaviors and activities, thus ensuring, besides a consistent internal spiritual/ humane personal functionality, an high external humane personal functionality. Qualities such as altruism, empathy, optimism, perseverance, idealism, faith, balance, positive thinking, moral power, pure consciousness, self-control, tolerance, soulfulness, cheerfulness, creativity, desirelessness, devotion, endurance, virtuous energy, enthusiasm and more are defining characteristics both of a humane, but by result, of a mature and autonomous person.

In the humanistic-ontological paradigm, which we use in this paper, the completion and the fulfillment of the process of personalization through ontification, does not concern only the mere adaptation and mechanical social integration of the subject but concerns also issues of subjective-eudaimonical or ontological-psychological order. The goal of the process of personalization, from this point of view, is that the person to reach to be fulfilled, humanly and personally, happy, of course, primarily through social affirmation/ achievement, stage where, therefore, the person is fulfilled in psychological-human and psychological-ontological terms, characterized by balance, complacency, self-acceptance, but also by high degree of self-control (Waldrop, 1993; Erikson &, Erikson, 1998; Bickhard, 2012). After crossing these phases are accomplished so the both processes, of proper personalization, as we call it in the paper, of forming of the person as a social being, as well as the overall process of personalization, of forming as a human (personality) and social being - as a PERSON.

In a general way, the soul, with all its areas and components, is the place and central source of the humane jouissance. Therefore, if in the case of the body, of the senses, instinct's jouissance we talk about libido and pleasure, in the case of the soul's jouissance we talk about eudaimonia and happiness, while in the case of the humane soul's eudaimonia of happiness through the other, or altruistic happiness and jouisance. There is, also, an altruistic eudaimonia of the spiritual soul, and an altruistic and spiritual eudaimonia of the self/ ego.

In the complex and profound phenomenon of beingnes and functioning of the person/ personality participate many inner, biological, sensorial, psychological, spiritual mechanisms, resorts. In this sense, all the onto-personal mechanisms probably conditionate, largely, the promergence and the imergence, the processual internal beingness of the person. There may be also many ontic-psychological mechanisms of production of existential sense and prontos, of transformation of the emotions, of the subjective experiences in prontos and resorts for beingness, for a high consistency and continuity of the "being". At the base of the processes standing innumerable mechanisms, montages, motivational sources and resorts, internal ontos-formative loops that "work" in infinite combinations to assure continuity, subjective existential meanings and the internal beingness of the person.

The socio-human adaptation and integration of the person is much more than a simple social/ professional structural-functional integration into a collective, organization, community, group, it is also a compathetical integration among humans, beings with souls, emotions, feelings, sufferings, happinesses, loves, tragedies, etc. This is the concrete, human world where integrates and lives the person. That is why there are essential features of the humane personality such as empathetic capacity, spiritual well-being, personal/ humane development, selflessness, intelligence, culture, idealism, humanistic vision, or features of behavior such as agreeability, tolerance, kindness, compassion, playfulness, cheerfulness, sociability.

In this context, one can speak also about human fulfillment and happiness of the person, through individual human development and by assuming of certain goals and ideals congruent with those of the community in which it lives. The humanistic-ontological personology joins thus the efforts of displacement the focus from the quantitative approach to the one qualitative/ intensive in the motivational-eudaimonical representation of the person (including of the professional), addressed, therefore, not so instrumental or symbolic, but by attributes relative to the quality of human being such as: personal fulfillment through humane development, plenary personality, happiness through the happiness of all and the common good, professional happiness, etc.

The therapeutic process begins, so, with what we could call spiritual-humanistic and psychological-transpersonal evaluation, that seeks to identify and diagnoses mostly the structural-functional and situational impairments of the customer relating its psychological-humane and spiritual development and beingness. In the spiritual-humanistic therapy the practitioner, through his complex and spiritual/ transpersonal personality, contributes crucially to the achievement of the humanistic established objectives, mostly those relating to the spiritual wellbeing of the client, to the reduction/ relieving the sufferings and anguishes, but also to those concerning the empowerment, autonomization, the social, socio-humane integration and adaptation in the community where the client lives.

THE INTRODUCTORY SECTIONS OF THE CHAPTERS

The humanistic paradigm/ way of representation of the person and personality prioritizes the role of the self and of the ego, of the psychological-existential/ experiential, psychological-spiritual/ transpersonal and socio-*humane* factors, in combination with the ones concrete social, cultural, moral factors, representing the process of **formation** of the person as a successive and concomitant, emergent and imergent, phenomenological and ideothetical constructions of personal onto-formations, spheres, etc., and less as a simple activation and enabling of certain existing structures, of certain universal patterns (less variable), recognizing, therefore, the self-determination, the ontogenetical autonomy, the role of the subject, or the importance of some ideographical, imergent and emergent psychological-ontological constructions as the ego, the conscience, or the soul.

Crucial there are, so, in the process of **formation** and **development**, in **the structure/ structuration** and **the beingness/ functioning** of the person/ personality, the unique subjective experiences of the subject, the feelings, the emotions or the ontological ego and the free will, the existential and the psychological-spiritual factors/ formations (especially the ego and the soul – affective, spiritual, humane), the self-generative internal dynamics, through culturalization and humanization, through emergence and superization, through spiritual/ human generalization/ abstraction of the psychological-compathetical (socio-humane) subjective experiences.

***

Even if, in the ontogenetic process of formation of the most important formations, spheres, persoms of the person and personality, are very important the body/ organism, the mind (intellect/ intelligence), the social-economic, material conditions, still, in humanistic perspective,

287

the human/ humane conditions are, in fact, those that contribute crucially to the formation of a harmonious personality, of a strong person, fulfilled and, socio-humanly, effective, adaptable and happy.

Each of the two major spheres of the person is the product of the interaction of the subject with specific factors, even if cannot be traced strict boundaries between them. The contingent-experiential social-personal and socio-affective factors are crucial for the formation of the ontological-psychological sphere, while the cultural, moral, professional conditions of learning, training and working are essential for the formation of the social-personal/ psychological-social sphere. Thus, in a purely humanistic perspective, the human-personal, the human-social, and the human-cultural factors are decisive in the formation and development of a strong, balanced, adaptable and authentic happiness person.

So regarding the formation of the most important formations, spheres, persoms, of the personality and the person as a whole, must to be highlighted, firstly, the crucial contribution of the psychosocial and socio-human/ humane environmental factors.

The essence of the humanistic-ontological conception regarding the person/ the human personality is given by the idea that these are ontological/ ontogenetical products of some gradual and stadial processes held with the crucial contribution of the concrete/ contextual/ contingent socio-human factors where the person grows and lives, mainly the *personal*-human/ humane factors, with the crucial contribution of the individual persons, concrete people from the proximate environment with intense and constant psychological (emotional) and spiritual presence and influence, especially the significant members from its family/ significant group. Important are also the socio-cultural factors.

Of course, as was mentioned, very important are also the contributions of the mind (of the memory, thinking and imagination, intellect and intelligence, of the noetic ontos), or of the conscience; the latter operating with more advanced tools, more developed and more personalized, conditioning, crucially, through feedback, the process of personalization. Very important are also the contributions of the biological/ organic factors (the nervous central system, the humoral and neuro-psychic mechanisms, the neuro-vegetative system, etc.).

***

The formation, beingness, functioning and development of any living being imply, obligatory, some processes, laws, and characteristics, as well as some energies, mechanisms, resorts which support, feed, determine, facilitate both its formation as well its beingness, functioning and development. These characteristics are extremely important and relevant in the case of the *human* beings, in the context of formation and functioning of some specific very complex formations, spheres, persoms, or of the person/ personality as a whole.

So, in contrast to the processes of formation, to the laws, stages and the energetic resorts from the inorganic physical world level the processes of formation, the laws, the steps and the energetic resorts from the organic, psychological, or spiritual world level are of infinite complexity, these transcend the contingent, entail the past and the future, exceeding the spatial and temporal limitations, working simultaneously in the same "space", having unpredictable evolutions, arising, emerging, randomly, some from others.

However, despite appearances, these processes, laws, stages, and resorts are, in our opinion, normal, natural dimensions, valences, properties of the objective existence, do not originate and do not belong to another (parallel, metaphysical) world, but, still, these must to be understood, modeled in a scientific-epistemological framework much wider and dialectical way than permit the rules of the sciences of physicist type, applied, often, almost mechanically to the biological, psychological, and spiritual processes and phenomena.

In our ontological-humanistic paradigm of formation, beingness and functioning of the person/ personality, of the individual human being, we will talk so about characteristics, properties, processes, principles such as onto-formatization and persomization, promergence and dismergence, emergence and imergence, transmergence and telegence, conmergence and sinmergence, about stages of the evolution, development, establishment of the personal ontological-psychological formations, of the persoms, of the person as a whole, such as of contact, of acquisition/ accumulation, of structuration/ centralization, of constitution/ holistization, of establishing/ networking, of ontification/ FULFILLMENT, and about psychological-ontological-subjective human and spiritual experiences and jouissances that represent the main "substance", motivational-energetical sources and resorts of forming of the personality/ person's formations, persoms and spheres, motivational-energetical sources and resorts from where these are "feed", with genetic/ formative or functional/ existential purposes and energies. Some categories of experiences and jouissances being destined, with a great accuracy, to certain formations, persons, spheres, or to the personality or the person as a whole.

***

In humanistic perspective, even if are also important the economic, material conditions, *the socio-personal, the human/ humane,* and *the cultural conditions* are, in fact, those that contribute crucially to the process of personalization, to the formation of soul, ego, personality, to the formation of the person as human being, those that have the determinative contribution in the psychological-ontogenetical process of spiritualization and humanisation, those that contribute, consequently, at forming of a harmonious and developed, ontological-psychologically and socio-humanly, personality/ person.

Each of the major spheres and formations of the person/ personality is, in great measure, the product of the interaction with specific human, social, cultural, moral factors, even if cannot be traced strict boundaries between them. Thus, in a purely humanistic perspective, the human-personal and the human-social factors are decisive in the formation and development of the person as a whole, in the process of *human/ humane* personalization, thtough the two great sub-processes, of formation of the ontological-psychological sphere and of the social-personal/ psychological-social sphere. The formation of the ontological-psychological sphere, of the (ontological) personality, is done especially during childhood and adolescence, while of the social-personal/ psychological-social sphere, of the person, is done especially together with, and after, the subject acquires social autonomy, profession, its own family etc.

The formation of the ontological-psychological sphere, of the (ontological) personality includes mainly the formation of the personal ontos, soul, and ego/self, while the formation of the ontological-psychological sphere implies the ontogenetical construction of the (social) conscience comscience, culture, the humane conscience), the character, and the (social) competences, skills, abilities, qualities and habitudes, through processes as ontosfication, spiritualization, individualization, holistization/ persomization, socialization, autonomization etc. All, therefore, as sub-processes of the general, teleological process of personalization.

***

In the humanistic-ontological paradigm, which we use, largely, in this paper, the completion and the FULFILLMENT of the process of personalization does not lead only to the mere adaptation and mechanical social integration of the person but concerns, especially, the establishment of, what can be named, *the mature person*, and *the fully functioning person*, as the main target of the ontogenetic process of formation and development with characteristics such as:

- Personal and human development;

- High degree of awareness, of self-knowledge and self-esteem (Maslow, 2011);

- High socio-emotional development, high control of the emotions;

- Emotional intelligence (Erikson, 1998);

- Realism and balance, powerful will, resistance to failure and frustrations;

- Moral development, professional development;

- Personal and social autonomy, mature personality, adaptability (Rogers, 1980);

- Interpersonal development (Erikson, 1998);

- Live with integrity;

- Responsibility;

- Flexibilility and openness to learning and to new experiences, etc.

***

Crucial there are in the process of formation and structuration of the person's ontological-psychological sphere the unique subjective experiences of the subject, the feelings, the emotions or the ontological ego and the free will, the psychological-spiritual factors/ formation (especially the soul – affective, spiritual, humane), the self-generative internal dynamics, through culturalization and humanization, through emergence and superization, through spiritual/ human generalization/ abstraction of the psychological-compathetic (socio-humane) subjective experience.

In the spirit of the emergent systems theory (which involves, among others, the chaos theory and the complex systems theory) regarding the formation of the personality a whole, of the human being, but also of the ontological-psychological sphere we speak about characteristics, properties, processes, principles such as onto-formatization, persomization and promergence, emergence and imergence, transmergence and telegence, conmergence and sinmergence, and about ontological stages of evolution, development, establishment of the personal ontological-psychological formations, of the person as a whole, such as of contact, of acquisition/ accumulation, of structuration/ centralization, of constitution/ holistization, of establishing/ networking, of ontification/ FULFILLMENT.

In the light of the emergent systems theory's principles the processes of formation of the person/ personality, in humanistic personology – the ontological-humanistic perspective, make possible the appearance of new entities, structures, properties, etc. from the previous ones, defined as sources, factors, premises, (pre-)conditions, the processes being based mainly on the dynamic, transmergent, telegent, imergent, conmergent and sinmergent interaction of the existing entities, on its intrinsic law-like developmental and transformative properties, manifested in the context of the specific environmental processes and phenomena, as well as of the systems which the subject belongs.

According to the emergent systems theory the resulting entities incorporate features of the *source-entities* but are presented yet as new existences, with them own features and ways of relating, adapted also to an environmental context, in turn, usually reformed.

The processes take place, largely, without limitations and physical barriers of space and organization, transcending the structures, the organizations, and the entities already constituted, attracting and involving them in the processes of forming, constituting and establishing of the new formations, without altering them.

In humanistic personology, the ontological-humanistic perspective on the process of forming of the person/ personality the degree of freedom/ action is very large, the number of combinations and the facilities of structuration and formatization being almost unlimited; one of the most important explanation is given by the fact that in the emergent and complex systems the processes have the extraordinary quality to permit the transcendence and the multiplication to infinit to the informational/ spiritual entities, taking place without time limitations and barriers, by the fact/ explanation that in the emergent and complex systems the processes have the tendency to organize and concentrate them "thematically" in formations, persoms, structures, spheres etc., reflecting the inherence, the objective necessity of some functions, beyond any limitations of "logistic" or temporal order, by the fact that the entities coexist, simultaneously, in the same personal "space", the functioning and beingness of some distinct entities, structures, relationships, processes on/ through the same material, biological, informational, spiritual support, framework.

At any moment a number of formations, dimensions or processes are in growing, advancement, forming, are promergent, and others are in degradation decline, involution (Bickhard, 2012), are dismergent; both the formation and the beingness/ functioning of every formation, person, sphere, of the personality and the person as a whole being crucially determined by the predominance and the intensity of the promergence, of the promergent processes, the humane and spiritual experiences representing the main "substance", motivational sources/ resources and positive factors of promergence, of the promergent/ functional processes.

The humane and spiritual experiences and the promergent processes are involved in complex, emergent, dynamic mechanisms and entities, every formation, persom, personality, the person as a whole being so a product of the ontogenetical incorporation, union, synthesis, of the conmergent, emergent, transmergent unitary organization of the sub-entities/ formations, structures, energies, mechanisms, of the processes of organization in new structures, formative entities, formations, persoms, usually upper structurally and axiologically.

Finally, as result of the global process of personalization, of the processes of ontosfication, spiritualization, individualization, persomization/ holistisation, autonomization, the person, as a whole, incorporates, unifies, synthesizes, emergently, conmergently, transmergently in a unitary organization the formations, energies, mechanisms, the processes, structures and constructions on the global/ maximal level, forming a holistic entity, with unique characteristics, qualities and conducts; in humanistic personology, the ontological-humanistic perspective on the person, very important being its humanistic/ humane and spiritual dimensions/ valences/ contents.

All, as we see, therefore, begins, personologically, in ontogenesis, with the process of formation of ontological-psychological sphere, and especially of the personal ontos, with the complex and miraculous process of ontosfication.

***

In the ontogenetic process of formation of the pshychological-social/ relational sphere of the person participate, dialectically, inter alia, the personal ontos, the soul, the mind/ intellect and the conscience, especially through comscience, determining, in the context of action of the ambiental social-moral and cultural-ethical factors, ample phenomena of ethical-socialization, culturalization, and humanization, essential for the processes of psychological-ethical structuring and holistic organization of the personality, and the person as a whole, of ethical superization of the feelings and behaviors, of the internal ethical constitution relating to the ancestral anthropo-generical human-psychological model, of the internal personal-psychological representation of the contemporary ethical model of person, specific psychological-moral configuration, characteristical for the community where the person grows, lives. Still, even if in the process of formation of the pshychological-social/ relational sphere of the person are important the formal-institutional and format-cultural and ethical conditions the concrete experiential and ideothetical-phenomenological moral-human and socio-cultural conditions contribute crucially to its structuration and orientation.

***

The person, after the ontogenetical construction of its constitutional formations as the personal ontos, the soul, the ego, the conscience, character, personality, etc, and after completing the two major sub-processes, and establishing the two macro-spheres - the ontological-psychological sphere and the social-personal sphere, will be, largely, a new construction, not only an ensemble/ collection of formations or the overlapping, the coexistence of the two sub-spheres.

Thus, we may speak, also, about a third process, and a third sphere, a mega-, pan-sphere, where all the formations, the two sub-processes and spheres will merge, unify, leading to what will be, ultimately, a certain human individual, a social human being, a personality, a PERSON.

So, the person as a whole exists and acts, at maturity, through each formations, through the two great sub-spheres but also as a unitary sphere and system (Maslow, 2011), as a whole and as a distinct element in ontological and relational-social plan. Nevertheless, this construction is dynamic, evolutive, alive and always remain under the influence of the variable internal and external, subjective and objective factors.

***

The ontological-personological paradigm/ approach prioritizes the role and importance of the personal ontos, in the beingness and the functioning of the person/ personality, which as it was shown, could be considered *the being* of the person, and comprises, in its broad and comprehensive acceptation/ sphere, in our opinion, mainly, ontos-formations such as the hedonic ontos, the phobic ontos-formation, the projective ontos, the prosentic ontos-formation, and the malsentic ontos-formation, but also the soul and the ego, determining especially its humane and spiritual dimensions, valences, content.

Regarding the internal psychological-ontological bengness and functioning of the person/ personality it is closely determined and linked, inter alia, to the existence, action and interaction of two ontological-psychological poles, located in the extremes of the psychological-personal assembly, respectively *the hedonic-phobic* pole and *the projective-aspirational pole*. Each of the onto-formations of the two poles, *the hedonic ontos* and *the phobic onto-formation* - from the hedonic-phobic pole, and *the projective ontos* and *the aspirational/ideal ego* - from the projective-aspirational pole, operates with autonomous functional role but very important, too, is the psychological-ontological balances, levers, mechanisms, tensions/ conflicts that form and operate by their involvement and through their interactions, as well, each pole, the hedonic-phobic pole and the projective-aspirational pole, works/ functions autonomously but is also, in the same time, part of a trans- and pan-personal mega-balance, mega-mechanism, mega-conflict/ tension with very important role/ contribution in the internal general, global functioning, beingness and dinamics of the person/ personality.

In the complex and profound phenomenon of internal beingness and functioning of the person/ personality participate many inner motivational, eudaimonical, and energetical resorts, many biological, sensorial, psychological, spiritual mechanisms. In this sense, all the onto-personal mechanisms probably conditionate, largely, the promergence and the imergence, the processual internal beingness and functioning of the person. In humanistic-ontological/spiritual perspective very important being, also, theirs *humane and spiritual dimensions, valences and orientations.*

***

Humanistic genetic personology promotes both the realization/ fulfillment of the person as an individual, with the atribut of free will, personal well-being and happiness, but also the realization as a human, with the atribut of humanity, as human among humans, as human who through his personal fulfillment and happiness not undermines the fulfillment and the happiness of the others, the common interests of the community, but, on the contrary, through his individual fulfillment and happiness contributes to the fulfillment and happiness of the others, to the promotion, affirmation, fulfillment of certain humanistic values or higher social ideals. one can speak so of human fulfillment and happiness of the person through individual human development and by assuming of certain goals and ideals congruent with those of the community in which he daily lives.

REFERENCES

AND CONSULTED BIBLIOGRAPHY

Ainsworth, M.D.S., Blehar, M.C., Waters, E., Wall, S. (1978), *Patterns of Attachment: A Psychological Study of the Strange Situation.* Hillsdale, NJ: Lawrence Erlbaum Associates.

Allen, K.E, (2015), *Developmental Profiles: Pre-Birth Through Adolescence,* 8th Edition, Cengage Learning.

Allport, G.W. (1961), *Pattern and growth in personality,* New York: Holt, Rinehart &. Winston.

American Humane Association (2004), *Helping in Child Protective Services: A Competency-Based Casework Handbook,* Oxford University Press.

Andrieux, C. (1973), Perspectives nouvelles de recherche en personnologie. In: *L'année psychologique.* vol. 73, n°2. pp. 681-707.

Antony, M. (2008), *Shyness and Social Anxiety Workbook: Proven, Step-by-Step Techniques for Overcoming your Fear Pape,* Second Edition, New Harbinger Publications.

Aristotle, Robinson, D.N. (1999), *Aristotle's Psychology,* POLOS Ltd.

Arnet, J.J. (2011), *Human Development: A Cultural Approach,* Pearson.

Arts, W., Muffels, R., Meulen, R. (2001), *Solidarity in Health and Social Care in Europe* (Philosophy and Medicine), Kluwer Academic Publisher.

Ashcraft, D. (2014), *Personality Theories Workbook,* 6 Edition, Wadsworth Publishing.

Barlow, D.H. (2007), *Clinical Handbook of Psychological Disorders,* Fourth Edition: A Step-by-Step Treatment Manual (Barlow: Clinical Handbook of Psychological Disorders), The Guilford Press.

Bandura, A. (1975), *Social Learning & Personality Development,* NY: Holt, Rinehart & Winston, INC.

Bandura, A., Locke, A. E. (2003), Negative self-efficacy and goal effects revisited. *Journal of Applied Psychology.*

Barbara, M.H. (2012), *Emergence: The Shift from Ego to Essence,* Hampton Roads Publishing.

Batson, C.D. (2011), *Altruism in Humans.* New York: Oxford University Press.

Baumeister, B.R.F., Bushman, B.J. (2013), *Social Psychology and Human Nature,* Cengage Learning.

Bean, J.S. (2013), *Finding Real Love through God's Word (Relationship Guide for Women Seeking Soulmates),* Kindle Edition, Amazon Digital Services, Inc.

Beaumont, H., Cobb Jr., J.B. (2012), *Toward a Spiritual Psychotherapy: Soul as a Dimension of Experience,* North Atlantic Books.

Beck, U. (1992), *Risk Society - Towards a New Modernity,* London: Sage.

Benner , D.G. (2011), *Soulful Spirituality: Becoming Fully Alive and Deeply Human,* Brazos Press (March.

Berger, P.L., Luckmann, T. (1967), *The Social Construction of Reality: A Treatise in the Sociology of Knowledge,* Anchor.

Bergin, A.E. (2003), *Casebook for a Spiritual Strategy in Counseling and Psychotherapy,* Amer Psychological Assn.

Bergson, H. (2007), *Mind-Energy ,*Palgrave Macmillan

Berkowitz, N. (1996), *Humanistic Approaches to Health Care: Focus on Social Work (Social Work in a Changing World),* Venture Press.

Bickhard, M.H. (2012), The emergent ontology of persons. In: Jack Martin and Mark H. Bickhard (eds.) *The Psychology of Personhood.* pp. 165-180.

Biestek, F.P, Gehrig, C.C. (1978), *Client Self-Determination in Social Work,* Loyola Press.

Bounds, M. (2010), *Welfare Policy: Feminist Critiques,* Wipf & Stock Pub.

Bowling, D., Ho attachments ffman, D. (2003), *Bringing Peace Into the Room: How the Personal Qualities of the Mediator Impact the Process of Conflict Resolution,* Jossey-Bass.

Bowlby J. (1999), *Attachment. Attachment and Loss* (vol. 1) (2nd ed.), New York: Basic Books.R. Brown.

Briar, S., Miller, H. (1971), *Problems and Issues in Social Casework,* New York: Columbia University Press.

Buechler, S.M. (2008), *Critical Sociology,* Paradigm Publishers.

Burkitt, I. (1991), *Social selves: Theories of the social formation of personality,* Sage Publications, London.

Byers, S.C. (2012), Perception, Sensibility, and Moral Motivation in Augustine: A Stoic-Platonic Synthesis, Cambridge University Press.

Bywater, I. (2010), *Aristotelis Ethica Nicomachea* (Cambridge Library Collection - Classics) (Ancient Greek Edition), Cambridge University Press.

Canda, E.R., Furman, L.D. (2009), *Spiritual Diversity in Social Work Practice: The Heart of Helping,* Oxford University Press.

Castiello, J. (1936), *A Humane Psychology of Education.* New York: Sheed & Ward.

Chardin, P.T (1959), *The phenomenon of man,* New York: Harper and Row.

Chansky, T.E. (2008), *Freeing Your Child from Negative Thinking: Powerful, Practical Strategies to Build a Lifetime of Resilience, Flexibility, and Happiness,* Da Capo Lifelong Books.

Chelf, C.P. (1992), *Controversial Issues in Social Welfare Policy: Government and the Pursuit of Happiness (Controversial Issues in Public Policy),* SAGE Publications, Inc.

Cicchetti, D., Carlson, V. (1989), *Child Maltreatment: Theory and Research on the Causes and Consequences of Child Abuse and Neglect,* Cambridge University Press.

Cloke C., Davies M. (1995), *Participation and empowerment in Chid Protection,* London, Pitman.

Cojocaru, S. (2013), *Appreciative Inquiry in Social Work: Theories and practices,* LAP LAMBERT Academic Publishing.

Collins, D., Jordan, C., Coleman, H. (2010), *An Introduction to Family Social Work,* Belmont, Brooks/Cole.

Comte, A. (2004), *Catéchisme positiviste ou Sommaire exposition de la religion universelle,* Kindle Edition, EbooksLib.

Corey, G. (2012), *Theory and Practice of Counseling and Psychotherapy,* Cengage Learning.

Crisp, B.R., Beddoe, L. (2012), *Promoting Health and Well-being in Social Work Education*, Routledge.

Gilligan, P. and Furness, S. (2006), *The Role of Religion and Spirituality in Social Work Practice: views and experiences of social workers and students*, British Journal of Social Work, 36 (4), 617 637.

Cross, M.C. (2001), *Becoming a Therapist: A Manual for Personal and Professional Development*, Routledge.

Cuin, C.H. (2006), The nomologic approach in sociology, *Revue suisse de sociologie*, Switzerland, Seismo Verlag.

Cummins, K., Sevel, J.A., Pedrick, L. (2011), *Social Work Skills for Beginning Direct Practice: Text, Workbook, and Interactive Web Based Case Studies,* (3rd Edition), Pearson.

Cusick, A. (2011), *The Psychology of the Soul*, CreateSpace, Charleston SC, an Amazon.com Company.

Danesh, H.B. (1994), *Psychology of Spirituality*, Paradigm Publishing.

DeVries, R., Zan, B. (2012), *Moral Classrooms, Moral Children: Creating a Constructivist Atmosphere in Early Education*, Teachers College Press.

Deurzen, E., Kenward, R. (2005), *Dictionary of Existential Psychotherapy and Counselling*. SAGE Publications.

Doherty, W.J. (1996), *Soul Searching: Why Psychotherapy Must Promote Moral Responsibility*, Basic Books.

Doise, W., Deschamp, J.C., Mugny, G. (1996), *Psihologie socială experimentală*, Editura Polirom.

Durkheim, E. (2004), *Sociologia - regulile metodei sociologice*, Editura Antet.

Edwin, L. (2007), *Projective Psychology - Clinical Approaches To The Total Personality*, Pratt Press.

Elkin, D. (2009), *Humanistic Psychology: A Clinical Manifesto. A Critique of Clinical Psychology and the Need for Progressive Alternatives*, Universities of the Rockies Press.

Elrefai, T. (2013), *Diversity to Unity: A journey to a vision of humanism*, Commoners.

Ellis, A. (1974), *Humanistic Psychotherapy: The Rational-Emotive Approach*, Mcgraw-Hill.

Ellis A., Abrams, M., Abrams, L.D. (2008), *Personality Theories: Critical Perspectives*, SAGE Publications, Inc.

Else, J.F. (1977), *Purposive social change: A radical humanist perspective*, Social Work Foundation, School of Social Work, University of Iowa.

Elson, M. (1988), *Self Psychology in Clinical Social Work*, W. W. Norton & Company.

Endler, N., Parker, J. (1992), Interactionism revisited: Reflections on the continuing crisis in the personality area, în *European Journal of Personality*, 6, pp. 177-198,

Erikson, E. H., Erikson, J.M. (1998), *The Life Cycle Completed* , W W Norton & Co Inc.

Feldman, R. (1985), Reliability and Justification, în *The Monist*, Buffalo, NY: Open Court Publishing Company.

Filip, J., McDaniel, N., Schene, P. (1999), *Helping in child protective services. A competency-based case-work handbook*, American Human Asociation, Englewood, Colorado.

Fox, P.J. (2011), *Heart of a Caregiver: Touching Lives with Compassion and Care*, Simple Truths.

Frankl, V. (2009), *Teoria şi terapia nevrozelor. Introducere în logoterapie şi analiza existenţială*, trad. în lb. română de Daniela Ştefănescu, Bucureşti: Editura Trei.

Freud, S., Strachey, J., Hitchens, C., Gay, P. (2010), *Civilization and Its Discontents* (Complete Psychological Works of Sigmund Freud), W. W. Norton & Company.

Friedman, H.S., Schustack, M.W. (2010), *Personality: Classic Theories and Modern Research* (5th Edition), Pearson.

Garfinkel, H. (2006), *Seeing sociologically*, Boulder, CO, Paradigm Publishers.

Game, A. (1991), *Undoing the Social: Towards a Deconstructive Sociology*, Toronto, University of Toronto Press.

Gammer, C. (2008), *The Child's Voice in Family Therapy: A Systemic Perspective*, W. W. Norton & Company.

Garrigou-Lagrange, R., Cummins, P. (1950), *Reality—A Synthesis Of Thomistic Thought*, St. Louis, Mo.: Herder.

Gerdes, K. E. Segal, E. A. (2009), A social work model of empathy. Advances in Social Work Practice, *Social Work* 10(2), 114-127.

Gill, D.W. (2000), *Becoming Good: Building Moral Character*, IVP Books.

Gill, M. (2011), Educating the Professional Social Worker: Challenges and Prospects, în *Revista de asistenţă socială*, nr. 4, pp. 30-41, Iaşi: Editura Polirom.

Ginsberg, L.H., Ginsberg, L. (2008), *Management and Leadership in Social Work Practice and Education*, Council on Social Work Education.

Goldstein, H. (1984), *Creative Change: A Cognitive-Humanistic Approach to Social Work Practice*, Routledge.

Goldstein, E.G. (1995), *Ego Psychology and Social Work Practice*: 2nd Edition, The Free Press.

Gonzalez-Mena, J. (2012), *Child, Family, and Community: Family-Centered Early Care and Education*, Pearson.

Goroff, N. (*1981*), *Humanism and Social Work Paradoxes*, Problems, and Promises, The Journal of Sociology & Social Welfare: Vol. 8: Iss. 1.

Hall, E., Hall C. (1988), *Human relations in education*. Psychology Press.

Hall, E. (1966), *The Hidden Dimension*, New York, Anchor Books.

Harel, I., Papert, S. (1991), *Constructionism*, Norwood, Ablex Publishing Corporation.

Hamblin, R. L., Buckholdt, D., Ferritor, D., Kozloff, M., Blackwell, L. (1971), *The Humanization Processes: A Social, Behavioral Analysis of Children's Problems*, Krieger Pub Co.

Hardcastle, A. (2011), *Theories and Skills for Social Workers*, 3 edition, Oxford University Press.

Hegel G. W. F., (1977), *Phenomenology of Spirit*, 1st Edition, Oxford University Press.

Heidegger, M. (1995), *Introduction in Metaphysics*, Humanitas.

Habermas J., Lenhardt, C. (2001), *Moral Consciousness and Communicative Action*, The MIT Press.

Helbo, A. (1987), *Theory of Performing Arts*, John Benjamins Publishing Company.

Hobson, J.A. (1933), *Rationalism and Humanism*, London: Watts & Co.

Hoffman, M.L. (2000), *Empathy and moral development: Implications for caring and justice.* New York: Cambridge University Press.

Howe, D. (1995), *Attachment Theory for Social Work Practice*, Palgrave Macmillan.

Hughes, D.A. (2000), *Facilitating Developmental Attachment: The Road to Emotional Recovery and Behavioral Change in Foster and Adopted Children,* Jason Aronson, Inc.

Humanistische Akademie. (1998). *Humanistische Sozialarbeit*, Berlin: Humanistische Akademie. Series: Humanismus aktuell, H. 3. Jg. 2.

Inderbitzin, M.L., Bates, C.A., Gainey, R.R. (2012), *Deviance and Social Control: A Sociological Perspective,* SAGE Publications.

James, W. (1981), *Pragmatism: A New Name for Some Old Ways of Thinking*, Hackett Publishing.

Jex, S.M., Gudanowski D.M. (1992), Efficacy beliefs and work stress: An exploratory study. *Journal of Organizational Behavior* .

Jones, C. (1993), *New Perspectives on the Welfare State in Europe,* London: Routledge.

Jones , D. (2014), *Using a Humanistic Solution Focused Approach with Parents and Families to Reduce Anti-Social Behaviour and Youth Offending: An Evidence-Based Approach for Professionals in Social Work Practice,* Lulu.com.

Jung, C.G. (1981), *The Archetypes and The Collective Unconscious* (Collected Works of C.G. Jung Vol.9 Part 1), Princeton University Press.

Kant, I. (2005), *Prolegomene*, Paralela 45.

Kellerman, H. (2012), *Personality: How it forms.* New York: American Mental Health Foundation.

Kelly G.A. (1991), *The Psychology of Personal Constructs*, London: Routledge.

Khan, H. I. (1981), *Spiritual dimensions of psychology.* Lebanon Springs, NY: Sufi Order Publications

Kierkegaard, S. (1981), *The Concept of Anxiety: A Simple Psychologically Orienting Deliberation on the Dogmatic Issue of Hereditary Sin* (Kierkegaard's Writings, VIII) Princeton University Press.

Kimakowitz, E., Spitzeck, H., Pirson, M., Dierksmeier, C., Amann, W. (2011), *Humanistic Management in Practice,* Houndmills: Palgrave Macmillan

Kirsley, D. (2010), *Personology*, Prometheus Nemesis Book Company.

Kosman, A. (2013), *The Activity of Being: An Essay on Aristotle's Ontology*, Harvard University Press.

Kostelnik, M. (2011), *Guiding Children's Social Development and Learning (What's New in Early Childhood)*, Cengage Learning.

Kotarba, J.A., Johnson, J.M. (2002), *Postmodern existential sociology*, Walnut Creek, CA, Alta Mira.

Kreeft, P. (1992), *Back to Virtue: Traditional Moral Wisdom for Modern Moral Confusion*, Ignatius Press.

Krill, D.F. (1978), *Existential social work*, New York: Free Press,

Kramer-Moore, D., Moore, M. (2012), *Destructive Myths in Family Therapy: How to Overcome Barriers to Communication by Seeing and Saying -- A Humanistic Perspective*, Wiley-Blackwell.

Kroeber, A. L., Kluckhohn, C. (1952), *Culture: A Critical Review of Concepts and Definitions*, New York: Vintage Books.

Lacan, J. (1991), *The Seminar of Jacques Lacan: Book II: The Ego in Freud's Theory and in the Technique of Psychoanalysis* , W. W. Norton & Company, 1991.

Langan, T. (2009), *Human Being: A Philosophical Anthropology*, University of Missouri Press.

Lerner, M. (2011), *Education And A Radical Humanism: Notes Toward A Theory Of The Educational Crisis*, Licensing, LLC.

Levi-Strauss, C. (1969), *The elementary structures of kinship*, Beacon Press, Boston.

Lock, A., Strong, T. (2010), *Social constructionism: Sources and stirrings in theory and practice*, New York: Cambridge University Press.

Lukacs, G. (1978), *Ontology of Social Being*, Volume 1, Hegel, Merlin Press.

Madanes, C. (2006), *The Therapist as Humanist, Social Activist, and Systemic Thinker*, Zeig, Tucker & Theisen, Inc.

Maddi, S.R., Costa, O.T. (1972), *Humanism in Personology: Allport, Maslow, and Murray (Perspectives on personality)*, Aldine•Atherton.

May, G.G. (1987), *Will and Spirit: A Contemplative Psychology*, HarperOne.

Maslow, A.H. (1993), *The Farther Reaches of Human Nature*, Penguin / Arkana.

Maslow, A.H. (2011), *Toward A Psychology of Being* - Reprint of 1962 Edition, Martino Fine Books.

Maslow, A.H. (2008), *Motivation and Personality*, Trei.

Masters, A., Wallace, H.R. (2010), *Development for Life and Work,* 10 edition, Cengage Learning.

Maritain, J. 1956), *Existence and the Existent: An Essay on Christian Existentialism*, trans. L. Galantiere and G.B. Phelan, New York: Image.

McAdams, D. P. (2009), *The person: An introduction to the science of personality psychology* (5th Ed.). New York: Wiley.

Mc Call, L.A. (2001), *The McCall Body Balance Method : Simple Concepts for Ageless Movement*, Lisa Mccall.

McLaren, N. (2010), *Humanizing Psychiatrists: Toward a Humane Psychiatry,* Future Psychiatry Press.

Mead, M. (2001), *Coming of Age in Samoa: A Psychological Study of Primitive Youth for Western Civilisation* (Perennial Classics), William Morrow.

Mille, S. (2009), *The Moral Foundations of Social Institutions: A Philosophical Study,* Cambridge University Press.

Miller, C. (2013), *Moral Character: An Empirical Theory*, Oxford University Press.

Miller, J.P. (1999), *Education and the Soul: Toward a Spiritual Curriculum*, State University of New York Press.

Miller, J.P. (2005), *Holistic Learning And Spirituality In Education: Breaking New Ground*, State University of New York Press.

Million, T. (1990), *Toward a New Personology: An Evolutionary Model.* New York: Wiley.

Minsky, M. (2007), *The Emotion Machine: Commonsense Thinking, Artificial Intelligence and the Future of the Human Mind*, Simon & Schuster.

Mjoset, L. (2009), The contextualist approch to social science metodology, în David, B., Ragin, C.C. (coord), *The SAGE hanbook of case-based metods*, London: SAGE Publication Ltd., pp. 39-68.

Moody R., Carroll, D. (1997), *The Five Stages of the Soul: Charting the Spiritual Passages That Shape Our Lives*, New York: Anchor Books.

Moghaddam, F.M. (1998), *Social psychology*, New York: W.H. Freeman end Company.

Moore, T. (1994), *Care of the Soul : A Guide for Cultivating Depth and Sacredness in Everyday Life*, HarperPerennial.

Moore, T. (1994), *Soul Mates: Honoring the Mystery of Love and Relationship*, HarperPerennial.

Moustakas, C. (1966), *Existential Child Therapy*, Basic Books Inc.

Moustakas, C. (1994), *Phenomenological Research Methods*, Thousand Oaks, California: Sage Publications.

Mowrer, E.R. (1972), *Family Disorganization: An Introduction to a Sociological Analysis*, Arno Press and The New York Times.

Mullaly, B. (2002), *Challenging Oppression: A Critical Social Work Approach*, Oxford University Press.

Murray, H. A. (2007). *Explorations in Personality*. Oxford University Press; 70th Anniversary Edition.

Muntean, A. (2013), *Adopția și atașamentul copiilor separați de părinții biologici*, Iași: Editura Polirom.

Myers, D. G. (2004, *Theories of Emotion. Psychology*, Worth Publishers, Găsit la adresa: www.scribd.com/doc/39094849/Emotion.

Nietzsche, F. (2013), *Ecce Homo*. Humanitas.

Noam, G.G., Wren, T.E. (1993), *Moral Self: Building a Better Paradigm*, The MIT Press.

Noddings, N. 2003, *Happiness and education*, Cambridge University Press.

Nolan, P., Lenski, G. (2010), *Human Societies: An Introduction to Macrosociology*, Oxford University Press.

Outhwaite, W. (2006), *The Future of Society* (Blackwell Manifestos), Wiley-Blackwell.

Panter-Brick, C., Smith, M.T. (2000), *Abandoned Children*, Cambridge University Press.

Parsons, T. (1978), *Social Systems and the Evolution of Action Theory*, New York: Free Press.

Pavlovich, K., Krahnke, K. (2013), *Organizing through Empathy* (Routledge Studies in Management, Organizations and Society), Routledge.

Patterson, C. H. (1973), *Humanistic education*, Englewood Prentice.

Pelzer, D. (1997), *The Lost Boy: A Foster Child's Search for the Love of a Family*, Health Communications.

Punalekar, S.P. (1983), *Deprivation, institutionalisation and development: A study of child welfare institutions in Gujarat*, Centre for Social Studies.

Hamilton, E., Cairns, H., Cooper, L. (2005), *The Collected Dialogues of Plato: Including the Letters*, Princeton University Press.

Plotnik, R., Kouyoumdjian, H. (2007), *Introduction to Psychology*, Belmont: Wadsworth Publishing Company.

Pound, R. (1996), *Social Control through Law*, Transaction Publishers.

Reamer, F. G. (1993), *The philosophical foundations of social work*, New York: Columbia University.

Reichmann, J. B. (1985), *Philosophy of the human person.* Chicago, Il.: Loyola University Press.

Rickert, H. (1986), *The Limits of Concept Formation in Natural Science*, Cambridge University Press.

Rifkin, J. (2009), The *Empathic Civilization: The Race to Global Consciousness in a World in Crisis*, Tarcher.

Rogers, C. R. (1951), *Client-Centered Therapy: Its Current Practice, Implications, and Theory*, Boston: Houghton Mifflin.

Rogers, C.R. (1959), A Theory of Therapy, Personality and Interpersonal Relationships as Developed in the Client-centered Framework. In (ed.) S. Koch, *Psychology: A Study of a Science*, New York: McGraw Hill.

Rogers, C.R. (1977), *On Personal Power: Inner Strength and Its Revolutionary Impact*, Delacorte Press.

Rogers, C.R. (1980), *A Way of Being*, Boston: Houghton Mifflin

Rogers, C.R. (2008), *On Becoming a Person*, Trei.

Ross, E.A. (2002), *Social Control: A Survey of the Foundations of Order*, University Press of the Pacific.

Rutter, S.M, Smith, D.J. (1995), *Psychosocial Disorders in Young People: Time Trends and Their Causes*, Wiley.

Saran, P. (1998), *Tantra: Hedonism in Indian Culture*, DK Printworld.

Schooler, J.E. (2010), *Wounded Children, Healing Homes: How Traumatized Children Impact Adoptive and Foster Families*, NavPress.

Schreurs, A. (2001), *Psychotherapy and Spirituality: Integrating the Spiritual Dimension into Therapeutic Practice*, Jessica Kingsley Pub.

Seidman, B.F. (2004), *Toward A New Political Humanism*, Prometheus Books.

Seligman, M.E., Csikszentmihalzi, P. (2000), Positive Pshyhology, în *American Psychologist*, vol. LV, nr. 1.

Seligman, M. E. P. (2002), *Authentic Happiness*. New York: Free Press.

Shebib, B. (2002), *Choices: Counseling Skills for Social Workers and Other Professionals*, Pearson.

Shemmings, D. (2011), *Understanding Disorganized Attachment: Theory and Practice for Working With Children and Adults*, Jessica Kingsley.

Sinnott-Armstrong, W. (2014), *Moral Psychology: Free Will and Moral Responsibility*. A Bradford Book.

Sousa, D.A. (2010), *Mind, Brain and Education: Neuroscience Implications for the Classroom*, Hardcover Solution Tree.

Stairs, J. (2000), *Listening for the Soul: Pastoral Care and Spiritual Direction*, Fortress Press.

Stangor, C. (2004), *Social groups in action and interaction*, New York: Psychology Press.

Steiner, R. (1996), *The education of the child, and early lectures on education*, Hudson, N.Y.: Anthroposophic Press.

Stern, E.M., Kramer, S.Z. (1995), *Transforming the Inner and Outer Family: Humanistic and Spiritual Approaches to Mind-Body Systems Therapy*, Routledge.

Stolorow, R. D. (2011), Toward a renewal of personology in psychotherapy research, *Psychotherapy*, 442–444.

Stone, J.D. (1999), Soul Psychology: How to Clear Negative Emotions and Spiritualize Your Life, Wellspring/Ballantine.

Storr, A. (1992), *The Integrity of the Personality*, Ballantine Books.

Stefaroi, P. (2012), *The Humanistic Approach in Psychology & Psychotherapy, Sociology & Social Work, Pedagogy & Education,*

Management and Art: Personal Development and Community Development, CreateSpace, Charleston SC, Amazon.com, USA.

Stefaroi, P. (2015), *Humanistic Personology: A Humanistic-Ontological Theory of the Person & Personality. Applications in Therapy, Social Work, Education, Management and Art (Theatre)*, CreateSpace, Charleston SC, Amazon.com, USA.

Stefaroi, P. (2016), *Humanistic Philosophy: Humanistic and Pro-Humanistic Ideas, Values, Orientations, Movements, Methods, and Representatives in Philosophy, Science, Society, and Social Practices*, CreateSpace, Charleston SC, Amazon.com, USA.

Stets, J. E., Carter, M. J. (2011), The moral self: Applying identity theory. *Social Psychology Quarterly*, 74, 192–215.

Tanzi, E.R., Chopra, D. (2013), *Super Brain: Unleashing the Explosive Power of Your Mind to Maximize Health, Happiness, and Spiritual Well-Being*, Harmony.

Tiryakian, E.A. (1962), *Sociologism and existentialism, two perspectives on the individual and society*, Englewood Cliffs, N.J., Prentice-Hall.

Vico, G. (1993), *On Humanistic Education: Six Inaugural Orations, 1699-1707 (Six Inaugural Orations, 1699-1707 : from the Definitive Latin Text, Introduction, and Notes of Gian Galeazzo Visconti)*, Cornell University Press.

Vincent, J-D., Hughes, J. (1990), *The Biology of Emotions*, Blackwell Pub.

Walsh, M. (2006), *Nurse Practitioners: Clinical Skill and Professional Issues*, 2 edition, Butterworth-Heinemann.

Ward, C.C. (2010), *Strength-Centered Counseling: Integrating Postmodern Approaches and Skills With Practice*, SAGE Publications, Inc.

Watson, D., Clark, L. A., Tellegen, A. (1988), Development and validation of brief measures of positive affect and negative affect, în *Journal of Personality and Social Psychology*, Washington: American Psychological Association. Găsit la adresa http://www.apa.org/pubs/journals/psp/.

Watt, I. (1957), *The Rise of the Novel*, Berkeley, University of California.

Webb, N.B. (2005), *Working with Traumatized Youth in Child Welfare (Social Work Practice with Children and Families*, The Guilford Press.

Weissman, D. (2000), *A social ontology*, London: Yale University Press.

Weisman, C. S., Nathanson, C. A. (1985). Professional satisfaction and client outcomes: A comparative organizational analysis. *Medical Care*, 23, 1179–1192.

Wheeler, G. (1991), *Gestalt reconsidered*, New York: Gardner Press.

Whitaker, C. W. A. (2002), *Aristotle's De Interpretatione: Contradiction and Dialectic* (Oxford Aristotle Studies), Oxford University Press.

Wilber, K. (2000), *Integral Psychology: Consciousness, Spirit, Psychology, Therapy,* Shambhala.

William K. F. (2012), *Opening to the Sacred: A Humanist Approach to Holistic Spirituality*, Premium Prose Publishing.

Whiteside, (1969), *Personology: The Dynamics of Success*, New York: F. Fell.

Wommack, A. (2010), *Spirit, Soul and Body*, Harrison House.

Yalom, I. (1980), *Existential psychotherapy*. New York: Basic Books.

Young, P.T. (1961), *Motivation and Emotion*, John Wiley & Sons Inc.

Zamfir. E. (2008), The new human model proposed by humanist pychology. Types of conflict resolution, in *Social Work Review*, nr. 1-2, pp 3-28.

Zheng, R. (Ed.). (2012), *Evolving psychological and educational perspectives on cyber behavior*, Hershey.

*** www.ohchr.org/EN/UDHR.

*** www.ourfutureenvironment.org/personality/wp-content/uploads/2010/08/endler_ interactionism.pdf.

GENETIC PERSONOLOGY:

The Formation, Functioning, and Development of the Person & Personality.

A Humanistic-Ontological Approach

by

Petru Stefaroi

Available on Amazon.com, Amazon Europe,
CreateSpace Store, and other retail outlets

---

http://www.amazon.com/
https://kindle.amazon.com

Author's email adress:
petrustefaroi@yahoo.com

The
HUMANISTIC
PERSONOLOGY
Project